"This book is an excellent resource for parents of children with self-regulation issues and the professionals who take care of them. It presents dozens of practical strategies for helping children with many kinds of dysregulation, from autism to Sensory Processing Disorder to ADHD. Therapists will appreciate the well-presented basic theoretical framework, but it is the careful and clear explanation of direct interventions that parents can do at home that is invaluable."

Sanford Newmark, MD
UCSF Osher Center for Integrative Medicine
Author of ADHD Without Drugs: A Guide to the Natural Care of Children with ADHD"

"With so many great ideas and on-the-spot solutions, this book is bound to become a marked-up, dog-eared reference for both established professionals and young therapists and teachers. Here in one book are techniques for helping a child calm, attend, and stay on task along with essential theoretical background to gain new insight and expand professional skills for working with children with autism, ADHD and sensory disorders."

Dr. Laurie Lundblad Clinical Psychologist Building Bridges Therapy Center

Self-Regulation Interventions and Strategies

*Keeping the Body, Mind and Emotions
on Task in Children with
Autism, ADHD or Sensory Disorders*

TERESA GARLAND, MOT, OTR

Copyright © 2014 by Teresa Garland, MOT, OTR

Published by
PESI Publishing & Media
PESI, Inc
3839 White Ave
Eau Claire, WI 54703

Printed in the United States of America

ISBN: 978-1-936128-77-8

PESI
Publishing
& Media
www.pesipublishing.com

Thanks to Mike Olson at PESI for giving me the opportunity to write this book; to Linda Jackson for help, encouragement and good advice at every step and to editor Marietta Whittlesey for help making the book more accurate and readable.

I am grateful to friends and colleagues who generously took time to read through and comment on these pages: Dr. Laurie Lundblad, Michelle Mintz, Brad Naberhaus, Stephanie Ramser, Laurie Similuk, and Jennifer Smith. Thanks to Sue Troutman for getting me started with the sensory therapy mentorship at the Center for Developing Kids in Pasadena.

Thanks to Therapy Shoppe and SensoryJunction for the use of photos from their sensory catalogs. Thanks also to SPIO, Vision Audio and the Qigong Sensory Training Institute for permission to use photos.

A final thanks to my dear husband Peter for his excellent advice and untiring help at all stages of the book.

Self-Regulation in Children

About the Author

Photo by Rose Widel

Shortly after graduation with her MOT, Teresa became intrigued with sensory integration and quickly obtained her certification. She avidly pursued theoretical and practical knowledge about the children she treated, trying in particular to understand their difficulty with self-control. As a child and young adult, Teresa herself had struggled with sensory issues and mild ADHD that had gone undiagnosed. As she conducted research and sought to make a contribution to this area of study, she produced a blog, http://otselfregulation.blogspot.com. Soon she was giving workshops on self-regulation for children with autism, ADHD and sensory disorders.

Along the way, Teresa worked with children in clinics and schools in New Mexico, California and Michigan and with children with autism in the office of a Defeat Autism Now (DAN) doctor. Teresa has a Master's Degree in Occupational Therapy from the University of New Mexico. She began her career with an MS in computer science from the University of Michigan, worked first in the field of artificial intelligence and then in business systems, consulting to Fortune 100 companies. Her hobbies include growing herbs and vegetables, riding her bicycle, reading, and dabbling in art. She is married and lives in Plymouth, Michigan. *Self-Regulation Interventions and Strategies* is her first book.

Introduction

What can be more satisfying than helping children find harmony with themselves, their families and the world around them? But helping them reach that peace or serenity can be daunting, especially when we work with children with autism, ADHD or a sensory modulation disorder. It is not unusual for such children to have trouble self-regulating at all levels: physical, sensory, mental, emotional and social. We can teach children with these disorders to learn to self-regulate, and we can do it in ways that are fun. The focus of this book is to share interventions that therapists, educators and parents can use to help children to engage successfully in all aspects of their lives.

PHYSICAL

Ideally, our physical bodies should self-regulate without our conscious intervention. But we are complex creatures who are affected by hormonal, sensory and physical issues and processes. These processes can affect our alert state, our sleep habits, our willingness to eat the foods placed in front of us, and our ability to sit still. The state of our physical self affects our mental, emotional and social selves. Think of the child who eats poorly. She is going to feel too weak to participate in play and too mentally sluggish to attend to class work. Likewise, a child with poor sleep habits will likely have poor attention. If sleep problems are chronic, she may become hyperactive. In fact, chronic sleep problems mimic ADHD and are sometimes misdiagnosed as ADHD.

A child with all types of self-regulation issues can become physically grounded with regular activity involving heavy work, exercise, play or by regularly getting deep pressure. These activities can help a hyperactive child to slow down. They can also help a child with sensory issues to become calmer and stay that way for longer periods. A child with autism can maintain better regulation as he transitions from one activity to another. Heavy work, exercise, play and deep pressure are also effective in helping children with bipolar disorder burn off manic energy, while enabling children with post-traumatic stress disorder to face the world.

SENSORY

Self-regulation at the physical and mental levels is impacted by our senses. There are two types of problems. First, the sense organs—eyes, ears, tongue, nose, skin, vestibular organs, and muscle spindles—may not function properly. In the case of eyes and ears, we can correct much of the problem by wearing glasses and hearing aids. But when taste buds don't work, we see picky eating problems that can take years to overcome.

Second, within the brain we must process information coming from all the senses. We integrate that information so that it gives us the coherence and orientation we need to navigate successfully in the world. Our right ear must be synchronized with the left if our auditory processing is to work correctly. Our ears must be in sync with the eyes in order for our brain to get the big picture. Think of watching a movie in which lips and sounds are out-of-sync. It takes extra effort to decipher the dialog, and we may lose track of what is being said. This is how children with poor sensory modulation can experience the world.

Sensory processing issues can be broken into different types of problems, the biggest being poor sensory modulation. There are three ways that we can have problems with modulation: oversensitivity, undersensitivity, and craving of sensory input. We can have any or all of these problems in any one of the senses. One or more of our senses may be oversensitive, in which case we may be easily irritated by shirt tags rubbing our skin or by loud voices. Other senses may be undersensitive: we may find food to be bland or we may not notice when our name is called. And we might struggle with sensory cravings, like the girl with ear buds listening to music non-stop or the boy with autism staring in a fixed manner at the moving parts of clocks and fans.

Of these three types of sensory modulation issues, sensory oversensitivity typically causes the greatest number of self-regulation issues. Children who are oversensitive to sound or touch live in a world that is too loud and intrusive and presses in on them, producing emotional and social problems.

We can counter these problems with strategies, therapies and lifestyle changes that can support their need for specific types and levels of sensory input.

MENTAL

School children need good attention and focus in order to be successful. This is a problem for the child with ADHD who is unable to focus and concentrate for periods of time. He may have difficulty attending to school work even when he has no difficulty focusing on a video game. His brain is motivated when activity or work is interesting, but motivation deserts him for what he feels is mundane work.

ADHD symptoms are the result of underdeveloped executive-functioning circuitry (located primarily in the prefrontal cortex portion of the brain.) ADHD symptoms are classified into three areas: inattention, impulsivity, and hyperactivity. When a child shows signs of inattention he may have difficulty organizing his thoughts or his school work. He may forget things, make careless mistakes, become easily distracted and perform work tasks with a half-hearted effort. In fact, he may balk at having to work at anything that requires thinking, claiming that it is too hard for him. Impulsivity may cause him to blurt out words without thinking them through. He is inclined to interrupt others while they are talking or, worse, take over what the other person is doing. Hyperactivity shows up as excessive movement and talking. Hyperactive children squirm in their chairs and sometimes bolt out of them inappropriately.

When a child is being impulsive, his poor self-regulation might also affect his emotional and social states. Think of the child who blurts out overly personal information and then, seeing that his peers have turned away from him, later regrets it.

Research tells us that children with ADHD make good progress when they receive nutritional support and/or a combination of medication and therapy. Once the child is doing well, we have a great opportunity to teach him new behaviors that can support him in a medication-free life. Therapies and techniques such as self-management, timing therapy and mindfulness meditation have shown good success in helping to increase attention and decrease impulsive and hyperactive behaviors.

A child with autism also has another kind of poor attention. She will have difficulty shifting her attention from one thing to another, and she will find it difficult to engage with others in joint attention to an object, activity or topic of conversation. Her ability to shift her attention is also poor. She may be settled in an activity and focused on it so intently that she is caught by surprise when interrupted. Asking her to change focus can cause a negative reaction or a tantrum.

For this child, focusing on methods that help her understand and organize the day's plans while communicating her needs can improve cognitive self-regulation.

EMOTIONAL

For a child to be emotionally well-regulated he needs a good foundation in physical, mental and sensory regulation. The sensory child who is irritated by clothing seams or tags every time he moves is likely to become cranky. Even when a child has a reasonably solid emotional foundation, he may have poor self-regulation due to other issues such as an oversensitive fight-or-flight reflex. He may also be inclined to overreact in an attempt to make others understand how difficult his life is.

A child with ADHD who is deep into a video game is not available for emotional interactions. When impulsive or hyperactive, he is out of touch with his body and emotions. He is liable to do or say things that will backfire, and he won't realize the effect or the consequences. A child with autism is also typically out of touch with his emotions and may lack the ability to express them. We often must teach children with autism how to show their emotions on their face and how to read emotions in another person's face. If the child is non-verbal, he may resort to meltdowns to gain some amount of control over his life.

We can support these children with art, music and powerful tools such as EFT (Emotional Freedom Technique) and similar therapies that help release negative emotions.

SOCIAL

Now we come to the challenge of maintaining good self-regulation in the social arena. The better the foundation of physical, sensory, mental and emotional regulation, the easier social self-regulation will be. A child with sensory issues may be too overwhelmed with noxious sounds, light glare or other sensations to pay attention to a friend. A child with ADHD may act out with hyperactivity or impulsivity, driving potential friends away. A child with typical autism may be happily engaged in her own world and not care about making friends at all. The child with an Asperger's form of autism will try to be social but is limited by a brain that does not pick up on emotions, gestures and social conventions. Both children see the world from their own point of view and have difficulty relating to another person's point of view.

We can teach children how to stay calm at the same time we give them strategies to make social situations more successful.

These children carry a heavy load. They stand a greater chance than their peers of having dual or multiple diagnoses such as sensory and autism or ADHD and sensory. In addition, they are much more prone to both anxiety and depression than their peers.

This book contains a wealth of ideas for helping children gain control over their life so that they can participate in it successfully. In this book are recipes (techniques, interventions and strategies) to be used by therapists, educators and parents to help children regulate their emotions and behaviors. Some of the recipes are therapeutic interventions that can enhance self-regulation skills. Other recipes are strategies to help the child function with greater ease in a given setting. The combinations of many skilled and sensitive approaches can give the child the best chance for a functional life.

About the book

The book has chapters devoted to the specific diagnoses of sensory modulation issues, ADHD/ADD and autism. In addition, there are chapters that cover material useful for all diagnoses: calming and alerting techniques, interventions for emotional and social regulation and supporting interventions such as timing therapy and the use of behavioral techniques. Since ADHD, autism and sensory modulation can co-occur with each other and with anxiety, it is likely that material in many of the chapters will be relevant for any given child's therapy.

CHAPTER 1

Autism Spectrum Disorder (ASD)

ASD is a broad spectrum disorder affecting the brain and physiological development of children. While ASD is diagnosed as a neurodevelopmental disorder, it affects the child at all levels: physiological, autonomic, motor, gastric, immunological, sensory, cognitive, executive function, language, communication, emotions and social systems.

The first part of this chapter looks at the symptoms underlying self-regulation issues in children with ASD. This is followed with a variety of approaches to engage and to communicate with children with ASD. Finally, methods are presented for helping to establish desirable behaviors in children.

Readers can find strategies for many other aspects of self-regulation in other chapters of the book. For the most part, the entire set of interventions and strategies in this book are useful for children with ASD.

SELF-REGULATION AND ASD

Children with ASD are challenged physically, emotionally, mentally and socially with self-regulation issues. Among factors causing their self-regulation problems are the following:

Physiological: Problems in three key physiological processes—antioxidation, energy production from mitochondria, and immune function—are associated with some cases of ASD. Along with genetics, these three areas are the prime focus of research in ASD.

> **Anti-oxidation:** High levels of toxins including heavy metals such as lead, mercury and cadmium have been found in the brains and bodies of children with ASD. Studies have found insufficient levels of antioxidants such as glutathione which clean up toxins in the body. The reasons for the insufficiency are not yet completely understood.

> **Cell energy production:** As readers know from studying biology, mitochondria are little organelles that live in our cells and produce cell energy. Five percent of children with ASD have a mitochondrial disorder and another 28% have poor mitochondrial functionality. This means the cells have less energy than what they require to perform their function. We do not yet understand all the ways this affects children with ASD, but it appears to be systemic.

> **Immune system:** Eighty percent of our immune system resides in the gut. Immune issues, such as decreased levels of immunoglobulin which fights off bacterial and viral infections, are common in children with ASD. Food sensitivities (such as the inability of

1

most children with ASD to digest lactose in milk) are also common in these children, to the degree that 6% of them have gut inflammation. This has led Kushak, et al (2011) to suggest that food sensitivities may contribute to the high rate of immune system issues. Questions remain concerning the reasons for food sensitivity and the role of other factors in the weakening of the child's immune system.

Physical systems: Children with ASD tend to engage in sedentary play and repetitive behaviors which do not challenge the body or allow muscles to build. As a result, they tend to have poor muscle strength, especially in the upper body. Sensory modulation problems are common in children with ASD (72%) and can affect their ability to tolerate tastes, smells and textures of various foods, as well as the feel of clothing against their skin, the sound of hair clippers near their ears and the sensation of nails being clipped. Sensory modulation is also a factor in their poor sleeping behaviors and poor bowel-and-bladder control, although other physiological factors may play a part as well. Visual processing is often a strength in these same children, and many successful interventions (such as visual schedules) make use of that strength. Sensory dysfunction symptoms often decrease naturally as the child develops. Many sensory strategies and therapies can successfully decrease remaining sensory symptoms. Some children with ASD have rigid eating behaviors. They may, for example, elect to eat only white foods such as pasta, chicken nuggets, crackers and yogurt. This is a separate problem from sensory-based picky eating. The sensory trained specialist can be confounded if she does not consider the child's rigidity as a key factor in his eating problems. Likewise, the behavioral therapist can have limited success with eating issues if sensory issues are not addressed.

Emotional: While children with ASD obviously experience emotions, they often have poor emotional affect. They do not show their emotions on their faces and similarly do not recognize emotional expression on the faces of others. Fortunately, they can be successfully taught a fuller emotional range through therapeutic approaches involving stories, mirrors, emoticons, and so on. But the process can take considerable time.

Non-verbal children with ASD lead emotionally challenged lives. They may have difficulty being understood and getting their needs met. They may act out painful behaviors, including tantrums. To help them, we can teach them visual methods of communication that regulate both emotions and behaviors.

Mental: Most children with ASD have an IQ of 70 or higher and are capable of learning. A child with ASD has excellent attention to an object or topic of his own choosing, but has poor joint attention (shared attention) to an object or topic of someone else's choosing. Sometimes the child will "stim" (engage in repetitive behavior) on sensory input such as watching a fan or watching himself repeatedly flick his finger. He may obsessively line up his shoes, toy cars or stuffed animals and refuse to move on until they are organized to his standards. Obsessive activities can interfere with the bright child's ability to acquire information about his environment and to find patterns in his experience that allow him to make useful generalizations about the world.

Social: Children with ASD lack crucial social foundation skills. They do not make eye contact, visibly express their emotions, read another person's facial expressions, understand hand and body gestures, or interpret other social cues. The problem presents itself early in life. Studies at Yale University's autism program showed that when babies with ASD look at a face, they watch the mouth move rather than, as a normal baby does, look into the person's eyes as a way of connecting.

A combination of poor imitation and face-recognition skills, along with a general lack of interest in people, prevents the child with ASD from learning information through mirroring (imitating) the movements of others. In addition, they are unable to learn vicariously (learning how to perform a task by watching others do it).

In terms of socialization, White and Robinson (2009) found that the child with Level 3 (low-functioning) ASD needs an emotional connection to his family, but does not appear to have an emotional need for friends. In contrast, children with Level 1 (high-functioning) ASD or Asperger Syndrome would like to have friends, yet they miss crucial social expressions, gestures and cues. They do not pick up the rules of social interaction and do not understand their role in carrying on a conversation.

Diagnosing ASD

ASD is a system-wide disorder. It is not unusual for a team of professionals to be involved in the diagnosis and assessment process. Diagnosing ASD in a child requires an in-depth look at the child's psychological functioning, speech and communication skills, socio-emotional development, motor behaviors and sensory-modulation skills. In addition, some doctors will complete extensive physiological exams including blood, urine and stool tests. The diagnostic criterion in the DSM-5 contains lists of common symptoms as well as additional criteria identifying the severity of the disorder.

A synopsis of the symptoms is provided below. The severity of the disorder is determined by the level of support needed by the individual (Level 1 = requiring support, Level 2 = requiring substantial support and Level 3 = requiring very substantial support).

Symptoms of ASD (simplified)

1. Persistent deficits in social communication and social interactions across multiple contexts:
   a. Deficits in social-emotional reciprocity, ranging from abnormal social approach to failure of back-and-forth conversation.
      i. Reduced sharing of interests, emotions or affect;
      ii. Failure to initiate or respond to social interactions.
   b. Deficits in nonverbal communicative behaviors used for social interaction.
      i. Poor eye contact;
      ii. Inability to understand and use gestures;
      iii. Poor or complete lack of facial expression and nonverbal communication.
   c. Deficits in developing, maintaining and understanding relationships.
      i. Difficulty with imaginative play;
      ii. Absence of interest in peers.

2. Restricted, repetitive patterns of behavior, interests, or activities with at least two of the following four symptoms:
   a. Stereotyped or repetitive motor movements, use of objects or speech such as lining up toys, flipping objects, echolalia, idiosyncratic phrases.
   b. Insistence on sameness.
      i. Inflexible adherence to routine;
      ii. Ritualized patterns of behavior.
   c. Highly restricted, fixated interests with abnormal intensity or focus (perseveration).
   d. Hyper- or hyporeactivity to sensory input or unusual interest in sensory aspects of the environment.
      i. Indifference to pain, temperature;
      ii. Adverse response to specific sounds, textures;
      iii. Excessive smelling or touching of objects; fascination with spinning or moving objects.

Early diagnosis

It is vital that children with ASD get intervention at the earliest opportunity. However, the above set of symptoms may not appear in a child until the age of two. The organization, Autism Speaks, has put together a list of some early indicators of ASD that can be used to help gain access to services prior to a formal diagnosis.

- No big smiles or other warm, joyful expressions by six months or thereafter.
- No back-and-forth sharing of sounds, smiles or other facial expressions by nine months.
- No babbling by 12 months.
- No back-and-forth gestures such as pointing, showing, reaching or waving by 12 months.
- No words by 16 months.
- No meaningful, two-word phrases (not including imitating or repeating) by 24 months.
- Any loss of speech, babbling or social skills at any age.

What about Asperger Syndrome?

While the DSM-5 no longer supports the autism sub-diagnosis of Asperger Syndrome, a preliminary blind EEG-coherence study was able to differentiate between children with "typical autism" and those with Asperger Syndrome. They found that children with Asperger's have greater brain connectivity than their ASD peers (Duffy, 2013). Here are common features of Asperger Syndrome.

- Good verbal skills, but poor communication skills. The child may engage in one-sided conversations on his own preferred topic of interest. He may be a non-stop talker. Some children with Asperger's speak in a monotone voice; some speak too loud or have other speech idiosyncrasies.
- Average or above average intelligence. The child may excel at math and science.

- Difficulty with executive-function skills such as planning and problem solving, especially in real-life situations. He is good at details but may miss the big picture.
- Obsessions with particular topics such as vacuum cleaners, old cars, rockets, Star Wars and so on.
- Poor coordination. He may have a peculiar walk with a wide-gait pattern.

Like his peers with autism, he has these additional characteristics.

- Poor social skills. He doesn't understand non-verbal cues such as facial signals (quizzical, smile, rolling eyes) or gestures (come here, thumbs up). He will typically lack empathy and have an inability to see a situation from another person's point of view, instead seeing the world from his experience and interest. He may have a poor sense of humor.
- Poor affect (a stiff face). Although he has emotions, he does not express them or understand what they are in himself or in another person. He may also have difficulty with emotional self-regulation. He has poor eye contact.
- He may display repetitive behaviors.
- Difficulty regulating sensory modulation.

The prognosis is often good for children with Asperger's when they get early and aggressive intervention. They benefit from therapeutic interventions in the areas of social skills, emotional skills, sensory processing and coordination. It is common for children with Asperger's to grow into independent adults. However, they may have continued difficulty with social relationships and personal interactions.

Causes and development of ASD

We know that a child's risk of having an autism spectrum disorder depends on environmental, biologic and genetic factors. However, the specific causes are not known, and the reasons that children with ASD are susceptible to various environmental factors are not completely understood.

Children with ASD fare much better today than in past years. Improved outcomes have been achieved with early intervention programs such as the Developmental, Individual Difference, Relationship-based Model (DIR® Floortime, a type of play therapy), Applied Behavioral Analysis (ABA) therapy, Pivotal Response Treatment, speech and language therapy and occupational therapy with a focus on sensory modulation. Medical doctors are now on the lookout for what they know are common deficiencies in vitamins, minerals, and other brain and body chemical compounds. Children with ASD have access to a wider variety of therapies, and they are greatly helped by teachers who are specially trained.

ASD statistics

The rate of ASD in the U.S. population is one in 88 children. For boys, the rate is one in 54. A parent who has a child with ASD has a 2-18% chance of having second child with ASD. The co-occurrence of another developmental disorder (such as ADHD or learning disabilities) is 84%.

Having ASD does not mean that a child necessarily has an intellectual disability. A study of eight-year-old children with ASD found that 62% had an IQ of 70 or higher. Some children with ASD have very high IQs (CDC, 2013).

BASIC INTERVENTIONS FOR ASD

This section presents a variety of communication methods that are well-suited to the strong visual skills of children with ASD. Good systems of communication like these work to keep down their frustration level. Here we look at visual schedules, "first this, then that" constructs, first-person stories, transition techniques and ways to prepare the child for coming events.

INTERVENTIONS: VISUAL SCHEDULE

Creating methods for communication is arguably our most important work with children with ASD. In the United States, our chief method for communication is the *visual schedule,* a set of pictures, photos or icons set in a row that indicate the steps to be taken in an agenda. Visual schedules show the micro-steps of getting dressed (see figure 1) or the macro-steps of the day's plans (see figure 4). The level of detail depends on the context and the child's needs for communication support. To help encourage literacy and develop sight words at an early age, many therapists include the word (or words) that describe the image.

Specialists trained in the technique teach a child to identify pictures and to understand the meaning of sequential lists. As the child learns to use a visual schedule, he finds that the images inform him of what is next on the schedule, what is expected of him, and when he will be done with a task (see figure 2). Training to use the visual schedule usually begins in preschool. Once the child has been taught, other teachers and therapists can put together a visual schedule at the beginning of their classes or sessions that guide the child through the time period.

A communication tool has limited value if communication is only one-way, from the therapist to the child. We want to provide the child with opportunities to assist in creating and changing the schedule. When possible, give the child the opportunity to select the activities on the list. For example, in a therapy session let her choose an activity from a few options. To do this, hand her a few pictures and say, "What would *you* like to do?" The non-verbal child is not able to ask for a treat or fun activities, so when possible offer options to the child. Let the child choose the last item in the visual schedule—the reward—from a choice of several treats that she enjoys. See figure 3.

Figure 1. A Visual schedule showing the order for putting on clothes.

Let the child pick a treat

"Next we do numbers, Tina."

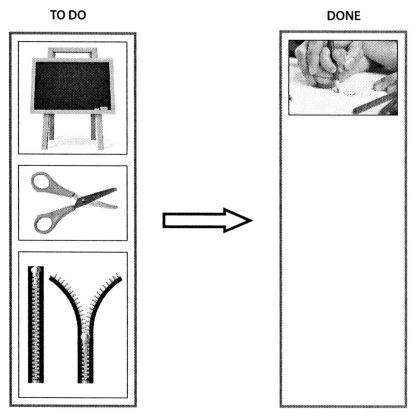

Figure 2. Here is an example of a visual schedule. It has two lists, one for pictures of activities to do, the other for pictures of activities that are completed. The child works on the activities represented by the pictures one-by-one, placing the picture on the "done" strip when it is completed.

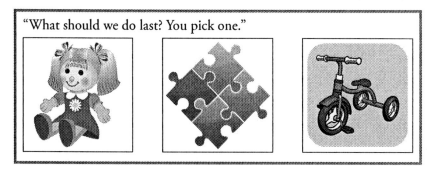

Figure 3. When making a visual schedule, we give the child opportunities to pick activities or to pick the order of activities whenever possible as a way of giving him increased control.

When it is time to get started, ask the child, "What's first?" She may say, "Writing." When she has finished her handwriting, she moves the handwriting image from the to-do list to the done list.

When the child gets older and becomes proficient in reading, the pictures can be replaced with a written list. For the young child, limit the number of activities presented at a time. Two activities may be sufficient: the task she is currently engaged in and the one that comes next. The two-item list also works well for "first this, then that" support, as in "first cutting, then iPad."

Getting images, icons and boards

Resources are listed below for finding images and icons for visual schedules, stories, and "first this, then that" constructs. Instructions for making your own images are also included.

Boardmaker: For those with access to Boardmaker software, many images are available for use in visual schedules and stories. Boardmaker also has free canned Social Stories™. The product cost is $399.

PECS: The Picture Exchange Communication System is a method for training children with autism in simple communication. You can find sets of images to use when making visual schedules, as well as boards to display visual schedules, at PECSUSA.com.

Apps: Look for inexpensive (or free) sets of clip-art in apps for your phone or tablet. You can upload the images to a computer for printing or use them in other apps. Organization apps that let you sort images into folders are also available.

Google Images: A wealth of images are available here, but be careful to note copyright limitations before selecting an image. See the instructions below for working with them.

Microsoft Word: Word has a large number of free clip-art images. Here is how to access them:

Figure 4. A visual schedule showing the day's plans.

1. While in Word, click on the insert menu tab at the top of the screen.

2. In the picture-icon menu that appears, select the clip-art icon.

3. The clip-art window will appear on the right of the screen.

4. Enter the name of the item you want an image for in the "Search for" text box, e.g. scissors, then click on Go.

5. A list of images appears. Scroll through the list until you find the image you want and click on it.

6. The image will appear. You can change its size before printing it.

7. To change the size of the image:

    a. Put the cursor over the image and click right.

    b. In the menu that appears, click on "Size and position."

    c. The number in the box labeled "Height" is a percentage. To make the picture 50% smaller, divide the number in the box by two and enter it into the box. For example, if the number is 100, replace that number with the number 50. To make the picture three times as big, replace the number with 300.

Create your own visual schedule materials

Consider making your own custom photos of people and objects in the child's environment to use in schedules and stories. Shrink photos to the appropriate size using any of the many photo-editing tools.

Materials: Camera, computer, printer, Velcro, stiff boards

Create images:
1. Photograph objects in the child's environment.
2. Resize the photo if necessary, perhaps 2 × 2 inches.
3. Print the image, cut it out, and laminate it if possible.
4. Adhere a piece of Velcro loop (the soft side) to the back of each image.

Make the visual schedule board:
1. Purchase a finished board or a piece of stiff poster-board (from a craft store).
2. If necessary, cut the board to size. For a visual schedule that holds 6-8 images in two vertical rows, the board will be about 18-22 inches long by 6-12 inches wide.
3. Cut two pieces of Velcro hook (the rough side) slightly shorter than the board.
4. Stick the Velcro strips to the board vertically, about four inches apart.

The first-then board

A variation on the visual schedule is the *first-then board*. First-then boards are used to provide visual motivation for a child to complete a non-preferred task. An example is shown below.

A first-then board

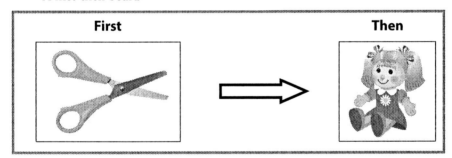

| First | Then |

Figure 5. A first-then board.

To use the board, place the image that represents the task under the word "first" and an image of the reward under the word "then."

Make a first-then board

First-then boards are easy to make.

Materials: Velcro, a stiff board, markers

Method:
1. Label the board *first* and *then*.
2. Draw an arrow below and between the two words.
3. Stick a square of Velcro hook under each word.

You can also purchase first-then boards from therapy catalogs. In addition, there are several excellent apps that provide this capability: *First Then*, *First & Then* and PECS apps from Pyramid Systems.

Keeping a routine vs. making changes

Children with ASD have difficulty with change. When we keep a child's schedule the same from day-to-day and week-to-week, he or she knows what to expect. This is the easiest course for them, and it lessens reactive behaviors.

That said, they can become very rigid and so it is important to introduce some changes on a regular basis. Consider putting a "Surprise!" card on the schedule in a different location or position every day so that they get accustomed to change in a manner that is not overwhelming. The surprise itself can announce a fun activity or a work activity. Make sure to use a first-person story like the one below to prepare the child for a more challenging surprise. Here are ideas for surprise cards.

SURPRISE!

In school we have a surprise every day.

Sometimes surprises are fun.

Sometimes they are not fun.

This is OK! No one has fun all the time.

When the surprise is not fun, I will stay calm.

I will count to ten slowly. This will help me stay calm.

1 2 3 4 5 6 7 8 9 10

It's okay to feel sad when the surprise is not fun.
Not all surprises are fun. But all surprises end.

INTERVENTIONS: SIMPLE AND COMPLEX STORIES

Stories are a helpful way to give the child with ASD information that he does not pick up on his own. Consider stories on the following topics: classroom rules, social rules, expected behaviors at grandma's house, and "Why Mrs. Daniels was unhappy when you picked her flowers." Stories are written in the first person so the child can more easily assimilate the information. The topic is described from the child's point of view and then from a larger perspective that deals with aspects of the situation he is missing.

Stories can be simple or complicated. Sometimes all the child needs is a set of rules, and a simple story is sufficient. Other times the child needs to understand social rules in context or someone's emotional reaction to an event. These situations call for a complex story. We look at both below.

The key points to remember when writing a story:

- Use words and phrasing that the child is able to read and comprehend. Add pictures to the story to help with comprehension. (See the "Surprise" story above as an example).

- Stories work best for the child with fair-to-good cognitive and language skills. Try picture stories or video modeling for very young children or children with poor reading comprehension.

- Write the story using the "I" pronoun. This helps the child internalize the story.

- Use easy-to-digest phrases such as "I will try," and avoid emphatic phrases such as "I will," "I must," or "I should" which put words in the child's mouth.

- Keep all aspects of the story positive.

- Put the story in a convenient location and encourage the child to read the story one or more times a day until the lesson is assimilated.

Simple stories

It can take just a few minutes to write a simple story that is just a list of rules. If you discover you have left out a rule, add it to the list for future reading. Simple stories are also useful for teaching rules for card games, board games and sports. Here is an example of a simple story. Note that the story ends on a positive note.

Rules for the TV

When I want to watch TV:

- *I ask mom if I can watch it.*
- *If she says "yes," I set the timer for 30 minutes.*
- *I turn on the TV.*
- *When the timer says 0, I turn off the TV.*
- *Sometimes it is not a good time to watch TV and the answer is no.*
- *That is okay. I must wait until later.*

Complex stories

When the child needs concepts and explanations along with rules, we craft a complex story. In this type of story, we give two viewpoints, the child's and ours. The child's view is represented in an objective rendering of the situation. Our view includes big-picture information, including the social context, lessons to be learned, and consequences of his choices when appropriate. To help round out the story, tack on a fun or interesting introduction. It does not have to be long. End with an affirmation of the child's strengths. Here is an example of a complex story.

I like candy.

Yesterday mom put a bag of candy on the table for us to eat. I ate all the candy in 15 minutes. I did not save any for Jeremy. He was upset because he did not get any.

I need to try and leave some so that others can enjoy treats, too. Next time mom puts out candy, I will try to take a small amount and leave the rest so that my family can have some. This is a way I can be nice to them.

That way mom can say that not only am I smart but I am also polite.

Here is the same story decomposed into its parts:

Introduction with a hook: I like candy.

Objective view of the situation: Yesterday mom put a bowl of candy on the table for us to eat. I ate all the candy in 15 minutes. I did not save any for Jeremy. He was upset because he did not get any.

Big-picture response: I need to try and leave some so that others can enjoy treats, too. Next time mom puts out candy, I will try to take a small amount and leave the rest so that my family can have some. This is a way I can be nice to them.

Ending with an affirmation: That way mom can say that not only am I smart but I am also polite.

Stories on a theme

If the child has a favorite topic such as Star Wars, Thomas the Train, vacuum cleaners or old cars, consider writing a series of stories using the favorite topic as a theme. These stories will have an extra appeal to the child and he may "get the message" a little faster. Here is a story about sharing with an underlying theme of Star Wars. It is a longer story and is written for a boy with Asperger Syndrome who has excellent verbal and comprehension skills.

Stars Wars with Angie

I like to pretend I'm Luke Skywalker. When my sister, Angie, asks to play with me, I let her play Princess Leia. We follow the script. I know all the parts by heart.

Yesterday, Angie said it was her turn to decide what to say. She used her own words and not the right words. I got upset. I screamed at her and went outside. Angie cried.

Dad said that I need to take turns with Angie. He said that making up new stories is fun and that I should pretend I'm George Lucas as I write it. He said that Angie and I could take turns play-acting our stories.

When I play with Angie, I will try to take turns with her. That is a way that I can be nice to her. Maybe we'll come up with a great story, and then dad will say that not only am I smart but I am also creative.

INTERVENTIONS: VIDEO MODELING

Video is a powerful medium for teaching children with autism skills and behaviors. In this section, we look at different approaches to using video with children with ASD.

Teaching the child functional skills

Mary Beth Palo, mother of a child with autism, created a novel video technique for teaching functional skills to her son. She uses the video camera to show the child's own view of a task. That means that the camera sees through the eyes of the child. The camera view moves as the child's head and eyes move, taking in the scene in front of him. The video clip shows hands performing a task but the rest of the body is not visible. A behind-the-scene narrator describes how to perform the steps.

This view is excellent for the child with autism who doesn't focus on instructions from his parents or teachers but loves to watch videos. Ms. Palo was able to teach her son skills involving dressing, eating, bathing, as well as safety rules and how to play with toys and games. As a side benefit, his language skills also improved.

Here is a script of medium complexity for a video showing how to make a bowl of cereal:

	Camera View	**Narrator's words**
1	A hand reaches out and opens a cupboard door. A box of cereal comes into view. The hand takes it off the shelf and places it on the counter.	"Open the cupboard, take out the cereal and put it on the counter."
2	Step one is repeated for the cereal bowl, milk and spoon in turn, until all are on the counter.	
3	Two hands open the box of cereal and pour it into the bowl.	"Open the cereal box and pour some into the bowl."
4	Two hands open the milk carton and pour some over the cereal.	"Open the milk carton and pour some into the bowl."
5	The hands put away the milk and the cereal.	"Put away the milk and the cereal."
6	The hands put the spoon into the bowl and then pick up the bowl.	"Put the spoon in the bowl and carry it to the table."
7	The hands and bowl move to the table and set the bowl down.	"Sit down."
8	The view of the table shifts downward (as the child seats himself).	
9	The hand picks up the spoon and brings it up to the camera (as if eating).	"Now you can eat your cereal."

For a video example of this technique, go to YouTube and search for my video, LightsOnTake2. My YouTube moniker is TGOTRL. It is relatively easy to put a video together. See the instructions in the next section. If you prefer to buy canned videos of common functional skills, you can do so at Ms. Palo's web site, WatchMeLearn.com.

Scripting a video of desired behavior

As children get older, the use of video can move from the instruction of functional skills to the demonstration of appropriate behavior such as social skills and how to ask for help in the classroom. You can continue to use the child-eye-view method described above for simple scenarios. However, when the child needs to learn to interact with others you will want to switch to scripted videos with actors.

Pick a topic: Target a single behavior. If you make the script too complex, the lesson might get lost on the child. Here are some sample ideas for topics and scripts:

1. Safety rules for crossing a street: hold Mom's hand, walk to the corner, look both ways, wait for cars, cross the street.

2. Leave the house: say goodbye, walk out the door, close the door, walk to the bus.

3. Find a seat on the bus: climb the steps, look for an empty seat, sit down.

4. The morning routine at school: hang up jacket, put away lunch, get work-folder, sit down.

5. Ask for help in the classroom: Have an actor (the student or a fellow-student) sit at a desk looking at a worksheet. He gets a puzzled look on his face, thinks for a few seconds, and then raises his hand. The teacher comes over and speaks with him. He nods his head in understanding and then continues his work.

For an older child, the videos of leaving the house and finding a seat on the bus could be joined together as a video about going to school.

Get signed waivers from the actors

In order to videotape with children, you must have signed permission from all actors and from the parents of all child actors. Waivers are often obtained by the school or clinic administration during the registration process, and you only have to be concerned with validating the signature. If the school or clinic does not have standard waivers, then a waiver must be created and the school or clinic's attorney needs to approve the waiver's language. Specify the circumstances for which the video is to be used, such as "For working with the child singly or in a group," or "For the education or training of others." There are multiple examples of video waiver forms online. To find them, do a search on "video waiver school."

Make a scripted video

I have laid out the steps for making a scripted video. If you have a simple script, you may be able to skip some of the steps.

Consider using the target child as the actor for his own film. He will get the benefit of practicing and acting the part, as well as watching it. However, find another actor if the child does not like to see himself on video

Steps in making the video:

1. Write out the script:
   a. Describe the location
   b. Identify props
   c. Identify acting roles
   d. Write up the action steps
   e. Write out each actor's speaking lines
   f. Determine the camera perspective or position for each scene
   g. Identify the device that will be used to show the video. If you are using older video equipment, be sure the device accepts and plays video from your camera.

2. Make plans:
   a. Find a shooting location with good light and room for the actors and the camera
   b. Identify actors
   c. Verify that the school or clinic has signed audio-video waivers for each actor
   d. Set a date for videotaping
   e. Gather the props.

3. Role-play the script, make corrections.

4. Videotape it!

If you have the time and energy to edit the video and make technical improvements, go for it. But rough videos work just fine. Send a copy of the video to a phone, tablet or computer that will be used for the showings.

Show the video to the child

Typically, you show the video to the child for about 10 days. At the end of that time he should be imitating what he has seen. Some children catch on more quickly, especially if they acted in the video. Save the video after the intervention is complete so that if the child regresses he can see it again for a few days.

Catch the child being good

Here is another approach: Make a video of the child when he is being good. Grab your video camera and catch the moment. Create a 2-3 minute clip. Now you have an excellent resource for teaching the child.

Other sources of clips

Before you go to the effort of creating a video, check to see if YouTube has a clip that suits your needs. YouTube has many such clips, including ones that show children getting their hair cut, visiting the doctor and eating new foods. You can also purchase canned video model clips from ModelMeKids.com.

Video and social skills

Make it a point to regularly create videos of a high-functioning child interacting with others. Show the child the videos so that he can acquire a sense of how he appears to others. As you watch the video with him, keep your comments about his behaviors upbeat and positive.

INTERVENTIONS: TRANSITIONS AND ENGAGEMENT

Children with ASD have executive-function impairments, especially their difficulty shifting cognitively from one thought, activity or plan to another. Asking a child with ASD to transition before she is ready can produce undesirable reactions. The therapist, teacher or parent may need to first gain her attention in order to stop her current activity. The next activity or process is explained, and the child is given time to process the information before the new activity is initiated.

Source: Therapy Shoppe

There are a number of techniques that can make transitions easier. Let's look at them.

Ways to give warning before moving to a new activity:

1. Use a visual schedule or a first-then board.
2. Use a timer (visual timers work best) to let the child know when it is time to move to the next activity.
3. Countdown: 5, 4, 3, 2, 1.
4. Count down very slowly when the child is playing hard: "Twen-ty, nine-teen, eight-teen . . . three, two, one."

How to signal that the activity is over:

You can train children to respond to cues. Here are some that work.

1. Ring a special bell.
2. Flick the lights.
3. Sing the cleanup song.
4. Clap hands in a rhythmic pattern.

Use an object of transition to move from one location to another:

1. Ask the child to help you carry something. A heavy object helps to calm her, and she will enjoy the opportunity to help you.
2. The child may select her own object of transition such as a favorite book or fidget. If it is a familiar object, it acts as a security blanket for her. Once in the new location, she must "park" the object by the doorway so that it is not distracting. When it is time to return to class, she takes the object with her.

3. If she is reluctant to leave the classroom, you could pick an object she likes and suggest that she bring it along with her. Have her set it down near the door when she gets there.

Have fun moving from location to location

1. Roller skate, ride a tricycle, use a scooter board, or bounce a ball to the next location.

2. Meet the child with a weighted ball and play catch from a short distance. With a small child, pass it carefully back and forth.

3. Sing a song (make one up) as you move from one place to the next.

Preparing for coming events and changes

Big changes—such as new outings, swim classes, getting ready for a new teacher or moving to a new house—call for serious planning. To ensure success you may want to make use of stories, photos, video, role-playing, drama skits and the internet as you help to prepare the child.

Examples:

1. A class outing to the zoo: Have the children look at the zoo's website. Are videos available? If not, create your own on a pre-trip visit. Make a list of the animals you plan to visit. Have the children find out about them in books and online searches. Consider making a video or story about the sights along the way to the zoo.

2. Changing to a new therapist or teacher: Put a picture of this new person on Mom's smart phone, the classroom bulletin board or the refrigerator at home. Better yet, have the new teacher or therapist make a short video saying *Hi* to the child (or to the class). Play it daily until the change takes place.

3. A new weekly activity such as swimming: Make a video of the route to the pool and of small children laughing and playing in the pool. Put the start-date of the class on the calendar. Create a story that explains the "when, what, where and what for" of the activity. Augment the story with pictures, especially if the child has poor reading skills.

Engaging a child

This is a fun technique devised by Dr. James MacDonald for getting the attention of children who are thoroughly engaged in their own world. Keep it playful and you will get attention and giggles.

Method:
1. Mimic whatever the child is doing, but playfully and with a smile on your face.
2. As the child notices you are copying her, she may react by moving away. Follow her, again playfully. You might try to change the pattern of her actions. For example, if she is moving her fingers in front of a light and watching shadows, try moving your fingers in different ways. See if she imitates you. Instead, she may do something completely different to see if you now copy her. Stay with her; she is looking at you and may break into giggles any second.
3. You have her attention. Allow the giggles to settle and then gently move her into the next activity.

INTERVENTIONS: WORKING WITH BEHAVIOR

Before you randomly try a technique for a problematic behavior such as hitting or tantrums, document what happened both immediately before and after the incident. You are trying to be a detective who determines the causes of the child's behaviors. Write down what you see. You want to collect information from several incidents to see if you can find patterns in the child's eruptions. Your goal is to identify triggers that set off the child's behavior, and you want to determine if the child is unintentionally being rewarded for bad behavior. When you can find these triggers and responses, you will know what to work on to eliminate the inappropriate behaviors. Three types of observations can be made for each incident:

1. Antecedent (or trigger): What happened before the behavior occurred. Here are two common triggers.
   a. The child is unable to wait patiently for what she wants.
   b. Desire for escape from the current task or the environment.
2. Behavior: The child's response or reaction. Here are some example behaviors:
   a. Hitting
   b. Self-injury
   c. Meltdown or tantrum
   d. Elopement (child runs off without permission)
   e. Hyperactive behavior
   f. Unresponsiveness, shutting down.
3. Consequences: What happened as a result of the child's behavior? Was the child rewarded, punished or ignored? Here is an example: Tony is shopping with his mother. He sees an action- figure he wants. His mother says *no;* they are shopping for groceries, not toys. He tantrums and will not stop. Here are ways she might respond:
   a. She acts neutral, takes his hand and leaves the store.
   b. She buys him the toy to get him to be quiet.
   c. She picks him up, cuddles him and whispers that he needs to stop screaming, thereby rewarding him with attention.
   d. She tells him he will lose a privilege if he doesn't stop.
   e. She gives him a light swat on his behind and tells him to stop.

After several incidents are observed in the same child, look for patterns that help to determine the triggers for the behavior. The pattern may suggest that the child is being rewarded (most likely inadvertently) when he acts out. For example, if every time a child hits someone he is removed from the room, consider whether escaping from the room was the child's goal. Now you have the triggers, you can try to eliminate them. In the next section we look at ways to change behaviors that can be triggered.

With a non-verbal child, we may have more work to do. We need to see if something in the setting made the child want to escape. This involves more detective work as we look for possible irritants in the environment (loud noises, bright lights, and so on) or in his body (a toothache or hunger, for example). A behavior plan is not going to help a child with an unmet physical or emotional need; we need to address his issue. However, we may be able to help his find ways to communicate his needs without him resorting to act-out behaviors.

This process can be challenging, and you may need the help of a behavioral therapist to sort it out.

Eliminating or replacing repetitive behaviors

Repetitive or ritual behavior is a common symptom of ASD. Some children "stim" on sensory input such as rubbing or shaking an object, others line up things such as shoes or kitchen utensils, and still others create new act-out behaviors such as biting on their arm in reaction to events around them. Eliminating a child's repetitive behaviors is difficult, yet some techniques can help in many situations. The most reliable way to eliminate a behavior is to replace it with a new benign or functional behavior. In this section, we examine a variety of ways to reduce, replace or eliminate repetitive behaviors. We start first by looking at harmless behaviors. This is followed by a technique to minimize hand flapping. Next, four case studies are evaluated. These four cases make use of a combination of techniques—from behavior therapy, play therapy and occupational therapy—to replace difficult repetitive behaviors in children.

Harmless behaviors

Some behaviors are harmless and should be left alone. Think of the girl who fiddles with her hair. If her mother tells her to stop, the girl may comply but her fidgeting could reappear as a different habit. That new habit can't be predicted and could be worse than the original. While the general rule is to leave harmless habits alone, one might attempt to replace a child's fidgeting behavior with another less distracting behavior. For example, an attempt could be made to replace chewing on one's fingers with chewing a chewable (food-safe) bracelet (see p. 75 on fidgets). If it appears that anxiety is part of the girl's problem, she can be persuaded or taught to engage on a regular basis in stress-reduction activities such as yoga, martial arts or meditation, all of which help to calm mind and body.

Hand flapping

Hand flapping is a special case of repetitive behaviors. It is a reaction to intense emotions such as excitement or fear. A child who flaps his hands typically does so as an alternative to expressing the emotions that do not register on his face. Some parents teach their children to clench their fists or push their palms together (as they would with isometric exercise) as a replacement activity. In this case, the children are trained to do the replacement behavior over an extended period. A child can practice the new hand movements in front of a mirror so that he can fine-tune them. As a way of spontaneous role-playing, a therapist or parent can try to trigger hand-flapping by surprising the child with fun events and jokes and then reminding him to use his new hand movements. Parents can also set up a silent reminder, such as a special signal, to be used when they see their son flapping his hands in public. As a child becomes more conscious of his hand movements and how they are perceived by others, he learns to catch himself and express the urge in a less conspicuous way.

Four case studies and techniques

Sometimes a child's repetitive behavior is directly linked to his lack of communication, play skills or functional skills. When the child learns to effectively communicate needs, play with toys, and perform functional tasks, he is less inclined to perform repetitive behaviors. The following case studies outline several effective methods for replacing repetitive and ritual behaviors.

Case 1 – Nate: Teaching a new skill using modeling and rewards

Nate "stims" by twiddling a crayon in his hand while watching the crayon's movement. He picks up crayons and shakes them, but he does not hold the crayons correctly or make an attempt to use them for drawing. His parents want to encourage appropriate hand usage in the hope that, once he learns interesting things to do with his hands, he will no longer stim on objects. Techniques from behavior therapy can help him to use the crayons purposefully.

Planning the intervention

His therapist plans to make use of classic behavioral methods to teach Nate. First, she models what she wants him to do and then gives him a small reward when he does it. Typically, a child needs multiple training sessions (multiple trials) to learn a new skill. If parents intend to perform the training sessions themselves, they will need to plan breaks in their day to allow for the training. Perhaps mom does the training at 7:30 a.m., 9 a.m., and 6 p.m., while dad does it at 12:30 p.m. and 7:30 p.m.

Rewarding the child

The types of rewards used are:

1. **Social rewards** such as tickles or hugs. Social rewards are especially effective and help the child to develop a socio-emotional response.
2. **Primary rewards** such as small pieces of food. Therapists typically use raisins, M&Ms or a bit of granola bar.
3. **Secondary rewards** such as a small toy to play with like a building block. These are used in formal Applied Behavioral Analysis therapy (ABA) settings in which the child is working for multiple hours at a time with play breaks scattered throughout. The child earns interesting parts of a toy set (such as a building block) to play with during the work sessions.

Steps in the behavior method

There are multiple steps in the process of teaching a functional skill. The steps are listed in order below, along with examples of the procedure. The child will stay on a particular step until he is able to successfully perform the task.

1. **Model the replacement behavior**. Demonstrate picking up a crayon and say, "Nate, pick up the crayon."
2. **Teach him to do the replacement behavior using hand-over-hand instruction**. Help Nate pick up the crayon and then say, "Good boy," and give him a tickle or hug.

3. **Remind him to perform the new skill with a physical cue**. Move Nate's hand toward the crayon and say to him, "Pick up the crayon." Give him a reward when he does it.

4. **Remind him with a verbal cue to perform the new skill**. This time, simply remind him to pick up the crayon and reward him when he does it.

5. **He performs the new behavior independently**. Nate comes to the table, sees the crayon and picks it up. Reward him for this and continue with the next step which could be to scribble or draw a line with the crayon.

This method requires that parents work with the child multiple times throughout the day, for multiple days in a row. They need to firmly establish a schedule for the intervention (i.e., set alarms in their phones). Consistent practice speeds the rate of success.

Case 2 – Antwan: Replacing a triggered behavior

Antwan is a child who lines up toys and other objects. He has better fine motor skills than Nate, but he lacks functional play skills. Antwan's behavior can be triggered by piling small cars in front of him on a table. When he sees the cars, he lines them up. His mother is frantic. She is delayed getting him out of the house in the morning because he is preoccupied in this activity.

Triggered behaviors

Research has shown that behaviors which can be consistently triggered by an external event are the easiest to eliminate. When you can trigger a behavior, you have a better opportunity to teach a new skill and to reward the child for learning that skill. Boyd, McDonough and Bodfish (2012) developed an intervention strategy that marries behavior therapy with play and occupational therapy for use in this scenario. With this strategy, the child is taught a functional skill, using a reward-based system, to replace the current behavior. Boyd, et al created a 12-week course for parents that taught them how to determine the driver of repetitive behaviors (why the behaviors are rewarding), how to select a functional replacement for a given repetitive behavior, and how to use both behavioral and play techniques to help the child learn the new skill.

Let's look at the details of this strategy as adopted for Antwan: In Antwan's case, he lines up toys instead of playing with them, and so a combination of behavior therapy and play therapy can be used as an intervention. His therapist and parents discuss which new skills to focus on with him.

Repetitive behavior: Antwan lines up or stacks shoes, books, toys, kitchen utensils, and so on.

Drivers of the behavior: He is triggered by the sight of a collection of objects.

Functional replacement: Antwan's mother thinks he would excel as a stock boy, and she suggests that he could help her organize her cupboards. His father thinks Antwan might be a builder someday, given his propensity to put things together. "How about building blocks," he says. They discuss the idea of teaching Antwan to create buildings and vehicles with LEGO® kits as a replacement for his repetitive behavior. His mother asks if they aren't creating a new problem in which Antwan will obsess on playing with LEGOs. The therapist says this could happen, and he describes how to use visual schedules, visual timers and stories to create the rules and structure for playtime.

Steps of the procedure

Antwan's parents follow the steps outlined for Nate (see Case 1) to help Antwan learn to play with the pieces. They need to first trigger the behavior. The first session or two might look like this:

1. **Trigger the behavior.** Dad puts some LEGO bricks on the floor. Antwan lines them up.
2. **Model the replacement behavior.** Dad demonstrates how to connect two bricks and says, "Look, Antwan, put the bricks together."
3. **Teach him to do the replacement behavior using hand-over-hand.** Dad then takes Antwan's hand and helps him to put two bricks together. "Good boy!" He gives him a hug. They do this a few more times.
4. **Give him a physical cue.** Dad puts the bricks on the table and gives Antwan's hand a nudge toward the bricks, saying, "Put them together." When he does, he's given a reward.

They continue on through the steps over multiple sittings. Mom and dad are taking turns with the effort so they can meet the demands of 4-5 training sessions a day. Once the initial skill of brick building has been learned, dad moves into a bit of play therapy. He shows Antwan a picture of a simple LEGO structure, tells Antwan that he is going to build it and does so, asking for Antwan's help every so often. Alternately, if Antwan is building a long row of bricks, dad can ask if he can help. In this way, dad builds their relationship and encourages cooperative play. Over time, Antwan develops a new way of occupying his time along with play skills and a deeper relationship with mom and dad.

Case 3 – Robin: Sensory stimming replaced with an appropriate fidget or game

Robin runs to the bathroom and plays with the water in the toilet whenever she gets the chance. Her behavior is triggered by the sight of the toilet and so she is a candidate for an intervention similar to Antwan's. Her parents could replace playing in the water with a fidget that she plays with instead. The new scenario goes like this: when she needs to go to the bathroom, they give her the fidget. Her parents are not keen on having her play with a fidget while using the toilet. They want her to have access to the fidget after she has used the toilet and washed her hands. This preferred sequence is challenging to implement because she must wait to get her reward. Since Robin is an impulsive child, her therapist has suggested starting with the first method (Robin gets the fidget when she goes to the bathroom) in order to break her habit of playing in water. Later, she is trained to wait for the reward until she has washed her hands. The case details follow:

Repetitive behavior: Robin is fascinated by water and will play in it whenever she sees it, including water in toilet bowls.

Drivers of the behavior: Water has several sensations: it is sparkly as it moves in the light, it feels pleasant to the skin, and it makes a gurgling noise. To determine the driver of Robin's behavior, her therapist ran a few experiments. First, he investigated tactile (touch) sensation. He let Robin play with a small dish of scent-free lotion and later in a bin of sand. While she liked both activities, she was not driven by them. Next he played music clips of a gurgling river and a running faucet. When she heard the sound of water, she turned her head to see it and was disappointed that real water was not present. Finally, the therapist let her play with a bead ring (see image). She was immediately captivated by it. The therapist deduced that the driver for Robin's behavior is visual: She likes to see the sparkle of splashing water.

The two-step solution:

1. Robin's parents purchased a few fidgets and rewarded her with the bead ring when she refrained from playing in the water (using the method described in case 1).

2. Next they placed the bead ring and several snow globes they found in resale shops on a small shelf in the bathroom. They took three photos (the toilet, the sink with running water, and a composite photo of the bead ring along with a snow globe and a visual timer set for five minutes).

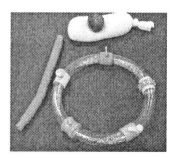

They made a simple visual schedule of the three photos and mounted the schedule on the bathroom wall. The schedule reinforces what Robin is told each time she uses the bathroom: she can play with the bead ring or a globe once she has flushed the toilet and washed her hands. Her parents use social rewards to implement the three-step schedule.

When Robin uses the bathroom, her mother points to the picture of the toilet on the visual schedule and asks her, "What do you do first?" Mom prompts Robin to say, "Toilet." Mom gives Robin a social reward (tickle or hug.) Once she has used the toilet, mom points to the photo of the sink and asks, "Now what do you do?" Mom prompts her to say, "Wash hands." That is again followed with a tickle or hug. Finally, mom asks, "Now what can you do?" Mom prompts her to say, "Play," and then asks Robin to point to the object (bead ring or globe) that she wants to play with. Mom sets a visual timer to five minutes and lets her play. When five minutes are up, Robin gives up the bead ring or globe.

The therapist tells the parents they can make use of Robin's craving for visual stimulation to reward her and to teach her new skills. Because Robin is so fascinated by visual input, she most likely will show better attention when rules and lesson material are presented in this manner.

Case 4 – Emilio: Triggered self-injury

Emilio had been seeing Ms. Anne for speech therapy for some time, and he enjoyed his sessions with her. However, Ms. Anne recently went on a two-month maternity leave and he now sees Ms. Peggy who he dislikes. When his mom says, "Emilio, put on your coat, we're going to see Ms. Peggy," he looks at her and begins pulling out eyebrow hairs. She reacts with a look of horror and tells him to stop. He has done this regularly for several weeks. She understands that his behavior is triggered by the trips to the clinic. But she doesn't know how to stop this cycle and worries that he may be developing a new habit that will spread to other areas.

As mentioned, any behavior that can be consistently triggered by an external event is especially amenable for elimination. Emilio's behavior is triggered when his mother tells him it is time for speech therapy. Obviously, Emilio is trying to communicate to his mother that he is distressed in those sessions with Ms. Peggy. His mother has acknowledged his self-damaging behavior with her expression of horror, but this is not solving the problem. It just rewards him for getting an intense reaction out of her.

How best can his mother respond to help Emilio change his behavior?

1. First, she can do her best to stop reacting emotionally when he pulls out eyebrow hairs. Her reaction presents him with a negative reward, and it fails to acknowledge his fear or anxiety. She needs to acknowledge to Emilio that she understands that he doesn't like Ms. Peggy. If he were verbal, she could let him speak or attempt to speak about these feelings without being judgmental of them. Since he is not verbal, she can put together a story with words, pictures and emoticons that describes the situation, his reaction to it, her perception of his feelings and how he can use the method below to express his emotions without pulling out eyebrow hairs.

2. She can try to replace his self-injurious behavior with a benign one so that he has a way to communicate with her without self-injury. This might involve a two-step procedure:

   a. She puts a loose-fitting rubber band or elastic bracelet on Emilio's wrist. Next, she uses the method (described in case 1) to replace one behavior with another. Emilio's self-injury is replaced with a mild stinging of himself by snapping the elastic. If Emilio has other act-out behaviors, she might try to replace them with the elastic as well.

   b. His mother does not want him to feel even a sting. Once he is using the elastic independently she can (with the help of a speech pathologist, play therapist or psychologist) replace the rubber band with communication or relationship skills.

CHAPTER 2

Staying Calm and Alert

What is driving negative or self-defeating behaviors when a child is acting out? These behaviors could be caused by many things: something someone said, tight socks, the memory of a fearful situation, fatigue or something the child ate. It might also be several such factors acting together.

Our ability to self-calm depends on the resilience of our nervous system. We begin this chapter with an introduction to Polyvagal Theory, Dr. Stephen Porges' theory of how the nervous system works. We then look at interventions that can be used as part of a child's daily routine to help develop and maintain a well-regulated nervous system that supports the child in a calm and alert state. The last section of the chapter describes a simple technique to teach poorly modulated children how to monitor and regulate their physiological, social, mental and emotional states.

The diagram below shows the components of the social-exchange: facial muscles, heart, organs, portions of the limbic system (in the brain), and myelinated fibers of the vagal nerve. The social-exchange system receives information from the senses and emotions.

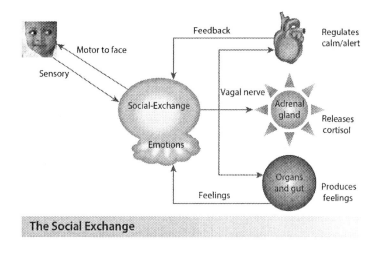

The Social Exchange

POLYVAGAL THEORY AND THE NERVOUS SYSTEM

A steady set of nerves is essential for a child to keep a calm demeanor in the face of change, social situations, and tribulations. In this chapter, we look at what is involved in getting the nervous system to regulate itself.

One of our nervous system's most important functions is to keep us safe. It responds to danger signals picked up by our senses and instructs the brain and body to either freeze, go into a fight-flight pattern, or use social skills to get out of the situation. Our most primal response is to freeze like a deer in the headlights. As our body freezes in alarm, our systems shut down. This is obviously not a healthy response. In our next level of response—the fight-flight pattern— adrenaline is pumped through our body, our heart speeds up and our organs slow down, diverting energy to our arms and legs for fighting or running. Our most evolved response involves interacting with other people using speech, facial expressions and body gestures. As we interact with others, our organs continue to work, our heart beats calmly and our face is responsive. This is a healthy response and offers the best opportunity to think clearly as we react to a situation.

Polyvagal theory is based on these features of nervous system activity. The theory, proposed in the 1990s by psycho-physiologist Stephen Porges, describes how our nervous system works anatomically, physiologically and behaviorally. Most aspects of the theory have been scientifically validated. The most interesting aspects of the theory involve the social response, what Porges calls the *social exchange*. We look at that here, but first let's consider an interesting scenario.

Adele's friends have thrown a surprise birthday party for her. Everyone is waiting as she walks in the door. Here is her nervous system's response as she hears, "Surprise!"

Nervous system's response	Senses	Her response
Neutral		She walks into her house.
	She hears shouts and sees a large group of people in what should have been an empty room.	She registers alarm.
Freeze		Her nervous system gives the command to freeze. She stops breathing. Her eyebrows lift, her mouth opens, then movement stops. Her middle ears open to listen for more sounds.
Fight-flight		Within a split-second, freeze is abated as fight-flight takes over. Her heart speeds up and her gut clenches. Her adrenals emit cortisol and her palms get slightly moist. She gets ready to run.
	She looks in the direction of the shouts and sees friends.	Her face which is once again mobile quickly expresses surprise.
Mixed fight-flight and social exchange		Almost immediately, the surprise turns to joy with recognition and engages the social-exchange system as it does. Her heart slows down and she begins to feel calmer. Her gut relaxes and continues to process food.
Social exchange		Her face is animated as she chats with her friends. Her heart, lungs and gut are relaxed and doing their jobs.

Developing the social exchange

Porges claims that the three subsystems—freeze, fight-flight, and social exchange—work together rather than in on-off states. Our nervous system's default mode is fight-flight, so when social exchange is activated it inhibits or puts the brakes on fight-flight. For the most part, we end up with gradations between fight-flight reactions and social-exchange reactions. For an example of how the mixture of the two works, look at the birthday-party surprise scene above and consider that split-second when Adele realizes she is the recipient of a surprise party. Her alarm turns to shock, then she feels joy, and moments later she is experiencing a pleasing, calm interaction with friends.

We learn how to respond to life's uncertainties and dangers based on our own ability to calm ourselves and the ability of our caregivers to stay calm. Those response patterns are hard-coded in our nervous system at an early age and are difficult to change. They affect our ability to handle stress and changing situations, along with our ability to interact with others (Porges, 2008). A skittish child who is asked to read in front of a group tends to go into fight-flight, whereas another child who is comfortable with her peers will instead react calmly. It is apparent that children with autism, sensory sensitivities or ADHD, who are all susceptible to increased anxiety, will not adapt optimally and easily revert to a fight-flight strategy in times of stress (Porges, 2008; Schaaf, et al, 2010). They are also at risk for health problems due to lengthy periods of intense heart rate and knotted stomachs.

A deeper look at social exchange

The social-exchange system relies heavily on the hard-wired connections between the face and heart. When you move your facial muscles to express emotion or to speak, the movement sparks a signal to the heart to regulate itself to match the face's expression. If the facial movement is a smile, the brain recognizes a safe situation and inhibits or puts the break on fight-flight. The heart and organs can now operate in a slow, well-regulated manner. If a threat is perceived, the fight-flight system is quickly engaged, the face expresses shock, and social exchange releases the fight-flight brake. The heart pumps faster, and organs are shut down to allow energy to move to the arms and legs.

All the components in the social exchange are connected in a feedback mode and interact with one another (see diagram). When the heart is beating calmly, the face is freer to smile. When the body is in fight-flight mode, the face displays tension or anxiety, and the person who tries to keep that expression off his face has to work hard to do so (Porges, 2008).

Sensory and hyper-vigilance

Children with sensory sensitivities who recoil from sound, touch, smell or taste often operate out of a hyper-vigilant mode. Here are two examples of two children with auditory and tactile (touch) sensitivities at a party.

1. Cory is eight. He has been "holding it together" at the birthday party through the screaming and bumping of other kids. But when one kid too many bumps into him, he turns to the child, punches him in the arm and screams, "You hit me!" His fight-flight reaction overrides his social-exchange response. Why is that? His sensory system put him

into a hyper-vigilant state because of the crowding. His body signals told him he was being threatened, and he responded accordingly.

2. Tamara is 10 and is doing her best to have a good time at the noisy, crowded party. After 30 minutes, she has difficulty coping, finds a chair in a corner, picks up a picture book and shuts down her social self while she looks at the book. This is, in fact, a good strategy because it provides her with time to recuperate.

It is important that children with sensory issues learn to navigate gracefully through the world of sound, touch, smell, taste, light and movement. We can teach children about their sensory self and how to honor the limitations of their senses. Teachers and therapists can gradually give them new challenges, exposing them to longer or more intense stimulation. We can also give them social strategies that allow them to participate in fun activities for brief periods before bowing out. For example, Cory may be able to say to the host that, although he has been looking forward to the event, he would only be able to stay for a short while.

The social exchange and autism

Children with a flat affect due to autism will have difficulty developing a social-exchange system. Without fluid facial movement, the remaining parts of the social-exchange system (heart, gastric system, pancreas, the hypothalamus-pituitary axis, as well as brain cortical processes) miss out on crucial feedback. Regulation will be compromised or disabled in all of those areas, potentially causing health issues. Early intervention in the form of games with smiles and giggles are important, no matter how simple the games. For example, if a child with autism doesn't share smiles with his mother but giggles when he sees his toe, his mother can make games of showing him his toe as a way of encouraging emotional expression and joint attention (Porges, 1993). Other methods for children with autism include prosody (sing-song speaking), singing, drama and breathing. We look at them next, along with standard interventions such as stress reduction and teaching to imitate.

How to encourage growth of the social exchange

Although the nervous system is set at an early age, Porges speculates that we can create a "fourth paradigm" for our nervous system by actively performing stress reduction and other activities. The following approaches can strengthen the child's social exchange.

1. Teach the child to use internal prosody (sing-song self-talk) and to use it often. This self-soothing provides input to the nervous system. For example, teach the child to self-soothe with words like, "I'm okay. He didn't mean to hit me, he was just running too fast to stop."

2. Conduct plenty of stress-reduction activities. These usually involve movement or soft sounds but can include meditation, drama and the arts as the child matures.

3. Have the child learn breathing exercises. The breath aspect of yoga can be included after the age of seven. Teach the child to play a wind instrument. A young child can play whistles, kazoos and harmonicas. Develop this talent so that it provides the cardio-vascular support that is used by the social-exchange system.

4. Encourage expressive singing that can help the face and heart to strengthen connections.

5. Try role-playing alternative responses to difficult social situations. The intention is to reinforce new socially acceptable responses that become engrained behaviors and override the impulse to fight-or-flight.

CALMING AND ALERTING TECHNIQUES

This section provides a wide variety of calming and alerting techniques. We first look at simple ways to quiet a child. Following that are fun ways for the child to get on-the-spot or long-term regulation. Our focus in the interventions below is on calming, but remember that most of these techniques are designed for simultaneous calming and alerting.

The basics: Let's calm down

Here are classic recipes for calming an overwrought child.

Amount of time: 5-15 minutes

Materials: A mat or a cushion, soft music, weighted blanket, therapy ball or pillow

Quiet time
Have the child lie on a mat or a cushion. Turn the lights low. Put on soft, calming music. Speak in a soft low voice or just remain quiet.

Resting with a weighted blanket

Quiet time with deep pressure

Deep pressure pulls energy out of the muscles and helps calm the body. Try any of these methods to soothe a tantrum. Lower the lights and add soft music for a larger effect.

- Cover child with a weighted blanket.
- Roll a therapy ball slowly up and down the child's back as she lies on a mat or carpeting.
- Gently squeeze shoulders and arms.
- Gently rock the child in your arms or in a chair.
- Swing gently in a platform swing or a Lycra™ (pocket) swing.

The hotdog

Tell the child he is a hotdog and you are going to put him in a bun and add catsup, mustard and relish. Have him lie on a soft cushion. As you roll a ball over him say, "Here's the mustard, here's the catsup, here's the relish." While saying, "here's the bun," press a ball or pillow on the child with deep pressure.

The burrito

Instead of a hotdog, the child becomes a burrito. Have her lie on a yoga mat or folded blanket. Speak aloud as you put on the imaginary toppings: "Salsa, cheese, meat, beans, lettuce." Then wrap the blanket or yoga mat around the child (head sticking out) with enough pressure to give the child a good hug. Hold it for a few seconds or until the child has calmed.

The basics: Timeouts

Classroom timeout

A timeout for the entire class is the teacher's old standby. Give the class a few minutes to settle after a movement activity or game or when less-regulated children in the class get overly excited.

Amount of time: 2 minutes

Method:
Have the children sit down with feet on the floor, heads resting on their arms on their desks (or if necessary, hands flat on their laps and heads on desks). No talking is permitted. Turn down the lights and put on calm music for two minutes of uninterrupted silence.

The mind jar

Here is a pleasant timeout for a child as she watches glitter settle in a jar for a minute or so.

Materials: Glycerin, clear dish soap, multiple colors of glitter, a small jar.

Amount of time: 1-2 minutes

Make the mind jar
1. Fill a small jar, half-and-half, with glycerin and dish soap. This will create a 2-5 minute descent time for the glitter. Other proportions of glycerin and soap will work. The greater the amount of dish soap, the faster the glitter will descend. Using just one tablespoon of dish soap in a small jar of glycerin creates a 15-20 minute descent.
2. Start with 2-3 tablespoons of glitter. Add more to the jar if desired.
3. Cap the jar tight and keep it on a protective plate. (If it leaks on wood, it will leave a stain.)

To use the jar
1. Turn the jar upside down and rock it gently. Once the glitter has spread through the glycerin, it will slowly drift back to the bottom.
2. Have the child sit quietly, no talking, as she watches the glitter descend.

The mind jar app

The mind jar can travel anywhere an iPod can, using the Mind Jar app from Wisdom Publications. You can find it at iTunes for free.

The basics: Breathing

Calm Breathing

This method is useful for children who are angry or having a tantrum. There are additional breathing techniques later in this chapter.

Amount of time: 1-2 minutes

Method:
1. Have the child put her hand on her belly.
2. Breathe in through the nose, counting to four. Feel the belly rise.
3. Hold the breath for a second or two.
4. Breathe out through the mouth, counting to five or longer. Feel the belly fall.
5. Repeat a few times, until the child has calmed.

Calm focus

This method is a quick exercise for re-focusing. It comes from Mary Jaksch (2011).

Setting: Room with a window

Amount of time: 1-2 minutes

Method:
1. Walk to a window. Look out as far in the distance as possible.
2. Take one slow, deep breath.

The basics: Massage

Massage: Infant

Massaging is an effective way to help a baby to calm down and sleep. There are a number of infant massage videos available. This massage makes use of Dr. Jane Forester's method in Parent's Magazine.

Materials: A teaspoon of grape-seed or sesame oil, computer or tablet, massage video instructions at http://www.parents.com/baby/care/newborn/how-to-massage-baby/

Setting: Put the baby on a blanket in a quiet place

When/How often: When he is alert at bedtime or when he needs extra soothing

Amount of time: A few minutes

Method:
1. Watch the Parents magazine video (see link above) to observe the technique.
2. Print out the massage instructions for a reference.
3. Sit on the floor with your legs in a diamond shape, feet together. Drape a blanket over your legs and feet.
4. Undress the baby and put him on the blanket.
5. Gently touch head, then toes. If the baby does not resist, continue with the massage.
6. Massage the baby's tummy, head, face, chest, arms, back and legs with the tips of your fingers for 10-30 minutes according to the instructions.

Loofah massage

A parent can massage their child with a loofah mitt or sponge in or out of the bathtub. The older child can do her own massage in the shower or bathtub. Loofah brushes can be purchased in drug stores or stores that sell skin-care products. If the child finds the loofah sponge irritating, soak it for an hour or so and then dry it. Or try a mitt instead.

Materials: A loofah mitt (preferable) or sponge

Setting: Quiet, private space such as a bathroom

When/How often: Everyday

Amount of time: 5 minutes

Method:
Use the loofah mitt or sponge on bare skin. Scrub firmly so the loofah flattens somewhat from the pressure, but take your cue from what the child can tolerate. You can do these steps in any order.

1. Before using the loofah, soak it for a minute or two to soften it.
2. Rub the loofah up and down the child's bare arm with pressure.
3. Rub up and down and side-to-side on the back.
4. Rub the bottoms of the legs slowly, as with the arms. The child can do upper legs if she desires.
5. Wash out the loofah with soapy water and let it dry thoroughly to prevent molding. Replace the loofah as needed.

Qigong massage

Louisa Silva, M. D., has developed a technique to help increase sensory regulation and overall function in young children with autism and poor sensory modulation. Her extensive published research shows that a 15-minute qigong (pronounced chi gong) massage significantly improves sensory modulation, self-calming, social skills, and bowel and bladder control.

Parents massage their child in the proscribed manner for 15 minutes before bedtime. This program is done for five months.

Dr. Silva teaches the qigong technique in a workshop setting for those who have experience working with children with autism. Parents can optionally learn the technique from her book, *Qigong Massage for Your Child with Autism*. An accompanying DVD shows the technique. Her web site is QSTI.org.

INTERVENTIONS: HEAVY WORK AND PLAY

A steady diet of heavy work, physical play, exercise and deep pressure is an effective way to keep a child calm and alert. Heavy work is also effective as an on-the-spot intervention when a child is having a difficult day. See the section on movement in the chapter on sensory modulation for more ideas (p. 77). Here is an example of one child's day.

Example of calming with heavy work
1. He starts out in the morning with jumping on a small trampoline.
2. He then walks to school wearing a backpack that weighs no more than 10% of his body weight.
3. At mid-morning, he takes part in a class movement break.
4. He plays during the recess after lunch.
5. He joins in another class movement break in mid-afternoon.
6. He walks home wearing the backpack. After a snack and outside play, he does his homework and then 15 minutes of chores.
7. He does 10 minutes of yoga before bed.

Play heavy ball

Playing with a heavy ball is a quick way to settle a child of any age. I have done this with children with autism as young as 2 ½ years, and they love it. As a bonus, the child with autism learns a functional hand skill.

With small children, use your hands to help them form their hands into a bowl. Help them shape their hands to hold the ball; do not hold the weight of the ball for them. This game, by the way, is perfect for a small office area.

Setting: This works in a small space like an office

When/How often: During transition or as needed

Amount of time: 2-3 minutes

Materials: A variety of weighted balls: weights of one, two, four, six, eight and 10 pounds should cover your needs with children ages 2 ½-12. I prefer small balls, like those shown in the illustration, because the child can manage the ball easier. Therapy catalogs are a good source for the balls. (See resources list)

Method:
1. Select the ball weight as follows: The ball should weigh him down when he catches it, but he should be able to manage the ball without falling. Age 2-3: Use a one or two-pound ball. Adolescent: Try a 10-pound ball.
2. Play catch for 2-3 minutes.

Group variation

Do this in a group of children using multiple balls if necessary: one ball per eight children. This is calming for children who have become over-stimulated with play or movement.

Body sock

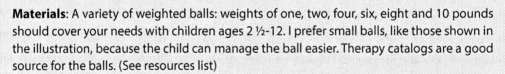

Children get plenty of fun and heavy work inside a body sock. Look for a body sock made of heavy Lycra™. They come in a variety of sizes.

Setting: Anywhere

When/How often: When the child shows signs of decreased modulation. Up to every 2 hours

Amount of time: 10 minutes

Method:
1. Set up the environment so the child has room to move about safely.
2. Have her put on the body suit and stretch as she moves.

Isometric stretch at school

This is a way for an older child to get calming while not drawing attention from others. The method can also be used as a replacement behavior for a child with autism who flaps his hands. Teach this to him while he is calm and remind him to use it when he gets excited.

Method:
1. Extend the arms with hands facing outward.
2. Cross the arms at the wrists.
3. Lace the fingers with palms facing each other.
4. Move arms straight down in front of the belly with knuckles pointing at the floor.
5. Cross the legs.
6. Squeeze shoulders, arms, hips and legs, and hold this position for a minute or so.
7. Reverse limbs and hold again.
8. This technique can also be done with arms behind the back.

MeMoves™

MeMoves™ is a multisensory interactive DVD demonstrating gentle rhythmic movement. The gentle exercises help to create a calm-alert state. Children can perform a 5-10 minute MeMoves™ routine in the classroom as part of a daily movement break. In a one-on-one setting, it could be used to increase attention prior to a difficult task.

There is some evidence that MeMoves™ can cause positive behavioral changes and activate the mirror neurons in children with autism. The product can be purchased at ThinkingMoves.com. Check out the videos on that site to see a sample movement routine.

INTERVENTIONS: BREATHING TECHNIQUES

Techniques for calm breathing are on p. 32. Here are additional techniques to help improve breathing and to reduce anxiety.

Melting

Try this with a child as a way to dissolve leftover anxiety.

Amount of time: 1-2 minutes

Method:
1. Have the child focus on the top of his head and imagine that a pool of warm, syrupy liquid is sitting there.
2. Tell him to let the liquid slowly move down his head and face and over his shoulders.
3. Does he feel calmer? Where is it calmer? (He should notice relaxation in the face, neck, and shoulders.)
4. Repeat this a few times.

Breathing into the back

There exists a vicious circle involving poor core strength and incomplete breath inhalation. Proper breathing helps keep the back firm. If the lungs do not fill to the back, then back muscles do not get exercised, and they become weak. When back muscles are weak, we do not breathe deeply enough to fill the back portions of the lungs.

This simple yet powerful morning exercise can help break that cycle. The exercise can help improve posture and breathing as well as decrease anxiety. This exercise is different from ones that focus on filling lungs deeply into the abdomen. In this exercise, the child consciously breathes into the back.

Setting: To be done at home

When/How often: Every morning

Amount of time: 5 minutes

Method:
Focused breathing can be alerting, and so it is best done in the morning.

1. Put a small piece of tape as a marker between the child's shoulder blades over the top of the spine. The tape should be about one inch above the bottom of the shoulder blade.
2. Have her lie on a bed or other padded flat surface with a pillow under her head.
3. Tell her to breathe so that she feels her breath expanding against the tape.
4. Do this for five minutes.

Method for teens

Once the method is understood, a teenager can do the above method while sitting with the back supported.

Method:
1. Have the child sit in a chair.
2. Tell her to keep her spine still by keeping the back neck muscles and pelvis muscles rigid as she breathes.
3. Breathe at a normal rate, deeply into the back.

Learning to breathe into the belly

Some children (and adults) breath from the chest. This shallow breathing is inefficient. At worst, it can contribute to anxiety and panic attacks. The best practice is to breathe deeply into the lungs, extending the abdomen and pushing out the belly in the process.

Setting: Anywhere

When/How often: Daily

Amount of time: 5 minutes

Method:
1. Have the child place one hand on his chest and the other on his belly.
2. As he breathes, he notices how his hands move. The hand on his belly should move the most.
3. Time the inhale and exhale so the exhale lasts longer than the inhale by a second or two.

Chest-breathing for teens

Here is an even better way to deepen one's breathing. It is a bit complicated, so use this procedure for older children. Be sure that the child is not wearing a tight elastic belt at the waist that might restrict good breathing.

Age: Adolescent or teen

When/How often: 3 times per day

Amount of time: A few minutes

Method:
1. Have the child put his hand on his belly and the other on his chest.
2. Tell him to breathe through his nose into his belly, extending the lower abdomen. The hand moves as the belly fills up. He should inhale slowly for 3-4 seconds and then exhale for 4-6 seconds.
3. As he breathes, he notices how his hands move. The hand on his belly should move the most.

INTERVENTIONS: STRETCHING AND YOGA

Yoga can be highly effective as a calming method for a hyperactive child or for a child who is too wound up to go to bed. It takes only a few minutes of work to pull the energy out of wiggly arms and legs and to calm the child in the process.

Daytime yoga

Setting: A quiet space

Group/Individual: Either

When/How often: In the morning or as a break. Wait 30 minutes after a meal

Amount of time: 10 minutes or more. A few minutes for small children

Materials: Yoga mat or carpeted floor, pictures of yoga poses, yoga cards, Wii Fit Yoga, or DVD program

Method:
1. Set up the yoga visuals (cards, DVD, or Wii).
2. Let the child choose 2-3 favorite poses. You choose 2-3 others to help round out stretches that both extend and flex the limbs and core. Don't forget the Tree pose which is good for balance. Finish by having the child lie on his back for a minute or two.
3. Hold each pose for 5-30 seconds, depending on the child's skill.
4. Repeat 2-3 times if child is unable to hold the pose for longer than a few seconds.

1. Cobra

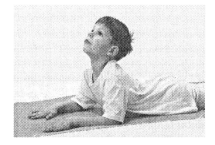

2. Bow Pose

3. Child's Pose

4. Tree Pose

INTERVENTIONS: AROMATHERAPY AND CALMING

Aromatherapy using essential oils (not scented oils) can reduce blood pressure and heart rate. However, they can trigger complications (asthma, for example) in exposures greater than 15-60 minutes. The National Cancer Institute (NCI), after looking at research done with cancer patients using aromatherapy to treat anxiety, concluded that aromatherapy can be effective with adults and children, especially when combined with massage. Here are some of the results.

1. Chamomile combined with massage appears to work well.

2. Various essential oils (selected by patient) appear to reduce anxiety.

3. Lavender and tea tree oils have been found to have some hormone-like effects. They have effects similar to estrogen (female sex hormone) and also block or decrease the effect of androgens (male sex hormones). Applying lavender and tea tree oils to the skin over a long period of time has been linked in one study to breast enlargement in boys who have not yet reached puberty. It is recommended that patients with tumors that need estrogen to grow avoid using lavender and tea tree oils.

Aromatherapy with chamomile

Evidence indicates that chamomile works for calming. Be sure to buy quality oils that are pure. Do not use scents or scented candles because they are typically artificial and allergenic. You can find essential oils at health food stores or online.

When/How often: As needed, but no more than every two hours

Amount of time: 15-60 minutes

Materials: 100% pure essential oils. Try chamomile for calming. Citrus may help with alerting. Optionally, use scented lotions. Make sure that the ingredients are pure. Some children are allergic to synthetic scents.

Method 1: Essential oils
1. Check for tolerance to the scent by putting some on a cotton ball and leaving it in the child's presence for five minutes.
2. Never use oils directly on the skin. Instead put them on a tissue or cotton ball near the child, or place a couple of drops into a cup of hot water and let the scent permeate the room.
3. Remove the source of the scent after 15-60 minutes.

Method 2: Massage with lotion scented with pure herbs
Use lotion and rub it on the arms of the child. A massage using chamomile lotion has been shown to improve relaxation. Check for tolerance to the scent first.

INTERVENTIONS: GETTING CENTERED

Each of us has struggled to maintain a good mood in spite of irritations such as anger, a headache, ill-fitting clothing or a poor night's sleep. Children have the same challenges. The problems some children experience (such as sensory sensitivities, social anxiety and hyperactivity) are chronic, and self-regulation is obviously a significant challenge. Children can learn self-regulation skills at the same time that we are working with them on other goals, producing children who have increased self-awareness and increased life skills.

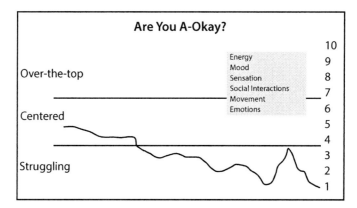

Here are some specific examples of how a child might demonstrate poor self-regulation or modulation:

- He shouts rather than speaking at an appropriate level.
- He runs laps around the room when he gets out of his seat.
- He has no energy to play with other children.
- He is emotionally reactive.
- He is grumpy much of the time.
- He is sensitive to the noise a sibling makes when chewing food.

We now examine three modulation states: centered, over-the-top (hyper-reactive), and struggling to perform (hypo-reactive). We look at the whole child: his energy level along with his physical, mental, emotional and social states. The terms "good modulation" and "poor modulation" are used to describe a child's ability to maintain emotional equilibrium and to recover from an event or situation that produces disequilibrium.

Typical children are more successful in staying centered throughout the day, and they often recover more quickly when they slip out of a centered state. A typical boy who gets very excited and wildly runs around the house, exhibiting poor modulation, can usually recover with a quick reminder to calm down. Another typical child who is sleepy after lunch, and feels as if he doesn't have the energy to participate in a class event, can with a little urging from a friend perk up and have a great time. Contrast these recoveries with the behaviors of children with sensory modulation disorder, ADHD or autism. Such children are unable to recover quickly from external (or even internal) stress factors, and they often spiral into more problematic behaviors before they crash or melt down. Another example involves a child who cannot engage successfully—physically, emotionally or socially—in her classroom. She might be deficient in several of the ways that others use to stay alert such as registration of movement and sensory input, interest in the world and people around us, proper sleep and diet, and an underlying good mood.

THE SIX PHASES OF GETTING CENTERED

A child goes through six phases as he learns to become centered. As a member of the child's village, we help to support him as he goes through each phase. The phases are described here. Exercises are at the end of this section.

1. **Identify the child's current state and a well-modulated state**

   a. Using a scale like the one in the illustration, have the child rate his modulation level with a number from 1-10.

   b. Have him practice trying to get to a five. He may need to use strategies that you teach him to get to that number. See the interventions below for ideas on how to do this.

2. **Learns strategies to get centered**

   The child will need strategies to get into a centered state. This tactic applies, as well, to healthy adults. If I am angry, my strategy may be to breathe slowly. If I have too much energy, I may do chair pushups, or push the heels of my palms together. If I am reacting to food I don't like, I may politely say, "I don't care for any more." We want the child to learn a variety of such responses whatever the issue.

   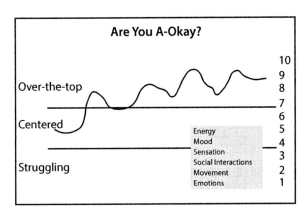

   a. Teach the child a strategy for moving out of the undesirable behavior and into feeling A-Okay.

   b. Help the child practice this response by triggering the issue. For example, offer him food he dislikes, and then role-play a polite response with him. Triggering must be done with care. Do not trigger an emotion or behavior unless you are confident you can get the child back to a well-modulated state.

3. **Uses the strategy with a verbal cue**

   Watch for opportunities to help the child get back into good modulation. It is this practice that helps him develop good skills. When he has hyper or hypo-reactive behaviors, we remind him to use the strategies he has been taught. Say to the child, "What level are you at? Show me what you learned for getting to five."

4. **Uses the strategy independently**

   With a strong village behind him reminding him to use his strategy, the child begins to remember to do so. This is a sign he is integrating the therapy. His support team should work with him to maintain the process.

5. **Learns to work without the strategy**

   Children will get triggered, of course, by strong emotions such as anger. We want them to learn a mature response. We can teach them to imitate good modulation and let the imitation process guide them to emotional equilibrium.

   As an example, Joey is easily angered. We want Joey to begin to take notice when his anger arises. We want him to monitor himself to see the ways in which he is beginning to act out. Next, we want him to exert control over himself and behave in a modulated fashion. While he is learning this skill, he may initially need "to bite his tongue" or restrain his verbal impulses as part of the process of staying calm. Eventually, he can learn to regulate and maintain control of himself, just as we all strive to do.

   a. Help Joey to create a checklist of what to look for in himself when he notices that he is losing good modulation.

   b. Practice it with him at various times, saying, "Let's get to a five!"

   Here is an example of a checklist for a child who angers easily:

   a. Look at your breathing. Is it too fast? Breathe a little slower.

   b. Look at your body. Is it still? Gently move your shoulders back and forth to get rid of stress.

   c. Consider your thoughts. Are you stuck at angry? Who or what are you angry at? Realize that the person you are angry at may be "pulling my strings again." Understand that, "I don't have to be her puppet."

   d. What is your face doing? Look into the mirror to see your reaction to the emotions you are feeling. Is this what you want to show people? If not, swallow once or twice and try to put on a neutral face.

   e. What is your reaction to others? Are you acting politely? Will you regret your actions? Swallow back mean words. Try to say as little as possible, and whatever you do say, say politely.

   This method does *not* replace addressing with a mental-health counselor the underlying issues of act-out behaviors and anger.

6. **Independently gets to a five**

   Performing Step 5 independently shows a high level of awareness and maturity. When a child realizes that he is slipping into a state of poor modulation, he monitors himself and consciously self-regulates.

Identify your level of modulation

Here is a way to for a child to learn to regulate his physical energy, as well as his responses to sensory input, along with his attention level, state of emotions and social interactions.

Setting: Anywhere

Group/Individual: Individual

When/How often: Daily or a few times per week

How long: 10 minutes

Materials: Make a scale labeled from one to 10 or use appropriate pictures

Method:
1. Teach the child to work with the modulation scale by demonstrating a modulation level.
2. Have her name the level she believes she is experiencing between one and 10, and give her your "reading," if necessary.
3. Have her register her experience of various levels so she can feel the difference inside herself.

Here are some example scenarios:

1. "How loud are you talking?" "Let's hear you talk at a 3, 7, 9, or 1."

2. "How fast are you moving?" "How fast when you run, skip, or crawl?" If possible, let the child do those activities before identifying the number that he is likely registering.

3. "How happy are you?" Have the child role-play other moods.

4. "How much energy do you have?" Again, go through the range of numbers for different energy states.

Use a strategy to get to a new state of modulation

Setting: Anywhere

Group/Individual: Individual

When/How often: As needed, or a few times per week

How long: 10 minutes

Materials: Make a scale labeled from one to 10 or use appropriate pictures

Method:
1. On a day when the child is poorly modulated, ask her to identify where she believes she is on the scale.
2. Teach her a strategy to help her self-regulate.
3. As she practices the strategy, ask her to identify where on the scale she feels she is as she increases self-regulation.
4. Practice this by triggering the problem (but only if you are confident you can do so without negative consequences).

OTHER TECHNIQUES

There are many other good ways to help a child get self-regulated. Listed below are methods described in other parts of this book.

1. Weighted vest *(p. 78)*
2. Pressure garment *(p. 79)*
3. Fidgets and sensory boxes *(pp. 72-74)*
4. "Wiggle" cushions and therapy balls *(p. 82)*
5. Mindfulness attention training *(p. 151)*

Source: SensoryJunction.com

CHAPTER 3

Sensory Modulation

Our brain constantly processes sounds, sights, tastes, smells, touch, and temperature from the environment, as well as itch, pain, head movement and other movement from our bodies. Sensory processing is a complex operation with many steps. Sensory input is gathered by our ears, eyes, nose, mouth, skin and muscle spindles. The input goes to our brain to be interpreted (as it is combined with other sensory input, thoughts, feelings, and memories) as part of our thinking and reacting processes.

Given the complexity of sensory processing, problems can arise in many ways. Some of us have glitches in our circuitry that make sounds seem too loud, or smells seem too sharp. Some of us barely notice degrees of pain or temperature. Others can't get enough of certain foods or music.

In this chapter, we look at what can go wrong with each of the senses. That discussion is followed with strategies, interventions and therapies for children with sensory-modulation issues. Interventions are organized by sense. At the end of the chapter, we consider methods to infuse a child's life with rich sensory input to assist with self-regulation.

THE SENSES

We have seven senses: touch, taste, smell, vision, auditory (hearing), vestibular (balance), and proprioception (the body sense). Some literature refers to an eighth sense, interoception, an internal sense that experiences physical pain, temperature, and organ sensation. The vestibular, proprioception and interoception senses are described below.

The vestibular sense

Our vestibular sense is our sense of balance and is located in our inner ears. It registers head movement up and down, side-to-side, back and forth, and clockwise or counterclockwise. It also measures the speed of movement.

If your vestibular system is impaired, you may feel dizzy or light-headed or get motion sickness. The head-movement information from the vestibular sense organs is fed to the vision and hearing systems to help them make sense of what they are seeing and hearing as the head moves. The vestibular sense provides a foundation for visual and auditory processing. When the vestibular sense fails to adequately process input, poor or inadequate data is produced. Vision and hearing can be blurred or compromised, giving the person a sense of dizziness.

The vestibular system has a total of 10 sensors, and it works with all planes of movement and all rotations of movement. Problems may be specific to just the linear axis or to the types of rotational movement. Some people get dizzy or car sick when their eyes are focused on reading a book. Others have trouble only with movements such as swinging.

The proprioception sense

Proprioception is our body sense. Our brain keeps track of the location and movement of every muscle fiber in the body. When you smile, your brain registers the upward movement of your lips. When you cross your legs, the muscle fibers involved in the movement send a message to your brain saying how much movement occurred. The brain does an enormous amount of processing to figure out direction and speed of movement. Ideally, we register movement and determine the location of everything that moves in our body, down to the little body parts—eyebrows, tongue, or lips. This is our sense of proprioception.

Proprioception is closely integrated with our sense of touch. When a child has defensive behaviors such as pulling away from a hug, it can be hard to sort out where the sensory problem lies. Is it with pressure on muscles and joints or with touch on the skin?

Intense proprioceptive input is self-regulating. We become alert or calm when we play hard, perform heavy work, exercise or get deep pressure such as a good massage. These forms of proprioceptive input provide the single most effective way to self-regulate. This input helps to burn off hyperactive energy, increase positive mood and decrease stress.

Proprioception combines with the vestibular sense to inform the brain and to sense movement. In fact, it can be hard to determine which sense is at play when a child tends to be in constant movement or is chronically sedentary. We look at this issue in the next section.

Interoception

Internal sensation has a formal name: interoception. As mentioned, it is sometimes identified as its own sense, an eighth sense. Interoception includes a combination of normal and abnormal sensations including temperature, breath, pain, itch, sensation from a bruise or from gut inflammation, nausea, hunger, satiation, and stomach cramps. As with other senses, the body may have difficulty modulating these sensations. For example, a small cut may produce an emotional overreaction in a child who is overly sensitive to pain. Contrast that with another child who is undersensitive to pain and experiences no symptoms of serious gut inflammation.

Sense interaction and integration

Our senses don't operate in an isolated fashion; they interact with each other and inform each other's processing. For example, the vestibular sense works with the body to keep us upright and balanced with good posture. It also shares its information with the eyes and ears so that they understand the stream of sensory information that moves past them as the head moves. The process of combining information from multiple senses is called *sensory integration*. This important function in the brain allows us to make better sense of what is happening in the environment and to successfully process our interactions with the world.

Sensory processing issues can come from one or more levels in the processing chain. Here are some of the more important locations of sensory processing:

1. The physical sense organs, such as the eyes or taste buds.
2. The nerves and tracks that carry that information to the brain.
3. The sensory cortex of each sense where raw sensory data is interpreted.
4. The association cortex that combines information from multiple senses.

5. Sensory-motor areas that process the automatic reactions and responses we make to sensory input.

6. Executive-function circuitry that regulates voluntary response to sensory input.

Common sensory-processing challenges include:

- Integrating the right and left signals from eyes, ears, nose and vestibular senses.

- Integrating the body signals of touch, proprioception and interoception.

- Adjusting for amplitude problems in any sense receptor. For example, weak hearing or a partial hearing loss in one ear requires sensory processing that smoothes over missing sounds.

- Syncing signals of all senses, at all levels, throughout the entire processing chain. For example, if there is a processing lag for a signal (the signal takes longer to transmit) across the corpus callosum, then that signal may not be present at a critical moment when other elements in the chain come together. This may cause the information in that signal to get dropped or cause processing of the entire circuit to be delayed. We see this latter problem in children with poor hearing or with auditory processing skills who struggle to make sense of what was said in the classroom. They may eventually understand what was said, but the poor-quality signals are garbled, and the children must sift through auditory noise to find words that make sense. Problems like these may be the cause of undersensitivity (see below).

- Integrating multiple senses that participate in a specific function. For example, the proprioception and vestibular senses combine to give us our sensation of movement, while the proprioception, vestibular, vision and auditory senses combine to give us posture.

- Too faint or too keen perception of sensory information. The child should notice sensory input at a comfortable "volume" within the brain so that it does not overwhelm the thought processes. Some signals may feel too soft or too loud, causing discomfort. As well, some children may have a very narrow comfort zone of perception.

Poor sensory modulation

When our sensory input processing is going well, we are able to engage in daily life without being bothered by sensation unless it is especially loud, bright, smelly, and so on. This is not the case for the person who is oversensitive or undersensitive to sensation or for the person who craves sensory input. These sensory-processing liabilities may cause self-regulation issues and, if serious enough, produce *sensory modulation disorder* or *SMD*.

Oversensitivity, undersensitivity and craving can affect an individual in the following ways:

Oversensitivity: Normal sensation from the environment (e.g. sound or touch) or from the child's own body (e.g., pain) seems strong or acute to the child. In some cases, the child enjoys the sensation; in most cases, it feels like a bombardment.

Examples include: He doesn't tolerate elastic in clothing; he pulls away when someone tries to hug him; he puts hands over his ears when an alarm sounds; he becomes disorganized in a cluttered room; he won't eat crunchy foods; he reacts to bright light.

Undersensitivity: The child does not notice certain sensations (ones that are important for self-protection and self-awareness) from the environment or from her own body.

Examples include: She doesn't react when her name is called; she tends to be sedentary; she does not care to eat because her poor sensitivity to taste makes food seem bland; she is insensitive to temperature or pain.

Craving: The child can't get enough of certain sensations, either because they feel good or because the brain is not registering the sensations and needs more input.

Examples include: He is in constant movement; he wants the TV on 24/7; he constantly touches things; he will only eat certain foods; he fixates on spinning objects such as clocks and fans.

A person may have symptoms of poor modulation in one sense, several senses, or in all senses. Any given sense may be oversensitive or undersensitive or cause craving. Any sense can struggle with all three modulation problems at different times. For example, a child may have difficulty focusing on school work when other children are talking nearby. But if she focuses her attention and gets back to her work, she may not hear someone calling her name. That same child may also be fond of humming, while also using humming as a strategy to block out other noises. She is oversensitive and undersensitive to hearing, while craving sounds as well.

Modulation problems

Here are examples of oversensitivity, undersensitivity and craving modulation problems for each sense.

Hearing

Issue	Signs & Symptoms
Oversensitive	Complains about noise; screams when loud noises are present; is easily distracted by noises in the room; has difficulty working in a group; places hands over his ears when there is a loud noise; avoids social situations.
Undersensitive	Does not hear his name called; is unable to follow oral directions.
Craving	Listens to music or watches TV constantly; sings, hums or whistles often.

Vision

Issue	Signs & Symptoms
Oversensitive	Complains about the sun or lights being too bright; is easily distracted by movement in the room including TV screens; sensitive to florescent lights; refuses to go outside on a sunny day; prefers the dark.
Undersensitive	Is unable to follow written directions; doesn't notice when work is left incomplete.
Craving	"Stims" on moving objects such as lights, fans or fingers; watches TV or sits at computer constantly; doodles during class; constantly reading.

Simple touch

Issue	Signs & Symptoms
Oversensitive	Dislike of crowds; says that brushing hair or teeth hurts; is sensitive to clothing; avoids crowds; avoids touching others; complains of gastric problems.
Undersensitive	Gets cuts and bruises easily without noticing.
Craving	Touches everything and everyone; constantly fidgets with things.

Body and touch

Issue	Signs & Symptoms
Oversensitive	A touch to the arm feels like being hit; muscles ache; avoids crowds.
Undersensitive	Sluggish, clumsy, poor handwriting.
Craving	Crashing, bumping; hugs people excessively; wears heavy clothes or blankets out of season; drops to floor (small child) in effort to be dragged; avoids exercise.

Vestibular: balance

Issue	Signs & Symptoms
Oversensitive	Dislikes moving head especially for tasks such as hair washing; gets nauseous easily. Refuses to participate in movement activities.
Undersensitive	Poor coordination. Falls out of seat; bumps into walls.
Craving	Constant movement: jumping, running, cartwheels, etc.

Smell and taste

Issue	Signs & Symptoms
Oversensitive	Finds smells and tastes overwhelming; has a poor appetite, gags easily.
Undersensitive	Finds foods bland, poor appetite.
Craving	Sniffs things. Craves particular tastes or smells.

Interoception

Issue	Signs & Symptoms
Oversensitive	Complains of gastric problems, feels warm and cool temperatures as hot and cold. May be a picky eater.
Undersensitive	May not register stomach pain, doesn't register heat, cold or pain.
Craving	

Development

Sometimes we see signs of sensory-modulation problems in infancy, especially in cases of premature babies. Such signs present themselves by the time the child reaches two or three years. When the child enters preschool he is challenged with new sounds, smells, and foods. He may be challenged and show poor adaptability when other children enter his space uninvited. The undersensitive child may have the opposite reaction. She may make use of the opportunity to get more sensation and take it to an extreme by touching things or by bumping into other children. Sensory-modulation problems can continue to grow until the ages of six-to-nine years. At ages eight-to-nine, two things can happen: first, some of the child's sensory issues may be resolved as brain and body development completes; second, the child develops abstract reasoning and puts together coping strategies for dealing with the noxious input around him. As a result of these two changes, the child's sensory symptoms decrease.

Co-occurrence rates

Small studies indicate that 5-16% percent of typical children have sensory-processing or sensory-modulation issues severe enough to be functionally debilitating. Children with special needs have a co-occurrence with sensory modulation at the rate of 20-30%. For autism, the co-occurrence rate is 72%. One study also reported a significant co-occurrence for ADHD (Rood & Miller, 1997; Miller, 2012).

Gifted children are more sensitive to the environment than their typical peers. Presumably, this sensitivity is a key aspect of the child's intelligence and provides that student with additional information about the world. However, the gifted child's sensitivity can be both a blessing and a curse. When a blessing, the child who has sensitive visual perception may spend hours learning to draw and become a gifted artist or architect. However, another child with visual sensitivities may find some normal environmental input (such as a classroom) to be too disorganized or intense and be overwhelmed by it. This child may avoid that type of input and resist going into a big-box store or an IMAX movie. If the child is oversensitive to sound or touch, he may avoid social situations and miss out on opportunities for social development (Dunn, 2009; Gere, 2009).

When a child is hyperactive or impulsive, it can be hard to distinguish between ADHD and SMD without testing, because the symptoms are similar. However, screening tests typically used for each disorder are effective at differentiating the two (Miller, 2012). Brain-imaging studies using a form of MRI called DTI (diffuse tensor imaging) are also successful at differentiating between ADHD and SMD. DTI images typically show abnormalities in the front of the brain (prefrontal cortex and frontal portions of the corpus callosum) in children with ADHD, while in children with SMD the abnormalities are primarily found in the back of the brain, including the corpus callosum and thalamic tracks (Owen, 2013).

Emotional and social issues

Children with sensory sensitivities have 37% greater anxiety than their typical peers (Reynolds & Lane, 2009). These children confront a vicious cycle: anxiety increases sensory symptoms and sensory symptoms increase anxiety. Children with SMD are more withdrawn, have poorer flexibility and do not adapt well to the environment. Attention levels are normal, and children with sensitivities may be hyper-vigilant as they await the next bombardment of sensory input. Children with SMD are also less socially mature than their peers (Miller, 2012). The child with sensitivities has significant issues with the environment, and so she may avoid situations with problematic foods and smells, loud voices, and crowded conditions that are mainstays of social events.

Creating interventions that work

Processing sensory information and maintaining good sensory modulation is a key task of the brain. As we have seen, problems can occur at any of many levels with individual senses or the combination of several senses. How does one begin to create interventions for the child? There is no single approach. We can create strategies for the child or alter the child's setting. Movement can be interspersed throughout the day in the form of play, exercise, heavy work, deep pressure and other types of sensory input. When possible, we design and build special break or rest areas for the child such as sensory rooms at school or home. This combined approach can provide the child with enough calming and alerting sensory input to satisfy the brain and body and allow her to develop and heal.

A multi-focused type of intervention was set forth by Dr. Patricia Wilbarger who developed the *Wilbarger Protocol* "brushing program" for children with sensory issues. Parents were taught to brush the arms, legs and back of their child with a surgical brush and then to give the child's muscles and joints soothing input by compressing the joints. Wilbarger found that when this was done regularly (every two hours over a multi-week period), the child's brain was often able to integrate the experience and develop natural skills for handling sensory input.

On the heels of that program, she created a second program called the *sensory diet* in which children were given strong sensory input such as heavy work and/or deep pressure every two hours to help stay regulated throughout the day. She encouraged her clients to do both programs together, and her informal studies indicated a 50% success rate. (Kimball, 2007) showed that the brushing technique decreases stress, as measured by cortisol levels in the saliva.

While large studies and strong case studies are still lacking for sensory diet, many therapists have found value in using the technique. However, implementing a sensory diet can be challenging unless the child is at home with a stay-at-home parent. The combined approach mentioned above allows us to fill the child's day with sensory input, thus creating a sensory-rich life for the child. We do this in a way that is natural for the setting. Once put in place, no one has to stop what they are doing to think about what the child needs to stay regulated. This approach was found to be effective for working with children with autism in a home setting. Woo & Leon (2013) showed that regular environmental enrichment, including daily olfactory and tactile stimulation, helps with self-regulation issues and also appears to decrease symptoms in children with autism.

We come back to this topic at the end of the chapter with an integrated approach to helping children with sensory-modulation disorder stay self-regulated throughout the day.

STRATEGIES AND ADAPTATIONS: HEARING/AUDITORY MODULATION

Poor auditory modulation can make it difficult for a child to make sense of the world. If he is oversensitive to sound, he will feel bombarded with noise. If he is undersensitive, he may not be able to follow directions from teachers or parents. In both cases, socialization could be a big challenge for him. When oversensitive, he may avoid social groups because they are too loud. If undersensitive, he may have trouble keeping up with conversations and plans.

Here are other ways that a child can be affected by poor auditory modulation.

Issue	Signs & Symptoms
Oversensitive	Complains about noise; screams when loud noises are present; is easily distracted by noises in the room; has difficulty working in a group; places hands over his ears when there's a loud noise; complains that movies are too loud; avoids social situations.
Undersensitive	Does not hear his name called; is unable to follow oral directions.
Craving	Listens to music or watches TV constantly; sings, hums or whistles often.

General advice

1. If the child has not had a recent hearing test, he or she should get one prior to using the strategies in this section. Also ask the parents if the child has tinnitus (ringing and other sounds in the ears), which can cause increased sensitivity to sound as well as block certain sound frequencies. You also want to know if the child has recurrent ear infections.

2. If the child has a fight, flight, or freeze response to loud noises, try programs that help with overall modulation such as sound therapy *(p. 56)*, a brushing program *(p. 51)*, qigong massage *(p. 33)*, a daily massage *(for infants, p. 32)* or daily acupressure (as done in the Emotional Freedom Technique, *p. 123*). Sound therapy is also useful for decreasing auditory sensitivity.

3. One school found that replacing fluorescent lights with halogen lighting and putting soundproofing in walls and ceilings increased attention and decreased behavioral issues. Students noted that it was easier to work because the light no longer hurt their eyes, and they found it quiet enough to think.

CHILDREN WHO ARE OVERSENSITIVE TO SOUND

Oversensitivity to sound is one of the most difficult modulation problems. Children with this problem are overwhelmed by noises that are not bothersome for others. Here are strategies to help them function:

Ear muffs and ear plugs

A child who is bothered by sounds in the environment may enjoy the relief of ear muffs or ear plugs to help decrease these sounds. But use them only as needed.

Materials: Ear muffs (available in teacher and therapy catalogs), a large clean supply of squeezable ear plugs, iPod or MP3 player

When/How often: In noisy settings

How long: Only as needed, let the ears rest and breathe otherwise

Method 1: Ear muffs
At the start of a noisy event, give the child heavy-duty (but light-weight) suppressor ear muffs to wear. Remove ear muffs once the noise subsides. Ear muffs may be stigmatizing for the older child, but headphones (not plugged in) are fashionable and can be a solution. Headphones do not have the same sound-dampening effect as ear muffs, so try them first before purchasing them.

Method 2: Ear plugs
For older children, try sound-protection ear plugs. But check with the child's parents and doctor before using them. Use them only as needed to block out loud or irritating sounds.

Method 3: Music device with ear buds or headphones
If ear muffs and ear plugs are stigmatizing, strip an iPod or MP3 player of all programs, apps and music except for calming music. Allow the child to wear the ear buds as needed. He can listen to the music or not.

Source: TherapyShoppe.com

School alarms

A child who is ultra-sensitive to alarms and bells needs to be told when to expect them. Here is an easy way to keep the child out of an "alarm" state.

Materials: Ear muffs

Setting: School

When/How often: Five minutes prior to practice fire, weather or other emergency alarms or drills.

Method:
1. Five minutes before a school-wide alarm is about to ring, the office calls the classroom and asks the hearing-sensitive child to come to the office.
2. At the office, the child is told an alarm is going to be sounded and is given ear muffs.
3. (Optional) Let the child press the alarm bell. This gives him a sense of control over it and makes it easier for him to adjust to the sound.

Variation: Start of school year
Have the child come to the school before the school year starts so he can press the alarms and school bells, and speak into the microphone. Gaining control over the sounds through play and repetition will help to decrease the shock of the alarm.

Taxing noises

Temple Grandin suggests this method as a way to help the child acclimate to difficult sounds:

Materials: Audio recorder, smart phone, tablet or tape recorder

Setting: School, home community

When/How often: Several times a day until the child has acclimated

Method:
1. Using an easy-to-use recorder such as a microphone app, record sounds that the child cannot tolerate.
2. Play the sounds back throughout the day at a reduced volume as a way of desensitizing.

Low-noise policy for the classroom

Try a low-noise policy. Keeping the sounds at a low volume in the classroom makes it easier for everyone to work.

Materials: None

Setting: School, home

When/How often: During heads-down work

Method:
1. Instruct children to raise their hands before speaking and to use low voices.
2. When working in groups, have children whisper when communicating with each other.
3. Voices are returned to normal (and ear muffs are placed on sensitive ears) for lively activities.

Option: Special seating
Place the sensitive child in the quietest part of the classroom and, if possible, close to the teacher so that he hears clearly and is not distracted by classmates.

Option: Find other space
Have the child do written work in the resource room or, if well-motivated, in the school library.

Cafeterias, gyms and other noisy places

Cafeterias, gyms and assemblies can be very noisy. Here are ideas for helping the sound-sensitive child stay at ease. The first method works as therapy.

Materials: None

Setting: School, community

When/how often: Daily

Method 1: Enter first
1. Have the child enter the room before other students arrive.
2. As the room fills up, she will acclimate to the sounds in the room.
3. Done daily, this can be an effective method for desensitization.

Method 2: Enter last
1. Have her enter an assembly last after other children are seated and quiet.
2. Just before the assembly ends, she leaves the room first and avoids the escalation of sound level as children exit.
3. Consider giving an older child a bit of autonomy. Have her sit in the back by the door and give her permission to leave if it gets too noisy. Chances are good she will "work through" the noisy sounds so she can stay for the entire event.

Method 3: Enter at the end (backward chaining)
Have her enter the public space (cafeteria or assembly) at the end of the event. Over succeeding days, have her enter earlier and stay longer as she is able to tolerate it. In this manner, escape behaviors are not reinforced by the student leaving before the event has ended.

Method 4: Avoid the cafeteria
Get permission for the child and a friend or two to eat lunch at the back of an empty classroom.

At the dinner table

Obnoxious sounds at the dinner table do not have to cause outbursts from sensitive children. We can tackle this issue from both directions by teaching the offending child (the noisy eater) good manners, while at the same time coming up with strategies and manners for the child with sensitive ears.

Materials: A book on meal-time manners

Setting: Home

When/how often: Mealtimes

The noisy eater:
1. Teach the noisy eater how to chew properly using these starter rules. This process requires patience while the child remembers to use these new skills. Tell the child to:
   a. Cut large pieces of food into small pieces and chew one piece at a time.
   b. Keep mouth closed when chewing.

    c. Refrain from talking with food in mouth.
    d. Use silverware quietly.
    e. Excuse oneself and leave the table to blow one's nose.
2. Make a list of the relevant rules and review them before meals.

The child with sensitive ears:
3. Teach the sensitive child techniques for handling irritations:
    a. Ask permission to eat at another table when noises arise that she can't tolerate.
    b. Look away when someone else is eating with mouth open.

Both children:
4. Role-play other situations that develop at the dinner table.
5. To keep the peace during this process, have children take turns eating at a nearby table or eating in shifts. Parents and older children need to be role models who are consistent in their good behavior.

Social situations

The older child with sensitive hearing risks being overwhelmed in a social situation. She needs to learn her limits and to act before she reaches them. Here is a way she can learn more about herself.

Materials: A stopwatch or clock

Setting: Practice social settings such as parties, restaurants, movie theaters, and sports venues

When/how often: Every week for an hour

Method:
1. Pick an event or setting. (Choose a different type of setting each week.)
2. Prior to the event, role-play a scenario in which she must leave an event before it is over. She needs to be able to offer a plausible excuse or reason to the host. The situation requires saying good-bye to present company or even apologizing to them for leaving early.
3. Upon arriving, set the stopwatch and have the child rate on a 1-to-5 scale how noisy and how crowded it is.
4. Let her participate in the event.
5. Every so often (every five minutes in very noisy settings) ask her to rate herself. Can she tolerate it? Is she becoming irritated?
6. When she feels she has reached her limit, look at the stopwatch.
7. Have her offer her excuse for leaving and then slowly make her way to the door.
8. When she is outside, look at the stopwatch again so that she understands how many extra minutes she needs to "hang-on" (as she says her good-byes) once she is ready to leave.

EASE SOUND THERAPY FOR SELF-REGULATION

Sound therapy can be a powerful remedy for the child with fight-or-flight response, auditory processing issues, autism and behavioral issues. Sound therapy is music that has been modified to exercise the brain's auditory processing, emotional processing and self-regulation circuitry. Sound therapy music is listened to with special headphones in a quiet setting such as home or clinic.

EASe is one product in particular that is especially good at improving poor self-regulation caused by auditory sensitivity. EASe also tempers symptoms of fight-or-flight. Think of a wiggly, inattentive sensory child with or without autism or a child who is alarmed by loud noises. This is the product's target population. EASe is available to parents and therapists in the form of CDs or an iPod app at Vision-Audio.com.

To see if this therapy will work for a child, get the $2 EASe Lite app for iPod/ iPhone/iPad. You can try it for a few minutes with standard headphones, but be sure to use good headphones (described below) once therapy begins.

Materials using CD player:
1. *Headphones:* You must use good headphones. Sony MDR7506, Shure SRH240 and Sennheiser 500A are recommended. The Sony and Shure are sound isolating, meaning that the child cannot hear sounds from the environment and so must be in a safe environment for listening. The Sennheiser model is open to air, which allows the child to hear environmental sounds, making it good for sensory integration. Do not use Bose headphones that filter sound.
2. *CD player:* Get a decent ($30 or more) CD player. Sony is recommended.
3. *CD ROM disks from EASe:* There are 10 EASe disks. EASe 1 and/or EASe 2 are good first choices. EASe 4 is good for auditory processing. The manufacturer suggests purchasing the complete collection (EASe1 to EASe10) and rotating them in a 10-day schedule.
4. *Instructions:* Download and print instructions for EASe CDs at http://www.vision-audio. com/CDplayer.html.

Materials using iPod/iPhone/iPad:
1. *Headphones:* Sony MDR7506, Shure SRH240 or Sennheiser 500A, as above.
2. *Music device:* iPod, iPhone or iPad.
3. *Music app:* You will need to buy either the Personal Listening Therapy app (for parents) or the Pro Listening Therapy app (for therapists who are trained on sound therapy.) You can purchase either app from iTunes.
4. *EASe apps:* EASe 1, EASe 3 and EASe 4 are available for the Personal Listening Therapy app. See the guidelines for CD ROM above.
5. *Instructions:* Download and print instructions for EASe iPods at http://www.audioforge. ca/downloads/User_guide.pdf.

Ages: 2-3 and older.

When/How often: Twice a day for 20-30 minutes. The two sessions should be three or more hours apart.

How long: Either follow the manufacturer's recommendations to rotate disks (see *Instructions* above) or use each disk/album for two weeks. Four weeks of music is often enough for self-regulation. Purchase additional EASe disks if you decide that the child has benefited from EASe yet does not appear ready to be weaned off the program.

Setting: School, home.

Cautions: Do not use EASe with children with a history of tinnitus, seizures or psychosis. Always try five minutes of the music and wait for 24 hours to see if there are any emotional or behavioral reactions. If reactions are observed, consult with an experienced sound-therapy professional before proceeding. If the child has an ear infection, wait for it to clear before doing sound therapy.

Method:
1. Try a 5-minute listening session. Wait 24 hours. Continue with the program if no unusual emotional or behavioral outbursts have occurred.
2. Follow the EASe protocol found at Vision-Audio. com. Have the child listen to music through proper headphones for 20-30 minutes at a time. Try for a protocol of twice a day, 5-7 days a week.
3. Use EASe when the child has relaxed attention and is otherwise engaged in simple activities. You can use this program in the classroom, but use it during the presentation of subjects that are easy for the child so his or her brain resources are not taxed.
4. Listening while playing is a sound strategy, but not while playing electronic games or watching TV. Again, these activities compete for brain resources. EASe makes PC games that can engage the child as she receives visual processing therapy that is coordinated with the EASE music. You can use standard headphones for listening to music. The games can be downloaded from Vision-audio.com.

Source: Vision Audio

CHILDREN WHO ARE UNDERSENSITIVE TO SOUND

Children with poor sound sensitivity may have problems with hearing, auditory perception, or both. If a child has good hearing, but does not pick up spoken instructions, he may have serious auditory-processing problems. He would benefit from working with a speech therapist or a developmental audiologist. If the problem impacts speech as well, excellent programs are available such as Linda Moody Bell, iLs or Fast Forward. These help the child to process sound and sound combinations. Sound therapy can help with distraction from sounds, sound discrimination, depth of auditory field and other processing issues. Good sound therapy programs include iLs, The Listening Program, Samonas, Berard AIT and Therapeutic Listening.

Poor auditory sensitivity in the classroom

Children with poor auditory processing skills who have trouble picking up on classroom directions can benefit from the same adaptive equipment used for children with hearing loss. A microphone and speakers can make a significant difference in the child's ability to comprehend oral directions in the classroom.

Materials: Speakers, lavaliere (optional)

Setting: School

Method:
1. Present lessons both orally and in written form. Seeing and hearing the same information simultaneously can help a child decode what was said and increase his auditory processing skills.
2. Face the child directly and speak clearly when addressing him.
3. Try putting speakers on the child's desk, with a lavaliere (wireless microphone) on the teacher's collar to increase the acuity of the sound quality. Optionally, put speakers on the wall so that all children can benefit from the amplified sound.
4. Train the child to position himself in the optimal location for sound. This may include sitting at the front of a room and sitting with the "good ear" nearest to others who are speaking.
5. Train the child to read lips (see below).
6. When watching TV, use the captions feature so that words are both heard and seen. Again, this helps with overall sound-processing skills.

Learning to read lips

Learning to read lips takes a bit of time and practice. Once mastered, the skill can help a person with oral comprehension through his or her entire life. Try these activities to master the process.

Materials: TV, smartphone or movie camera, mirror, as needed

Setting: Home and school

Method 1: Articulation in the mirror
1. Have the child look in the mirror while she recites nursery rhymes, poems, sounds and sentences.
2. Have her notice how she moves her mouth and lips. You do not need to get too technical with this approach, unless she also has visual processing problems.

Method 2: Make it a game
Play "Read my lips" game. Players take turns silently pronouncing words, directions or silly phrases to each other.

Method 3: Videotape
1. Videotape an adult reading a story that the child knows.
2. Have the child watch the video with the sound off.

Method 4: Do it live
1. Have the child start to practice reading lips "live" whenever possible.
2. Have her take a break from watching the speaker's lips every few seconds in order to make eye contact with the speaker. In this way, she learns to follows good social protocol.

Method 5: Using TV
1. Have the child watch TV with the sound on low for 15-20 minutes at a time. Pick shows such as children's news or talk shows where the host and guests are facing the camera. Look for speakers with good articulation.
2. Do not try this with cartoon shows and characters (instead, turn on captions).

Children who crave sound

Sound craving in children can be linked to both undersensitivity and oversensitivity. If the child has auditory undersensitivity, his brain may crave sounds because it is not registering them sufficiently. The child may constantly listen to music or insist that the TV be on when he is not watching it. He may enjoy the hum of the vacuum cleaner or other noisy devices and use them excessively. A small child may constantly play with noisy toy cars or talking dolls. If the child is oversensitive to sound, he may thrill to the sound of music because of a rich auditory processing system that brings music to life.

The child who talks, hums or whistles may be craving sound. More likely, though, he is using strategies to stay regulated. The humming acts as white noise to drown out other sounds in the environment. If he talks to himself while working, he may be using a strategy that helps him to amplify his mental processes. We are complex creatures, and sensory cravings illustrate just how true this is.

The strategies for auditory cravings are primarily the same as those listed for over- and undersensitivity. A bigger issue with making sounds or noise to satisfy internal craving is the lack of sensitivity to others in the environment. The child who makes inappropriate noises of any type needs education with respect to others' needs, as well as reminders that there is a time for quiet.

STRATEGIES AND ADAPTATIONS: VISION

Over- or undersensitivity to visual input is less common than to auditory or touch. Yet the problem can still wreak havoc on children who are easily distracted, bothered by light or overly fascinated by moving and spinning objects. This section gives ideas for modulating the impact of visual input.

Issue	Signs & Symptoms
Oversensitive	Complains about the sun or lights being too bright; is easily distracted by movement in the room including TV screens; sensitive to florescent lights; refuses to go outside on a sunny day; prefers the dark.
Undersensitive	Is unable to follow written directions; doesn't notice when work is left incomplete.
Craving	"Stims" on moving objects such as lights, fans or fingers; watches TV or sits at computer constantly; doodles during class; constantly reading.

General advice

If the child has not had a recent vision test, get one, along with new glasses if necessary, prior to using the strategies in this section. Also ask that either an occupational therapist or developmental optometrist assess and provide interventions for problems with visual perception.

Getting organization habits at home

The four or five-year-old child with the messy room could easily become the child who, in grade 7, can't find his homework in a messy locker. Educating parents on the need for good organizational habits at an early age can help improve the child's prospects. See the chapter on ADHD for additional interventions for organization.

Materials: Small labels and markers, sound cue such as a bell

Setting: Home or school

Age: 2 and up

When/How often: Multiple times daily on a schedule

Method:
1. Make a place for all the child's belongings, and label everything with a small caption or picture. Keep the caption small so it is not distracting.
2. Throughout the day, ring a bell for cleanup. At the sound of the bell, everything stops and messes are tidied. For the child who creates a whirlwind of clothes and toys, the cue to clean up could occur every 10 minutes, with the parent overseeing the process for a week or two until habits are formed.
3. As the child gets older, make house rules such as:
   a. "Before you move to a new activity, you have to clean up after the old one."
   b. "You don't leave the house until your things are put away."

4. Create a daily reward program for completing a list of organization tasks, using a chart to track to-do items completed. For the best compliance, pick rewards that can be given immediately each day after the work is completed.

	Joey's To-do List	Mon	Tues	Wed	Thurs	Fri	Sat	Sun
1	Hang up clothes	x						
2	Dirty clothes in laundry	x						
3	Make bed	x						
4	Homework in book bag	x						
5	Fun things stashed	x						
6	Dishes in dishwasher	x						
7	Desk clear	x						
	Total checks	7						

Reduce distractions in the classroom (and at home)

Some children look away from their school work to watch any activity in the classroom. Here are a few ways to help reduce distractions.

Materials: Carrel, poster board and tape or two pocket folders

Setting: School, home

When/How often: During heads-down work

Strategies:
1. Provide the child with visually quiet space by putting a carrel on her desk. Carrels can be found in teacher catalogs and online. You can construct one out of poster board or improvise one using two open-pocket folders.
2. Optionally, place a table and chair facing an undecorated wall in the classroom. The child does her written work facing the wall. She turns around in her chair to face the class during lessons.
3. Keep unneeded items, especially items the child craves, in closed cupboards or curtained shelves to reduce visual distractions.
4. In the child's study area at home, choose a simple, uncluttered décor with soft or neutral colors. Select pictures for the wall for neutral emotional content.

Calm cravings: visual fidgets

Some children with autism can become fixated on turning or spinning objects such as clocks or fans. Try providing them with visual fidgets to look at during a break. A good fidget calms the visual craving.

Materials: Kaleidoscope, lava lamp, mind jar

Setting: School, home

How long: For 5-15 minutes, as there is time

When/How often: As needed or scheduled every two hours

Method:
Test a variety of items for visual interest. Put the items that the child enjoys in a safe place to use for occasional sensory breaks, and then allow the child to have access to them during the day as needed or on a fixed schedule. If the child has a sensory box (as described at the end of this chapter) the items can go in that box.

Calm cravings: visual activities

The child who craves visual input will enjoy these activities. Items such as video games can be used as rewards, but sprinkling other activities into the day can help reduce craving and increase self-regulation.

Materials: Jigsaw puzzles, colorful magazines, picture books, colorful crafts, coloring books, mazes, word search, mosaics, pin ball, video games.

Setting: School, home

When/How often: As there is time

Use colors to reduce glare

Some children are sensitive to glare. For example, white paper reflects overhead light and hurts sensitive eyes. Two different solutions can be helpful: have the child use colored paper instead of white paper for school work, and have tinted glasses available.

Materials: A pack of multi-colored paper; tinted glasses (in the local drug or discount store).

Setting: School, home

When/How often: As needed

Method:
1. Using a computer, print a paragraph or two onto different colors of paper. Use pastels and also print on white paper. Make the font size of the words in the paragraph the same as in the child's workbooks.

2. Have the child read the paragraphs on the white and colored sheets. Is there a color that is easier to read? If so, use this color for written work.
3. Next, take a trip to a drugstore or discount store and have the child look through various tinted glasses to see if any of them help to reduce glare. If so, these could be worn as needed.
4. If this appears to be a good solution for the child, consider asking for permission to wear the glasses in the classroom.

Change room lighting

Children may be sensitive to glaring bright light or to flickering fluorescent lights. Here is a guide for room and task lighting. Experts say that we should move to LED lighting for all tasks as it becomes affordable.

Type of lighting	Comments
LED light emitting diode	This is easy on the eyes and is energy efficient. Lighting experts recommend moving to this option as a general solution for lighting as the price of LED lights comes down.
Energy efficient bulbs (Compact Fluorescent)	These bulbs give bright light in the blue spectrum which is alerting. Do not use this type of lighting before bed. It can keep the child awake by resetting the melatonin cycle. The bulbs may be too bright for children with light sensitivity. Consider replacing with LED lighting.
Halogen	This is the most expensive option, but gives bright, even lighting for an entire room. Make sure that bulbs are covered (to avoid glare and burns) and safely installed in the room (to avoid fires).
Fluorescent	Flickering fluorescent lighting can be irritating to those with sensitive vision. Worse, it can trigger seizures in those who are prone to them. Filters that mask the flicker are readily available and easy to install. Filters are a cost-effective alternative to replacing lights. Like incandescent bulbs, fluorescent bulbs are being phased out by manufacturers in favor of LED lighting.

STRATEGIES AND ADAPTATIONS: TOUCH

Poor tactile modulation can make it difficult for a child to operate within socially accepted personal boundaries. The oversensitive child pushes away from uninvited hugs and touches. Yet she will touch the soft hair and clothing of people in her environment for the pleasure of feeling the sensation. If she is undersensitive, her brain may crave touch sensation, causing her to constantly touch objects and people. It is common for both types of children to fidget inordinately.

A child who is oversensitive may have difficulty tolerating clothing, haircuts and manicures. The undersensitive child may be unable to register food on her lips or mouth.

Modulation strategies for internal sensation, pain, itch, and temperature are presented later in this chapter.

Issue	Signs & Symptoms
Oversensitive	Dislike of crowds; says that brushing hair or teeth hurts; is sensitive to clothing; avoids crowds; avoids touching others; complains of gastric problems.
Undersensitive	Gets cuts and bruises easily without noticing.
Craving	Touches everything and everyone; constantly fidgets with things.

General advice

Giving the child an appropriate object with which to fidget is an overall good strategy. A good fidget helps to calm the hands and allows the brain to stay focused.

Children who are oversensitive to touch

Being oversensitive to touch is one of the most difficult types of sensory-modulation issues. The child is bombarded with unwanted touch input, and this in turn can make her anxious. We can teach her calming and coping strategies or implement a skin-brushing technique such as the Wilbarger protocol (see the resource guide in the back of the book) which is known to alleviate touch-modulation issues.

Getting past defensiveness

Some children are sensitive to the point of being defensive. This condition is called "tactile defensiveness." Such children are easy to recognize. A small child will lash out when touched. An older child will pull away quickly. We can reduce the defensive reaction in a child by approaching him correctly.

To manage the child:

1. When taking a child by the hand, put firm pressure on his wrist. This is calming and reduces the chance of him reacting.
2. When giving a child a hug, open your arms, but let him do the work of walking into the embrace so that he has a sense of control over the event and does not feel threatened.

Touches and bumps with the young child

In crowds, the touch-sensitive child may become hyper-vigilant and fearful of being bumped.

Gently explain the nature of touch sensitivity to the child at an early age. Tell him that being touched and bumped startles or surprises him and makes him jump, but that he can learn to feel safe. Also show him ways that he can self-soothe.

Staying safe around other children:
1. Walk at the back of the line.
2. Sit on the side of the room.
3. Keep a little distance from others.
4. Though startled or surprised, try to smile when touched on the shoulder, hand or arm.

Practice self-soothing with touch:
1. Make a game of "touch and rub it in." Touch the child and have him rub the touch into his skin. The pressure of the rub will soothe him.
2. Have him say in a sing-song voice that is self-soothing: "She touched me on the shoulder because she likes me," or "I'm okay, he was just being friendly," or "She likes me."

Gradual exposure to touching and bumping:
1. Create a bumping game with the child and another (gentle) child or adult. Start by pushing fingers together, then hands, and then forearms and shoulders.
2. Do this often so that the child gets gradual exposure to touching and bumping.
3. At the end of the game, reward the child for his hard work.

Play a touch game with letters and symbols:
Using one's finger, make a game of drawing letters, symbols or other simple figures on the child's palm or back. Have the child try to identify what was written.

Preparing for a party or social event

Mingling with children in a social situation may be frightening for the touch-sensitive child. But as the child matures, we can give her a head-start on developing social strategies that allow her to engage more successfully with her peers. (See also the method "Social situations" in the auditory strategies section of this chapter.)

Method:
1. Role-play with her on how to react during a friendly touch. Use soothing prosody (sing-song, self-talk) as a way to help her calm. Try the scripts below a few times and then again when she is not expecting the touch, so that she gets practice.
   Adult: Touches child with medium weight on the shoulder and says "Hi!"
   Child, in sing-song voice: "It's okay, it's just a friend. No one is trying to hurt me."
   Child, out loud with a smile: "Oh, hi! You surprised me!"
   When she knows her lines, tell her to do the prosody to herself.

2. Role-play with her on how to react when a child who is teasing or provoking is bumping into her. The technique is the same as above.

Adult: Gives child a small push.
Child, in sing-song voice: "It's okay. He's teasing me, but I'm not afraid."
Child, out loud with a smile: "Oh, hi! You surprised me! Whatcha doing?"

3. Create a story (like those described in the chapter on autism, *p. 12*) that explains what to expect at a party. Here is a portion of a story about a birthday party that addresses the problem of getting bumped.
I'm going to William's birthday party next Saturday. There will be many kids there. We will sing songs, play games and eat birthday cake. It'll be fun. Sometimes kids get excited at parties and bump other kids. I may get bumped, too. If a boy bumps me, I'll try to remember that it's an accident, and he's just having fun. I can move to another part of the room where it's safe and quiet. That way I can have fun too, without worrying about being bumped.

Tickles, itches and clothing tags

Touch-sensitive children can react frantically to stray hairs and clothing tags on their skin. One boy was able to say where a stray hair had landed under his shirt and, without looking, pull it out. Clothing tags were especially irksome to him.

Method: (young child)
1. Manicure scissors and seam rippers work well for pulling tags off new clothes. Teach the older child how to use these tools, using old clothes.
2. Teach the young child to give his shirt a quick inspection for itchy or ticklish things before the shirt goes on.
3. Role-play this scenario: When he feels a hair in a private place, he learns to excuse himself to use the restroom.
4. If his clothing makes him itch, try detergents for sensitive skin and do an extra rinse cycle on his clothing.

When she can't wear clothes

Some children do not tolerate certain fabric or clothing seams and elastic. Here are some strategies:

Comfort clothing

1. Look for soft breathable clothing. In winter, have the child wear soft luxurious clothing such as corduroy and fleece. In summer, try sports jerseys and natural cottons.

2. Smaller children can wear clothing inside-out so the seams don't abrade them.

3. Replace elastic with a waist cord that ties. Cut the elastic out of the waistband. Open the waist seam three inches at the front. Place two metal grommets into the front of the waist using a grommet tool. String a cord through the

waistband and through the grommets. Tie knots in the ends to keep the cord from slipping out.

4. Cut the tops off socks.

5. Buy or make knitted clothing without seams or elastic. SoftClothing.net is a good source for clothes, from socks to coats, for children of all ages.

6. Try moccasins instead of shoes. In winter, get fleece-lined moccasins, shoes and boots.

Pressure garment

Pressure garments made of breathable, heavy Lycra™ and worn under the child's clothing have calming pressure that can override clothing annoyances. The gold standard is the Washington-based manufacturer, SPIO (SPIO.com). The company sells onesies (leotards), tees, shorts, long-sleeve shirts and long pants, both off-the-rack sizes and customized-for-fit pieces, for children of all ages. If you decide to look for clothing in local stores, consider UnderArmour or replicas of it, but be aware that the compression is much less than that of SPIO. Be sure the cloth is breathable and the fit is snug.

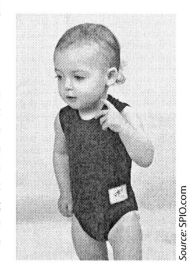

Source: SPIO.com

CUTTING HAIR AND NAILS

The sight of scissors or "snippers" can lead to fearful reactions and protests. There may be a primal fear of being cut. Remember that children respond favorably to the influence of a calm adult. I have seen a child scream in terror when her mother tried to cut her hair, yet sit with perfect aplomb when her special-needs teacher cut it. The teacher stayed calm while the mother reacted emotionally to the child's behaviors.

Try deep pressure to reduce a child's distress.

Method: small child
1. Nails: put pressure on the finger and keep it there while cutting. Nail clippers can be more efficient and less scary looking than manicure scissors. Or try an emery board which may be easier to tolerate. For additional calming, place a weighted blanket or weighted boa around the child's shoulders.
2. Hair: massage the head firmly with fingers or a plastic brush to help desensitize it before washing or combing the hair.
3. Long hair: use hair conditioner to make hair easier to comb. No More Tangles™ conditioner does not sting the eyes and comes in a pump-spray bottle that can be useful for dry, tangled hair. Use a wide-tooth comb to get through snarls with ease.

Method: older child
1. Nails: Practice using nail clippers or manicure scissors on slivers of plastic first until she gets used to the cutting action.
2. Hair: When it comes time to visit a hair-stylist or barber, have the child watch one of the many "Sammy" goes to the barber YouTube videos. Or ask a friend (or a parent in a salon waiting-room) if you can videotape their child getting a haircut. For more tips on video modeling, see p. 14. Consider writing an accompanying story titled, "It's time for my haircut."

GOOEY FINGER FOODS, GLUES AND FINGER PAINTS

Children with touch sensitivities are often intolerant of gooey paints, paper glue and finger foods. There are two general approaches to solving this problem. The first—desensitization—is sensory-based; it targets general sensory skills. The second—gradual exposure—is behavior-based; it targets a specific function such as putting on sunscreen before going out to play. Both methods work well when the child practices them regularly.

Desensitization

In this method, the child plays with increasingly gooey materials. Desensitization is done playfully and slowly so that the child does not become alarmed by the process. Allow the child to use gloves, sticks and utensils until he becomes braver at touching the gooey substances. Try to incorporate desensitization regularly into the child's day so the benefits are maintained.

Materials: A can of fragrance-free shaving cream, water, corn starch, natural food coloring, lunch foods

Setting: Kitchen, therapy room, classroom

When/How often: 1-3 times per day

How long: A few minutes

Possible activities:
1. Play in shaving cream: Have the child shake a can of shaving cream, spray it on a table and then draw pictures in it. Add a touch of food coloring and do this again.
2. Make glue: Put a few drops of water and a small amount of corn starch on a plate. Have the child mix them with a stick to the consistency of thin glue. Fold a piece of paper and, using a stick for spreading, glue the insides of the paper together.
3. Make beads: Put a few drops of water and a small amount of corn starch on a plate. Have the child gradually mix them together and roll the mixture into a bead. Paint the bead (using a brush) and let it dry.
4. Help make lunch: Have the child wash fruit, make a jelly sandwich (have him put a clean finger in the jelly) and handle other lunch foods.

Gradual exposure

This method comes from behavioral therapy and is typically used with children with autism in a discrete trials setting. The following example comes from an article by Ellis, et al (2006). *The method is done playfully so as to reduce fear.*

Materials: A bottle of sunscreen

When/How often: Several times per day

How long: A few minutes

Method:
1. Break the task into a series of short steps. For the task of putting on sunscreen, the first several steps are for acclimation. The therapist instructs the child to do the following:
   a. "Pick up the bottle";
   b. "Turn it upside down";
   c. "Squeeze sunscreen into my hand";
   d. "Put my finger into it and put it on my nose";
   e. And so on, including steps in which the therapist puts a dab of lotion on the child's arm, counts to three and then quickly wipes it off.
2. The last steps of the above task are functional. Once the child has moved past the problem of the gooey sunscreen, she now needs to put the substance on independently when told, "Get the sunscreen from the dresser and put it on your arms."
3. Model each step for the child and ask her to do it.
4. Reward her with a tickle, hug or small treat when she does it.
5. When she performs a step successfully, move to the next step.

Compressing joints with or without isometric exercises

Here is a method that can alleviate modulation issues for touch and proprioception (body) senses. The technique is to gently compress and release joints of the body using isometric exercises.

The protocol is quite easy to perform once you understand the proper pressure compressing the joints.

Materials: None

Setting: Quiet, private space

When/How often: Every day

How long: A few minutes

Compression using isometric exercises

You can train a child age seven or older to compress his own joints using isometric exercises. He can do the steps below in any order.

Tell the child to:

1. Lace fingers and press firmly on the crown of the head, then release. Do this 10 times. (This compresses the shoulder, hip, knee and ankle joints.)
2. Perform wall pushups 10 times. (This compresses the shoulder and elbow joints.)
3. Press palms together 10 times. (This compresses the elbow and wrist joints.)
4. Hold the fingertips of one hand with the other hand and gently pull on them 10 times.
5. Place the palm of one hand at the center of the back below the shoulder blades and the palm of the other hand in front just below the collar bone. Press gently but firmly three times.

Alternate version—compressing joints

A therapist can compress the child's joints using the following method. Do each compression a few times, firmly but gently. Do them quickly. Try to keep one hand on the child's body at all times so that he feels your connection. You can do the steps in any order.

1. Press downward on both shoulders at once, then let up.
2. Crook the elbow. Hold the shoulder with one hand and put the other hand on the bottom of the crooked elbow. Press upward into the shoulder from the elbow.
3. Crook the elbow. With one hand, hold the back of the crooked elbow. Position your other hand to shake hands. Press this hand toward the elbow, and then release it.
4. With one hand, hold the child's palm. With the other hand, hold all of the finger joints (skip the thumb). Gently pull on the fingers and release them.
5. Have the child sit on the floor or on a chair. Put one hand on the hip, the other hand at the front of the bent knee. Press the two points of contact—hip and knee—together.
6. Continue sitting. Put one hand on the knee, the other on the sole of the foot. Press up from the foot into the knee. If the child is seated on a chair, press down on the knees into the ankle and floor.
7. Place the palm of one hand at the center of the back below the shoulder blades and the palm of the other hand in front just below the collar bone. Press gently but firmly three times.

Children who are undersensitive to touch

Children with poor sensitivity are often fidgeters. The child seeks more sensory input than is being registered through the brain, and so she touches people (and objects) to the point that they become irritated. A child with poor sensation may not be aware of food remaining on her face or know when her jacket is crooked. She might not sense finger pressure and thus have difficulty holding a pencil or a fork.

A bigger problem for undersensitive children is poor sensitivity to pain or temperature. These problems put the child at risk for injury.

Looking in the mirror

Help the child with food on her face develop a habit of checking herself in the mirror, especially after meals. She will also need to remember to wipe her mouth often as she eats.

Materials: Mirror

Setting: At the table

Methods:

1. For the older child, a watch with a timer can be a cueing mechanism for her to look in the mirror.
2. Have her practice eating in front of a mirror to help her to see that lips are touching as she eats. (This is even more important if she has poor muscle sensation around the mouth.)
3. While eating in front of a mirror, play this game: Have her close her eyes and touch her mouth and lips in three or four places. In some of these places, put a dab of catsup or drop of water. Have her count the number of places you touch. Can she identify the location of the substance by wiping herself in the correct place before she opens her eyes?

Children who crave touch

Fidgets

Fidgets work well for children who are chronically restless, as well as for those who are constantly touching objects in their environment. Take a little time to select the proper fidget. You will want to consider appropriateness, distractibility and safety issues. Fidgets can be found in therapy catalogs (see Resources, pp. 186-188), at dollar stores—and you can make them!

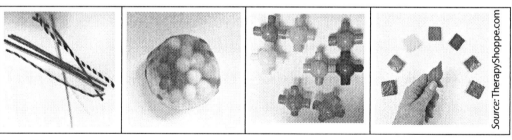

Source: TherapyShoppe.com

Tactile fidgets

Keeping distraction under control

Pick fidgets that are suited to the environment. Make sure that the fidget you choose is not distracting to others.

1. Pin fidgets of all types to a small child's clothing or attach them to the child's waistband.
2. In the classroom, put fidgets inside the pockets of a hoodie sweatshirt where children can toy with them out of sight. In warmer climates, cut off the hood and sleeves of the hoodie so that children don't get too warm.

3. Stick the long bristle edge of a piece of Velcro™ under a desk top or chair rungs. The child can rub the Velcro™ for rough tactile input. Fidgets can be attached to the Velcro under the desk so the child does not distract others as he toys with them.

4. Balls and other projectiles are a poor choice of fidget for the classroom.

Safety concerns

If the child puts things in her mouth, look for fidgets that are made of FDA-approved materials and free of latex, phthalates, PCBs, BPA and lead.

Fidgety jewelry

A wearable fidget is often the best solution. You can attach ribbons of silk, suede and plush to the clothing of a sensitive child. Jewelry works well for many children, too. Consider spin rings, string bracelets and chewable jewelry (found in therapy catalogs).

Other options

1. Theraputty™ is excellent as a fidget but can stick to clothing and electronics.

2. Kneadable erasers including artist's erasers are functional fidgets. They can be found at artist-supply shops.

3. Homemade fidgets work well. A homemade, ugly fidget is less likely to sprout legs and disappear. An effective fidget, made from an unsharpened pencil with a soft eraser and two inexpensive pencil grips, is illustrated here.

4. Create a fidget bin of rice, beans or sand with small cups and toys placed inside. Rice and sand are silky and soothing. Beans give rougher input. Let the child play in the bin for 10 minutes at a time.

STRATEGIES AND INTERVENTIONS: ORAL MOTOR CRAVING AND FIDGETS

Oral motor craving, as seen in constant licking and chewing, is a special situation in sensory modulation. Children who chew constantly are typically craving oral sensation or deep pressure (heavy proprioceptive input) to the oral cavity. This is normal behavior in teething babies and fades with time. For the child with this sensory dysfunction, the craving and the constant movement around the mouth can be managed. There are two main types of craving:

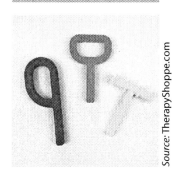

Oral craving: This involves chewing, licking, sucking behaviors of foods, fingers, clothes or "chewies." Clipping food-safe (FDA-approved) chewies to the small child's shirt (see image) or having her wear chewable jewelry are sound strategies for keeping her safe.

Pica: This involves ingestion of non-edible substances. It includes eating dirt, licking windows, and chewing such things as chair legs or toys. The behavior is thought to be caused by a mineral deficiency and a trip to the child's pediatrician is recommended.

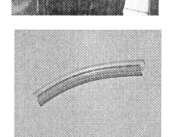

Finding safe things to chew

Look for FDA-approved materials. These include:

1. Plumbing tubing approved for drinking. You can purchase this at hardware stores or online.
2. Chewable jewelry such as Dr. Blooms' Chewable Jewels and Chewelry.
3. Ps, Qs, and Ts.
4. Gum with xylitol, an ingredient that repairs cavities.
5. Carrots and celery.

Source: TherapyShoppe.com

Source: TherapyShoppe.com

STRATEGIES AND ADAPTATIONS: INTERNAL SENSATIONS, PAIN, TEMPERATURE AND ITCH

Internal sensation has a formal name: interoception. It involves a combination of normal and abnormal sensations including temperature, breath, pain, itch, sensation from a bruise or from gut inflammation, nausea, hunger or satiation, and stomach cramps. As with the other senses, the body may have difficulty modulating these sensations. For example, a small cut may produce a big reaction in a child who is oversensitive to pain. Contrast that with another child who shows no symptoms of serious gut inflammation.

Issue	Signs & Symptoms
Oversensitive	Complains of gastric problems, feels warm and cool temperatures as hot and cold. May be a picky eater.
Undersensitive	May not register stomach pain, doesn't register heat, cold or pain.
Craving	

GENERAL ADVICE

Gastric-related issues

1. Be alert for medical issues. If the child has regular symptoms of stomach aches, this could be a sign of anxiety and/or gastric issues, including inflammation.

2. Recommend testing for possible food sensitivities, especially if they run in the family.

3. Remember that a child with a gut inflammation and poor sensitivity in the gut may not demonstrate pain but act-out the gut disturbance with other behaviors.

4. Note that a small or non-verbal child who resists moving out of unusual body positions or becomes highly agitated when moved may be in pain.

Temperature-related issues

Oversensitivity

1. For the child with temperature sensitivities, use gradual exposure and desensitization methods (as described in the section on touch, *p. 65*) to help him accept a broader range of temperatures.

2. The "getting-centered" techniques described earlier in the book will also be helpful.

Undersensitivity

1. Safety is the primary concern for a child with poor temperature sensation. Parents will want to regularly drill safety skills until they are assimilated. Children with autism can be trained in temperature safety with videos and written stories.

2. Place a mark on the wall and on the faucet showing how far to turn hot water handles. Test this with the child until you are sure that the procedure has been learned.

Itching-related issues

1. Lotion for itch: anti-pruritic and colloidal oatmeal lotions are good.

2. Rectal itching can be relieved with over-the-counter hemorrhoid creams and ointments.

3. Children who have messy stools and sensitive touch will find relief by thoroughly cleaning themselves after a bowel movement. A half-shower after the bowel movement does the trick. Use soft flannel or extra-large cotton balls to wipe the rectal area afterwards. (Make sure that the skin is very dry.) Another option is to use moistened wipes as long as they do not cause irritation.

4. If the child has eczema, consider having her tested for food sensitivities, especially dairy-related.

Pain-related issues

Oversensitivity

1. Have the child practice switching focus to a different part of the body. For example, if she cuts her finger, focus attention on her foot instead.

2. Consider a calming or stress-reduction program for a child who is oversensitive to aches and pains. Anxiety can increase sensory symptoms and so staying calm may help to reduce pain.

Undersensitivity

1. Safety is the primary concern, and so educating the child using drills, videos and stories is important.

2. Help to sensitize the child's skin and muscles with massage, joint compressions and yoga.

Strategies and Adaptations: Movement

Our physical movement relies on the vestibular sense (located in our head) and the proprioceptive sense (located in the body). These two senses provide feedback to the brain as we move, thereby keeping our movements coordinated and our posture upright. Both the vestibular and proprioception senses can, when dysfunctional, exacerbate the modulation problems of oversensitivity, undersensitivity and craving. These categories of dysfunction can cause children to be in constant motion or, conversely, to become sedentary and reluctant to move. Some children appear to be hyperactive, and their agitated movements can mimic ADHD at times.

When movement modulation problems occur, it is either a dysfunction of the vestibular sense or the proprioceptive sense. The two senses are so deeply entwined that we can have difficulty sorting out which sense is most dysfunctional, or the biggest problem, in a given instance. This complicates the choice of remedy. Fortunately, some of the best therapies are those that provide sensory input to both the vestibular and proprioceptive senses simultaneously, while doing so in a fun way with play. In this section we look at strategies and interventions that tackle problems involving these two senses in isolation to one another and in combination.

Strategies and Adaptations: Proprioception (body sense)

When the brain is unable to modulate input from the body, a myriad of problems can ensue. These include poor coordination, hyperactivity, and abnormally sedentary behavior. In the chapter on calming, we saw how a combination of heavy work, deep pressure, exercise and play helps to regulate the body. We looked at a number of ways to utilize those strategies. In this section, we revisit those ideas, beginning by looking at heavy work using weighted vests, and then considering the effectiveness of deep pressure using pressure garments. Finally, we consider interventions utilizing exercise and play.

Issue	Signs & Symptoms
Oversensitive	A touch to the arm feels like being hit; muscle aches; avoids crowds.
Undersensitive	Sluggish, clumsy, poor handwriting.
Craving	Crashing, bumping; hugs people excessively; wears heavy clothes or blankets out of season; drops to floor (small child) in effort to be dragged; avoids exercise.

General advice

1. A key to good physical modulation is a steady dose of heavy work, play, exercise and deep pressure. Try to incorporate physical activity into the child's day every two hours. Have the child engage in structured movement, climbing on play equipment, yoga and stretching and other physical play. These activities encourage development of coordination skills and enhance the brain's ability to modulate that input.

2. Timing therapy can correct coordination problems, which in turn can decrease proprioceptive modulation issues.

3. Traditional massage, qigong massage, brushing and joint compressions can provide modulating deep pressure to muscles.

Helping bodies to be still

Here are a variety of approaches that employ heavy work, exercise and deep pressure as the underlying principle. Often it is not clear which method is the better choice for a child, so a trial-and-error approach may be necessary. Additional strategies are provided in the vestibular section.

Two protocols for weighted vest

Place small weights totaling 5-10% of the child's body weight into the front and back pockets of a weighted vest, and follow one of the two protocols below. If the vest does not have enough weight packets, you will need to add more. You can find weights in sporting goods shops or make your own.

The evidence for the effectiveness of weighted vests is primarily based on two small studies using protocols described below (Fertel-Daly, 2003; Collins, 2011). According to those studies, vests work about half the time.

Setting: Anywhere

When/How often: Every 1½-2 hours

Amount of time: See Method

Materials: A weighted vest, additional weights, as needed

Source: TherapyShoppe.com

Method:
1. Weigh the child.
2. Distribute weight equaling 5-10% of child's body weight into the vest pockets. Adjust as needed so the child is working against the weight but not struggling. Use no more than 10% of body weight.

Protocol 1
3. Put the vest on the child for 15-20 minutes every 1½-2 hours.

Protocol 2
3. Have the child wear the vest two hours on, two hours off, throughout the day.

Variation: Older child
Weighted vests with brand names and team names can be found in sporting-goods stores. They are a good option for calming a boy with high-functioning autism who needs to stay calm as he navigates middle-school hallways.

WEIGHTED BLANKETS, LAP WEIGHTS

Lap weights designed as turtles and bears can help wiggly, small children stay still during circle time or centers. An older child can also hold a weighted object such as a heavy book or backpack on her lap.

Weighted blankets (homemade or those found in therapy catalogs) are useful for calming. Make sure that the child is comfortable with the weight of the blanket and is not struggling against it. As with vests, the child should wear no more than 10% of her body weight.

Make your own weighted blanket: Instructions for making weighted blankets, lap weights and boas are easily found online. Remember to use washable fill material such as poly pellets. Rice, beans and corn mold when they get wet.

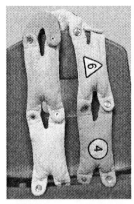

PRESSURE GARMENTS

Wearing a pressure garment made from heavy Lycra® or neoprene helps keep a child's body calm by providing deep pressure to the trunk, arms and legs. Pressure garments are sold by a number of manufacturers, including Benik, TheraTogs and SPIO. Benik and TheraTogs make neoprene garments which are oversized and then made to fit snugly with Velcro™. SPIO garments are made of heavy, breathable Lycra and come in one-piece suits, short and long-sleeve tees, and short and long-leg pants. Most manufacturers provide a trial wearing period. Parents might also consider purchasing snugly fitting UnderArmour™ shirts and pants, as well as bicycle clothes.

Although manufacturers have solid case studies on the benefits and usage of pressure garments, there is no published, evidence-based protocol at this time. Manufacturers recommend wearing the garment underneath the child's clothing all day long.

Source: SPIO.com

EXERCISE AND PLAY

Play is an excellent way to modulate the body. Choose activities that exercise the entire body and make the child work hard. Some children become "wired" with movement and need a cool-down period following play. In the classroom, a 1-to-2-minute timeout should suffice. Have children sit at their desks with feet on the floor and their heads lying on their folded arms. Turn off lights and put on calming music. Optionally, pass a weighted ball (five pounds for third graders) around the classroom.

Setting: Anywhere

When/How often: Every 2 hours

Amount of time: 10 minutes or more

Materials: As needed

Types of activities:
1. Animal walks, including frog jumps, bear walks, and crab walks.
2. Outdoor play on climbing equipment and monkey bars.
3. Jumping on an indoor or outdoor trampoline.
4. Tug-of-war with a long knotted rope.
5. Hop-scotch with variations that include touching the floor with the hops.
6. Jump rope.
7. Relay races.

TEACHER SAYS

Children can get a good workout with this variation of "Simon Says." Follow the activity with a short cool-down period.

Setting: Classroom

When/How often: Morning or afternoon break

Amount of time: 10 minutes

Materials: None

Types of activities:
1. Have children stand and follow your directives for the game of "Teacher Says."
2. Say: "Teacher says, 'Climb a rope! Pull that rope!'" Demonstrate pulling an invisible rope that hangs from the sky. Pull it hard.
3. Have children do an assortment of exercises such as rowing a boat, swimming, hopping, and jumping. Include 2-3 minutes of jogging in place and then finish up with jumping jacks.

STRATEGIES AND ADAPTATIONS: VESTIBULAR (BALANCE)

The vestibular sense is quite complex. Both inner ears have five movement sensors: three measure the x, y and z axes of linear movement (up-and-down, side-to-side, and back-and-forth), and two measure clockwise and counterclockwise rotation. Speed of movement is also measured. With so many sensors, there are many ways the vestibular sense can fail to modulate its input. During vestibular processing the brain feeds information to the body, eyes and ears about the head's movement. The body, eyes and ears use that information to help the body to move, the eyes to aim correctly and the ears to understand where auditory information is coming from. In addition, the body, eyes and ears provide input to the vestibular sense to help it understand context so that the head moves properly. For example, we might need to tilt the head forward to get a better look at something the eyes want to clarify. The body moves the head forward, and the vestibular sense keeps the head in the correct upright position.

If the body, eyes or ears fail to do their jobs correctly, the child's internal impression of what he is currently doing is confused. This may make his world spin, causing him to be anxious or fearful.

When a child is oversensitive to head movement, he may become fearful or nauseous when washing his hair or riding in a car or on a swing. Alternatively, he may become stimulated by head movement and crave it. A child who is undersensitive to the vestibular sense may bump into things or fall out of his chair. His brain, sensing the lack of input, may crave movement, sending him into constant motion.

Children with poor vestibular modulation are sometimes misdiagnosed with ADHD. The constant movement is mistaken for hyperactivity. The accompanying dizziness may cause the child to act without regard to others and, to the untrained observer, the child may seem impulsive. Here are two brief examples of ways that the vestibular system can malfunction.

Example 1: When Jon is riding his bike and sees a bump on the road, his senses share information that allow him to adjust his body for posture, steady his head to avoid being jostled, and understand why his head moved up and down over the bump. Without this sensory input coming together, he could lose focus when his head is jostled and fall off the bike.

Example 2: Adele is normally a quiet child, but whenever she gets too much vestibular input such as jumping on a trampoline she starts to scream with excitement. Without help, she is a whirlwind in constant movement, disrupting everyone around her. It can take her 20 minutes to calm down and sit still.

Issue	Signs & Symptoms
Oversensitive	Dislikes moving head especially for tasks such as hair washing; gets nauseous easily. Refuses to participate in movement activities.
Undersensitive	Poor coordination. Falls out of seat; bumps into walls.
Craving	Constant movement: jumping, running, cartwheels, etc.

Vestibular issues can be treated by an occupational or physical therapist. Therapy may include exercise with a therapy ball, a balance beam, listening to sound therapy, or working with special equipment such as the Astronaut Board. Given that there are so many forms of vestibular dysfunction, the therapist needs to do some detective work to sort out the issues and then prescribe exercises for clinic and home.

Strategies for vestibular modulation issues

Here are a variety of quick strategies for improving vestibular modulation.

Wiggle cushion to stay seated

Air-filled "wiggle" cushions provide children with movement and decrease the need to get up and move around. They are effective with approximately 50% of children who try them. Cushions come in two different shapes and in multiple sizes. One side of the cushion has bumps and can be used by a child who needs additional tactile stimulation. The other side is smooth. Have the child try out several cushions to find the most comfortable option.

Source: TherapyShoppe.com

Therapy ball for increased attention

Source: SensoryJunction.com

An alternative to a "wiggle" cushion is the therapy ball. Evidence shows that children with sensory issues or ADHD have better focus in the classroom and improved attention to homework while sitting on a ball.

Moving to a ball that has no back support is not for everyone, and so plan on a trial-period over a few days with a backup chair nearby. Special strategies are needed for impulsive children and for children with poor core strength:

1. Children with poor core strength and poor posture should not use a therapy ball as long-term seating. They can, however, use a therapy ball-chair as long as the feet touch the floor while seated and the back rests comfortably on the back support.

2. If the child is impulsive or hyperactive, make sure that the ball has a stand (or legs) to discourage its use as a toy.

3. If the child is unable to sit quietly without bouncing on the ball or playing with it, behavioral strategies may be needed.

Getting past dizziness

Ear infections and Meniere's disease can cause the vestibular system to act up for a few days at a time. While it may be necessary to treat the child's ear infection, a parent might be able to wait out Meniere's. Sometimes consumption of a small amount of caffeine, as in weak green or black tea, can help the brain push past vertigo symptoms. Movement is preferred over lying in bed since the vestibular system is best kept activated. Once the child can walk without nausea, he can do exercises that challenge his eyes while moving, such as the exercise below.

Vestibular exercises on stairs

The following exercises help calm a dizzy vestibular system. Start slowly, doing only what the child can tolerate. Gradually move to two or more repetitions of each exercise.

Materials: A pencil or fingertip, rubber-soled shoes for safety

Setting: A stairway (preferably uncarpeted) with six to 10 stairs and a handrail

When/How often: A few times a day, or for severe symptoms, every 2 hours

Amount of time: 5-10 minutes

CAUTION: *Stay behind the child while ascending the stairway, in front of him when descending, climbing with him to keep him safe.*

Method:
Here are the instructions, as presented to the child:

1. Stand at the bottom of the stairs. Place a finger about 10 inches from your nose (or whatever is comfortable) and keep both eyes fastened to your fingertip. Hold tightly to the handrail with your other hand.
2. Walk up and down stairs slowly, keeping your eyes on your fingertip.
3. As you walk, move your head slowly to each side, back and forth, watching your fingertip as you climb up and down the stairs.
4. Move your head slowly up and down, watching your fingertip as you climb.

Additional exercise

Once the initial scary symptoms are gone, the child can engage in fun vestibular play to complete the healing. Games such as play ball, ping-pong, badminton, tennis, and kite-flying exercise and encourage the reintegration of vision and vestibular.

SWINGING

Swings are a fun way for children to get all types of vestibular input. The following swings are useful at home, school or clinic. It is important to select the right swing for the right situation. Be sure that the child can tolerate the specific action of a given swing before investing in it.

Lycra Swing

Setting: Hang in any room.

Uses: Calming, alerting, vestibular therapy.

Heavy Lycra™ swings such as the Airwalker or Cuddle Swing are large enough to lie in, making them effective for calming a distraught child. But Lycra™ swings are great for alerting too, since the springy action of the Lycra™ responds to bouncing and shaking. In terms of vestibular response, the child can get rotational or linear input with eyes closed or open.

Platform swing

Setting: Hang in any room. Some models fit in a door frame or on a stand-alone frame.

Special feature: Soft bumpers can be added to the sides to prevent infants and small children from falling off.

Uses: Acclimation to vestibular input, calming, vestibular therapy.

The platform swing is a therapy staple used for many purposes with infants and children of all ages.

Inner tube swing

Setting: Outdoors or indoors with a mat on the ground or floor beneath.

Uses: Heavy work, alerting, calming, vestibular and proprioception therapy.

The inner-tube swing is highly versatile. A child can punch or kick it, providing him with fun heavy work. A child can swing side-saddle or traditionally. To help satiate rotational craving, the child can be spun on it in large or tight circles (see method and cautions below).

Hammock swing

Setting: Outdoors or indoors with a mat underneath.

Uses: As part of a sensory nest, calming.

The hammock swing can be placed over a child's bed, in the den or attached to trees. In a quiet place, it is a safe space for retreat. Its side-to-side movement is excellent for calming.

Source: SensoryJunction.com

Tolerating rotation: platform swing

For a child with low tolerance for swinging, the platform swing is a good first choice.

Put toys in the center of the swing, encourage the child to get on, and then hold the swing steady while she plays on it. Move the swing slightly at first and then gradually in bigger arcs. Take care not to alarm her.

Optionally, gently hold the child in your arms as you slowly sway on the swing.

SATIATING ROTATIONAL VESTIBULAR CRAVING

One boy I observed, a first grader with vestibular craving, would perform, after rising from his desk, one or two cartwheels in the back of the classroom or in a hallway. Such sensory craving can be reduced with satiation. Here the child is regularly given large doses of the stimulation he seeks. For vestibular satiation, I find that one to two such experiences a week for 6-8 weeks works well. But be warned, this method is not effective for all children. And use caution.

Materials: Frog or tire swing

Setting: Therapy room

When/How often: 1-2 times a week, until the child regularly senses the rotation (see Step 5 below for explanation). This is typically done for 1-2 months.

Amount of time: See "Caution"

CAUTION: *This is strong input; use it only for children with poor vestibular modulation who crave rotational vestibular input. Start slowly, for just 1-2 minutes at a time, until you understand the child's tolerance for rotational input. Nausea may not show up for 20 minutes or more after spinning. Gently increase spinning over time.*

Method:
1. Ensure that the child is seated safely and is holding on tightly.
2. Slowly push the child in a wide circle.
3. Reverse direction and repeat step 2.
4. If the child is craving more, try a few rotations in each direction. You can increase the speed (but keep it safe).
5. In future sessions, increase the number of rotations and the speed of movement. Stop after 10 minutes or when you see a look of surprise or alertness in the child's face that indicates registration of vestibular input. Children with vestibular craving have a very high tolerance for input because they do not easily sense the stimulation. Satiation therapy provides a strong enough input that a child's body can sense it in the pit of the stomach.

The Astronaut Board

Another way to reduce craving (and to repair other vestibular problems) involves having the child work methodically through vestibular input programs. One such program, called Astronaut Training, consists of a series of vestibular-sound-ocular motor exercises that are done on a padded spin-board called the Astronaut Board. The vestibular aspect of the exercises is straightforward. The child sits or lies in different positions on the Astronaut Board. As the board is rotated, the vestibular sensors in each ear are activated. Rotation is done slowly in each direction.

Mary Kawar, designer of the program, sells the boards on her site, AstronautBoards.com. Information about her training program can be found there as well. You can also build your own board with plans found online.

Getting linear movement

Linear vestibular input is easy to produce through the use of bicycles, roller skates, zip lines, and skate boards. Also consider using glider swings which are calming.

Using more than one vestibular aspect at a time is a good approach since it helps to integrate input from multiple sensors. Some examples of activities that exercise multiple sensors are:

1. Swinging on a trapeze.
2. Sliding down a slanted zip line or a slide.
3. Swinging on the playground.
4. Riding skate boards and bicycles on hills.

Up and down

Getting vertical input to sensors is easy with jumping games, trampolines, Hippity Hops, and pogo sticks. Jumping on a trampoline provides heavy work as well as vestibular input. Mini-trampolines are viable in many settings, including small offices, since they store sideways.

Scooting

Scooter boards are fun ways for children to get both heavy work and vestibular input. They come with and without padding and in a variety of sizes. You can also make your own scooter board from build-it-yourself plans available online.

Source: TherapyShoppe.com

HOW TO CREATE A SENSORY-RICH LIFE

In this chapter, we have discussed strategies that can keep children with poor sensory modulation self-regulated in a given setting, along with therapies that can help resolve certain sensory issues. Now we look at additional ways to provide self-regulation using approaches that involve sensory boxes, chores and adaptations (to the home or school environment). Later, we examine how these approaches can be combined to create a sensory-rich life for the child.

Approaches to a sensory-rich life

1. Sensory strategies for the child.
2. Sensory adaptations to the environment.
3. Sensory boxes and bins.
4. Heavy work, play, exercise, and deep pressure.
5. Chores for home and school.
6. Sensory nests for calming.
7. Sensory rooms and spaces.
8. Therapy.

Make a sensory box, rice bin, bean bin or sand bin

Sensory boxes and bins contain items that can satisfy a child's tactile, auditory and visual cravings for input. Children are given access to the items in the box during scheduled breaks. Choose items that are appropriate for the child's environment. Make sure that you think through safety issues and the mess that the items can make.

Rice, bean, and sand bins

Materials: Plastic bins, rice, beans, sand

Setting: Use anywhere. Store safely in a cupboard, drawer or on a shelf

When/How often: Every 1 ½-2 hours or as needed

Amount of time: 5-15 minutes

Make a bin of rice, beans or sand:
Give the child the opportunity to immerse her hands in rice and to feel its silky texture. When she pours a cup of rice into the bin, she also stimulates her vision and hearing.

1. Find or purchase a plastic container the size of a dishpan. Ensure that the lid fits tightly. Label it.
2. Rice bin: Fill a bin with rice. Add objects such as small cups and spoons that the child can use to scoop rice and watch it fall. Add large beads and small toys for additional interest.
3. Bean bin: Fill a bin with dried beans of all sizes. Hide toys in the bin.
4. Sand bin: Fill a bin with clean sand, small shovels or spoons, cups, toy cars, and other small items such as beach toys. Sand is messy, so plan to store it (and use it) in an appropriate place. Remember that sand may stick to plastic surfaces, causing additional messes.

Fidget bins

Materials: Fidgets of all sorts and plastic bins

Setting: Use anywhere. Store safely in a cupboard, drawer or on a shelf

When/How often: Every 1 ½-2 hours or as needed

Amount of time: 5-15 minutes

Make a sensory box:
The child plays with items in the box as a way of soothing the senses.
1. Find a large shoebox or a plastic bin. Label it.
2. Fill the box with items that can stimulate and calm each sense in turn.
   a. Tactile: fidgets, textured materials (both soft and rough), stuffed animals, putty, dough, Theraband™ or other stretchy material, textured balls.
   b. Visual: kaleidoscope, magazines, coloring book and crayons or markers, and colorful dough.
   c. Auditory: an iPod or MP3 player with calm music, toys with musical sounds, small instruments.
   d. Olfactory: scented cotton balls. Add scent to cotton balls using a few drops of naturally scented essential oil. Place the cotton balls in a zip-lock bag. Citrus and vanilla are good choices for the scent. Label the bag. Do not use artificial scents, since children might be allergic to them.

How to use the boxes and bins

1. Store the boxes and bins in a safe place so the materials are not lost.
2. Determine the child's schedule for using the box. It could be as often as every 1.5-2 hours, or just once or twice a day.
3. When it is time to use the box, the child can take the full box or a few items to the play site. You will need a special arrangement for rice or sand bins since they can be quite messy.
4. The child uses the items for 10-15 minutes or as time permits.
5. Consider letting the child use the sensory box every 1.5-2 hours so he gets sensory input at regular intervals.
6. Once a schedule is established, stick to it as much as possible. In any event, the child does not earn the sensory box, nor is it given on demand.
7. For young children, or children with autism or children with poor cognition, consider using a timer or visual timer to schedule use of the box. Also use the timer to set a time limit on the use of the box. When the timer rings to announce play time, let the child choose items from the box. The timer is then set for 10 minutes. When the timer rings, the child returns the items to the box and the timer is set for the next scheduled use of the box.

Variation for middle school and high school

Older children can carry sensory items in their backpacks or stash them in their lockers for use between classes. Consider using small malleable items such as pipe cleaners, Tangles™, small Koosh balls, artist erasers, a plastic coiled wrist keychain, modeling clay and barrettes.

Make a sensory nest

A sensory nest is space that is safe, quiet and comfortable. It may consist simply of a hammock swing over a bed. Or it can be quite elaborate: a tent with pillows, iPod, lava lamp and plush toys. The nest becomes a child's refuge after a hard day at school or when the world is pushing in too close. Sensory nests can also be set up in the back of a classroom where highly sensitive children and children with autism can take refuge for a few minutes.

Options for the nest:
- Pup tent, cardboard box, sheet thrown over a table.
- Pillows, bean bag chairs.
- Blankets, a weighted blanket.
- Soft lighting, flash light, lava lamp.
- Music device with headphones.
- Quiet toys and fidgets.
- Music device with headphones.
- Stuffed animals, plush toys.

Sensory spaces at home and school

A space in the house, yard, or at school can be used for active sensory play. Purchase or make equipment that allows the child opportunities to engage in heavy work. The following list offers ideas for equipping the space. Check out therapy catalogs and see Resources in the back of the book for additional ideas.

- Hang a trapeze in a doorway. Install a zip-line on a slant when 20 feet or more of open space is available.
- Hang a swing or inner tube in the basement, den or backyard. Put a mat or soft cushions on hard floors.
- Make a ramp from an 8-foot sheet of plywood for use with a scooter board. This play provides lots of fun and heavy work.
- Install an outdoor swing-set or climbing structure.
- For the emotionally reactive child, hang a heavy Lycra™ swing from an 8-foot ceiling or a hammock swing over the bed to allow for self-comforting.
- Purchase therapy balls as exercise aids. Many online sources have suggestions for how to play on them. SuperDuperInc.com sells a 60-card deck of activities called the Therapy Ball Activity Cards Fun Deck.
- Make space for small children to ride a tricycle in school halls or at home.

Chores at home

Chores give a child a chance to get heavy work as well as an opportunity to learn life skills. A small child can carry items for mom and dad, sweep with a toy broom, push chairs into place, put away toys and throw clothes in a hamper. An older child can make a bed, carry laundry and garbage, scrub a pot, sweep or vacuum a room, and dust. Select chores that involve lifting, pushing, or sweeping. Remember to include yard work.

Chores at school: movement and responsibilities

At school, children can benefit from movement breaks in the morning and afternoon. In addition, fidgety children can be honored with picking up books at the end of a class and passing out books for the next class. Movement and heavy work help to burn off energy and keep children regulated.

STEPS IN CREATING A LIFE FILLED WITH SENSATION

How does a therapist figure out what activities, strategies and therapies to recommend to parents and schools to improve a child's ability to modulate sensory input? Below is a three-step process that serves as a guide. Use the forms provided on pages 187-189 to structure interviews and to list strategies, adaptations, activities and therapies for the child.

Step 1: Assess the situation

a. Have both the parents and school personnel complete a sensory questionnaire such as the Sensory Profile, Short Sensory Profile or the SPM (Sensory Processing Measure). This screening helps to determine which sensory systems and environments to focus on.

b. Interview the parents and school personnel to determine what situations and times of day are most difficult for the child.

c. Summarize the issues in a few paragraphs.

d. List your observations. To do so, consider making a copy of the form on p. 170 called Sensory Observations Throughout the Day. This form is set up to track times when the child needs help with modulation.

Step 2: Create a plan

a. List helpful adaptations that can be made to the child's environment. (Make a copy of the Sensory Adaptations form on p. 172.)

b. List strategies that teachers, parents and the child can use to increase the child's modulation. (See the Sensory Strategies form on page 171.)

c. Would the child benefit from therapy? If so, list the therapy programs and the time required to do the programs. (See the Therapy Schedule form on p. 173.)

d. Make a copy of the Heavy Work/Play/Exercise Schedule on p. 174 to set times for heavy work, play and exercise.

Step 3: Put the plan into place

a. If the plan is not too complex, put it in place all at once, so that the child has a single lifestyle change.

b. If the plan contains several new activities that significantly change the family's schedule, such as yoga in the morning and gymnastics during the week, then break the plan into stages so that no one is overwhelmed.

CASE STUDY: SARAH

The following case study illustrates the three steps.

Sarah is an 8-year-old child attending third grade public school. Her parents requested a sensory assessment due to picky eating at home and inappropriate behaviors at school.

Assess the situation

Sarah's parents described her as generous and willing to please. However, she tends to be crabby, and occasionally she has a tantrum after getting home from school. She likes school and gets good grades without too much effort. However, she often claims to be too tired to do homework and, most nights, she fights with her parents about doing it.

Sarah spends her free time in her room listening to music and drawing. On weekends she stays busy with hobbies and spends time online. She also likes to ride her bike and hang out with her best friend, Toni. However, Toni does not live close by, and they get together only a few times a week. She does not have other close friends.

On Sunday, the family goes to church and then to her grandparents' house for dinner. Each week, Sarah begs to stay home by herself. She had stopped attending Sunday school the previous year because she found it too noisy. Now she attends the adult church service but finds that boring. She resists going to her grandparents' house because she doesn't get along with her rowdy cousins, and she is perpetually in fear they will run into her as they play. In addition, she does not like her grandma's cooking.

Sarah's Sensory Profile indicated "definite" oversensitivity to sound and touch. (That means she has a "definite difference" from her peers.) In addition, she demonstrated oral sensory behaviors: she avoids "squishy" foods including stews, casseroles and most cooked vegetables. She craves salt and sugar. She also exhibits emotional behaviors including nightmares and occasional tantrums. She seems unhappy most of the time.

The Sensory Processing Measure (SPM) was completed by school personnel, including Sarah's teacher, her bus driver, gym teacher and an aide in the cafeteria. Those results showed that Sarah had oversensitivity to sound and touch. Her teacher noted that Sarah, though a good student, had occasional emotional outbursts. Sarah's outbursts were most likely to occur in noisy environments such as the gym, cafeteria and music class.

The gym teacher said he encouraged her to take an active part in games, yet she tended to stand by at the edge of the action. The bus driver noted that she frequently complained about the noise on the bus and about other children bumping her. The cafeteria aide wrote that Sarah spent some of her lunch period with her hands over her ears. Some students teased her for this. Two students had been disciplined for targeting her; they made a game of bumping into her to watch her reaction.

A summary of the issues

- Sarah is able to stay self-regulated when on her own in a quiet environment. But she is easily irritated in noisy and crowded environments such as her school bus, music class, the gym, the cafeteria, Sunday school and her grandparents' house.

- She becomes reactive to being touched when jostled by other children during school line-ups and when playing with her cousins at her grandmother's house.

- During gym, she has developed a strategy of staying on the edge of play so that she does not get shoved.

- She does her best to be good all day at school. But she lets out her frustrations when she gets home.

- At church, she avoids the lively children in Sunday school by going to the adult service. But there she fidgets constantly and tries to engage her mother in conversation.

- She craves snacks and prefers not to eat healthy foods. She does not like the texture of "squishy" foods such as stews, casseroles and most cooked vegetables.

Sensory and Behavior Observation Form

Once Sarah's OT had interviewed parents and teachers, she filled out the Sensory and Behavior Observation form to get a better understanding of Sarah's struggle to stay self-regulated. (This form is provided on page 170.)

Getting up and getting to school: *Sarah is fine until it is time to get on the bus.*

When	Problem	Behaviors	Mood	Calm/Alert	Comments
7:40	Noisy, crowded	Whines	Crabby	C	Doesn't like bus

During the school day: *Sarah has problems throughout the day.*

When	Problem	Behaviors	Mood	Calm/Alert	Comments
10:00 Tues	Too loud	Refusal	Crabby	C	Doesn't like music class
10:00 Wed	Noisy, kids shoving	Stays at edge of play	Hyper-vigilant	C	She is using some strategies
11:15	Noise in cafeteria	Hands over ears	Anxious	C	Are there options?
	Junk food lunch	Silly on playground	Giddy	-	Won't eat healthy food
12:30			Sleepy	A	Due to junk food?
2:00	Another child Bumped her	Tantrum	Angry	C	During lineup for restroom

After school: *Sarah is irritable at home in the evening.*

When	Problem	Behaviors	Mood	Calm/Alert	Comments
4:00	Left-over anxiety from school	Slams doors, screams	Angry	C	She held it in all day
6:15	Doesn't like most foods	Whiny	Unhappy	C	Picks at food
8:30	Not sleepy	Whiny		C	Doesn't want to go to bed

Saturday: *Typically a good day for Sarah. She spends time in her room reading or playing with her friend Toni. Dinner is usually pizza which she loves.*

Sunday: *Sarah does not like to go to church or to her grandparents' house for dinner. She wants to stay home on her own.*

When	Problem	Behaviors	Mood	Calm/Alert	Comments
10:00	Church school is noisy	Refusal, arguing	Crabby	C	Does not want to go
11:15	Church service is "boring"	Fidgets, talks		A	Prefers the service, but fidgets constantly
1:00	Does not like Sunday at grandparents' house	Refuses to eat, whines	Unhappy	C	Behaviors around food. Rowdy cousins.

Create a strategy: adaptations, strategies and therapies

Here are suggestions for strategies, adaptations and self-regulating activities such as heavy work, play and exercise.

1. Education
   a. Educate Sarah about her sensitivities and how they affect her. Learning about herself will help her to develop coping strategies and allow her to participate more fully at school and in outside activities.

2. Noisy environments
   a. Provide Sarah with an attractive headband that is padded at the ears, and suggest she wear it during music, gym and cafeteria to dampen sounds.
   b. If necessary, ask Sarah's doctor if she could wear ear buds or ear plugs under the headband.

3. Touching and bumping issues
   a. Let Sarah walk at the back of the line so she is not bumped.
   b. Role-play ways in which she graciously asks others to give her a little space so she is not bumped.
   c. Arrange for Sarah to get sufficient heavy work, play and exercise throughout the day so she is better able to tolerate her sensitivities. (Her teacher was planning on adding two 5-minute movement breaks to the day to help the class stay alert.)

4. Staying on the sidelines in gym
   a. Sarah has already developed a strategy in the gym to avoid being bumped or shoved. Staying on the edge of play is working for her, but this strategy could ultimately be maladaptive since she loses opportunities for play and social-skill growth. Unless the therapies below solve the problem, she needs to be encouraged to work hard in individual sports as a way to make up for the loss of the benefits of team play.

5. Addressing after-school behaviors and tantrums
   a. Meet her at a local park and let her release her frustration through play.
   b. Create a nest at home for her to use after school. (Her parents suggested installing a hammock over her bed where she could lie and listen to music.) On arrival home, let her relax with a snack and unwind before putting any demands on her.
   c. Put out paper and paints and ask her to draw a picture of her day.

6. Touch therapy
   a. Initiate a brushing program at home and school. Or wait until summer break to do it at home. Sarah may be willing and able to do her own program, with someone helping to brush her back. Brushing may decrease her defensive behaviors.

7. Sound therapy
   a. Try an introductory sound-therapy program for a few weeks to see if it reduces sound sensitivity.

b. If some improvement is observed, consider a full sound-therapy program for her, based at school, home or in a clinic.

8. Picky eating

   a. Parents have suggested getting help with Sarah's picky eating from a local pediatric clinic.

   b. No starchy snacks within 90 minutes of mealtime. Healthy snacks like cheese or raw veggies are okay.

   c. She should engage in heavy work activities about an hour before dinner to help with appetite.

9. Sunday service

   a. Give her fidgets or appropriate books to read in church to help keep her engaged. This does not address the issue of attending Sunday school with her peers.

   b. Try a rewards-based program for attending Sunday school. In addition, she could wear her headband and use seating strategies such as sitting at the back or to the side of the room.

10. Sunday at her grandparents' house

    a. Bring a dish to share. Sarah can help select the dish and prepare the food.

    b. Organize a play activity for Sarah and the cousins with adult supervision. Consider games such as badminton, croquet or lawn darts that do not involve bumping. Or go roller skating or skate boarding.

The plan

Sarah's parents have opted to try an introductory sound-therapy program for a few weeks. They decided to wait until summer to try a brushing program, but will regularly incorporate some form of heavy work, play, exercise or deep pressure into her schedule. They plan to phase in an after-school activity, as well as yoga in the morning and at-home chores, over a period of two months.

Sarah agreed to an after-school activity from a choice of gymnastics, martial arts and swimming. She opted for karate and asked to go twice a week. Karate is a good choice because it builds social skills, provides fun, grounds the body and enhances self-confidence.

Her teacher started doing short movement breaks twice a day once she realized that several children in the classroom would benefit from the activity. The teacher conducts simple exercises (while standing) in the morning. In the afternoon, they play a game called "Teacher Says" (based on "Simon Says") in which children imitate movements such as rowing a boat, climbing a tree, jogging and doing jumping jacks. This vigorous activity helps the children stay calm and focused.

At home, Sarah was given new chores that involve heavy work. These new responsibilities are accompanied by her first allowance and by guidance in using the money wisely. Her main chore is sweeping the dining-room floor after moving the dinner chairs away from the table each evening. In addition she helps her father take garbage to the curb and load the car for the trip to church and to his parents' house on Sundays. Her father now takes the cousins for a walk to the park near his parents' house each Sunday where the children play in the playground. He helps Sarah to socialize with her cousins by directing play activities. If the brushing program helps to decrease her touch sensitivities, her father is hoping to interest Sarah in playing basketball at the park with her cousins.

Sarah and her mother decided to bring a plate of raw vegetables, sliced meat, crackers, and dip each week to her grandparents. Sarah helps to wash and slice the vegetables.

Therapy schedule

Day(s)	Time	Where	Activity	Comments
M-Su	7-7:30	Home	Sound Therapy	
M-Su	4-4:30	Home	Sound Therapy	See if it works right after school. Other possible time is 6:30

Adaptations to the environment

Day(s)	Time	Where	Activity	Comments
M-Su	4:00	Home	Hammock over bed	Dad will order and install

Sensory Strategies

Day(s)	Time	Where	Activity	Comments
TBD	TBD	Therapy	Educate Sarah about sensory	
M-F	As needed	Music, gym, cafeteria	Headband to deaden sound	Mom and OT will look for one.
		Music, gym, cafeteria	Ear buds	If necessary
TBD	TBD	Therapy	Role-play social skills	
Sun	11:30	Church	Fidgets or book	
Sun	1:30	Grandparents' house	Bring food to share	

Schedule for heavy work, play, exercise and deep pressure

Day(s)	Time	Where	Activity
M-F	6:30	Home	Yoga with mom
M-F	8:00	School playground	Play for 15 minutes
M-F	9:55	Classroom	Movement break before "special classes"
M-F	11:45	Playground	Recess
M-F	2:15	Classroom	Movement break - 5 min.
M-F	4:00	Home	Sensory nest (+ sound therapy)
Wed	4:30	Karate	Beginner level karate
M,T,TH	4:30	Home	Practice karate
M-Sat	6:00	Home	Prepare dining room – chore
Sat	10:30	Karate	Beginner level karate
Sun	9:00	Home	Yoga with mom
Sun	10:30	Home	Help prepare veggies
Sun	11:30	Home	Help dad load car, take out garbage
Sun	1:30	Grandma's	Play in park

CHAPTER 4

Eating, Sleeping, Bowel and Bladder

In this chapter we look at the physical regulation of eating, sleeping and bowel and bladder control. Each of these functions is controlled by autonomic processes and should work properly. However, problems with sensory systems, hormones and willful or stubborn behaviors can confound function and make self-regulation difficult.

PICKY EATING

There are many reasons a child may elect not to eat, and it can take detective work to tease out the underlying issues of a picky eater. A good investigation tool is the Oral Sensory Processing portion of the Sensory Profile (parent/caregiver version). This parent questionnaire asks about the child's eating preferences with regard to tastes, textures, and smells. Additionally, teachers and therapists can conduct a parent interview that covers the topics below. Here's a look at some common problems.

Sensory aspects: The child may be oversensitive to smells and tastes and resistant to eating foods with strong odors or flavors. The textures of certain foods may feel slimy or gritty and unpleasant in her mouth. The sight of certain foods such as oatmeal or scrambled eggs may make her nauseous. The sounds of eating and conversing at the table may be grating to her ears and make her too irritable to eat.

Conversely, she may be undersensitive to taste and reject food because it tastes bland to her.

Oral motor skills: A child may have poor oral motor skills such as inadequate lip closure, poor movement of her cheek muscles, an inability to move her tongue around in the mouth sufficiently to handle certain foods or a lack of jaw-power to grind meat.

Inflexibility: She may be unwilling to try anything new. Seen in the extreme in a particular child with autism, she eats only four foods in total, refusing to deviate from that set. When other foods are presented, she throws the food, pushes it off her plate or tantrums.

Food intolerances and allergies: Unknown to her parents, she may have food sensitivities that cause gut inflammation and other symptoms. She may not notice that these foods cause problems until much later, when inflammation occurs. By then the inflamed areas may become irritated by otherwise non-problem foods and she may associate the symptoms with the non-problem food rather than the true source of the inflammation.

As a result, when choosing foods that decrease symptoms, she may avoid foods that cause burning but not avoid the food that causes the inflammation.

Emotional issues and eating disorders: A child may be struggling with emotional problems such as depression or anxiety, and, as a result, either eat too much or too little. He may be so out of touch with himself that he doesn't recognize his hunger. In this case, suggesting to the child that he try to feel sensations of hunger or fullness in his belly can possibly solve the problem.

Cermac, et al (2010) found that adolescents with Asperger syndrome are at greater risk for eating disorders such as anorexia and bulimia.

Poor appetite: He may have a medical issue that affects his appetite. Zinc deficiency is known to cause food to taste bland. As well, some prescription medications, including some ADHD medications, cause a decrease in appetite.

Behavior-related: Occasionally poor eating is related to behavior issues. The child may use food and eating as a weapon in a pitched battle with his parents, either to force them to give in to him in an unrelated matter or to punish them.

Consider asking parents to make a video of their child eating a meal. Much can be learned from watching a picky eater in action. You will want to analyze behavioral interactions between parent and child, especially noting when a parent inadvertently reinforces poor behavior choices. Also observe the type of structure the parents have in place for meals, the child's reaction to being at the dinner table, his sensory reactions, and overall family dynamics. You may find that small adjustments involving sensory strategies and parental responses can make a big improvement.

Also check to see just how picky an eater the child actually is. Sometimes parents count the number of foods the child won't eat instead of the number of foods he does eat. Have the parent make a list of accepted foods in the categories of fruit, veggies, carbs/starches/grains, dairy, and meat or fish. Several reasonable foods in each category can give the child a workable diet. Moreover, the child may eventually learn to eat a wider variety of foods over time—most children do. Parents can be helped with strategies that get children to try new foods.

In the sections below are interventions for picky eating based on sensory techniques, behavior therapy and common-sense strategies. While it is common for eating problems to contain both sensory and behavioral aspects, the problems are unique to each child. Compare the child who is unable to tolerate gritty textures to the child who has rigid behaviors and eats only four foods. These two children benefit from completely different strategies, one that is primarily sensory with additional behavioral techniques as needed; the other that is primarily behavioral with supporting sensory techniques. The well-prepared feeding therapist has a wide array of techniques ready to implement during a feeding session.

Picky eating: Sensory strategies

When the problem is oversensitivity to smells, tastes, sights or textures, disguising the food may be a remedy. Along with the strategies below, consider reading Jessica Seinfeld's book, *Deceptively Delicious: Simple Secrets to Get Your Kids Eating Good Food.* Remember to include calming techniques such as 15 minutes of heavy work, deep pressure, exercise and play prior to eating therapy.

Masking tastes

1. Catsup, sauces, and salad dressings such as mayonnaise or ranch dressing are excellent for softening or masking flavors. I introduce these items early in a feeding program because, once accepted by the child, a variety of foods can be successfully introduced.

2. New meats are more likely to be accepted when they are breaded or wrapped in bread of some sort.

3. Add small quantities of new foods to pizza and tacos. The flavors and textures of the pizza and tacos limit the sensory impact and improve tolerance of new foods. Be careful about hiding a new food from sight. Unless the child has a good sense of humor, you might lose his trust if he discovers he has been deceived. Instead, put a small amount of the new food on the pizza or other dish in full view of the child. Optionally, hide it, but make a guessing game of where it is.

4. Cream-based soups and gravies are excellent for masking strong tastes. Try cream of chicken soup or a cheese soup straight out of the can and heated.

Masking smells

1. When food smells are noxious to the child, try masking them with other smells. For example, if you plan to present fish or broccoli, bake cookies or boil a pot of cinnamon tea as a way of covering the strong scent of the cooked food.

2. Fish presents a triple problem: smell, taste, and sight. Fish sticks are easier to tolerate and can be made up as fish tacos. Once fish sticks are accepted, try a very mild fish next. Mask the smell while cooking it, and then mask the taste with tartar sauce or mix a small amount in with mashed potatoes and gravy, cheese or garlic to mask the sight.

Getting past noxious sounds

When the child is set off by table noises such as the sound of her sister chewing, try one of these ideas:

1. Allow the child to wear earmuffs or headphones (not plugged in) at the table.

2. Put on quiet music that can mask sounds at the dinner table.

3. Give her separate seating just far enough away from others to dampen the noxious sounds.

4. To counter noxious sounds at the dinner table, consider using the strategies described in the auditory section of the sensory chapter *(p. 52)*.

5. Consider incorporating a behavior strategy such as self-management (chapter 6), in which the child self-monitors and self-rewards for not complaining about dinner sounds. This works when she feels satisfaction from the feeling of being in control of her behavior.

Hiding messy foods

1. When the sight of certain foods makes a child recoil or gag, try disguising the foods. For example, scrambled eggs can be incorporated into a breakfast burrito.

2. Some children can't bear to see different foods touching each other or being mixed together. The problem may be multi-sensory, meaning the child may dislike the sensation of mixed textures in his mouth while at the same time being averse to the sight of different foods touching each other. A gradual exposure approach—involving, say, one piece of corn in a serving of peas, followed later by a piece of corn and a piece of carrot in the peas—with or without a reward for success, can help to resolve this problem.

Picky-eating basics

Here is a brief look at a couple of successful methods for getting children to eat new foods. If you are new to picky-eating, consider attending a workshop on the topic.

Method 1: Slowly explore new foods
This idea comes from Kay Toomey and her excellent workshop titled, The SOS Approach to Feeding. She encourages children to explore the sensations of a new food prior to trying to eat it. She has a set method for doing that exploration, and other therapists have made additional contributions to the method. Try a subset of the steps below when you offer a child new food.

1. Touch the food
2. Sniff it
3. Kiss it
4. Bite the food
5. Put food into the mouth and spit it out
6. Chew and then spit it out
7. Chew and swallow the food
8. Eat it and swallow it

Method 2: Food Chaining™
A popular approach to picky-eating, known as Food Chaining™, comes from Cheri Fraker and Laura Walbert. The method involves increasing the child's repertoire of foods by targeting new foods that are similar in taste, smell, color or texture to currently accepted foods. Foods are tried in rapid succession.

Here is an example of a child who eats only Goldfish crackers.

1. Give the child Annie's Cheddar Bunnies and Cheez-It Crackers in succession and then move to Ritz crackers which are colored similarly but with no cheese.
2. Next, move in several directions simultaneously: Offer other types of crackers, including healthy crackers and other cheese-coated crunchy foods such as cheese popcorn.
3. Try a new texture such as cheese spread like Cheez Whiz on plain crackers.
4. Then try cheese soup.
5. At the same time, try different types and textures of cheese.
6. Use cheese spread as a dip to coat non-cheesy foods, allowing the child to branch (slowly) into new foods like veggies.
7. Regular cheeses can be melted and put on a cracker, and then on pita. This can create a branch with pizza and tacos that allows for the introduction of meats.

The problem of the white-foods diet

Some children with autism elect to eat only white foods. Interventions for them can be approached in two complementary ways. First, gradually add small amounts of new foods with only a small change in color. Note that this can be risky: the child may react by refusing to eat that food again. Therefore, never modify primary foods such as milk. Second, behavior-based feeding techniques can get past food rigidity. See the discussion in the section below titled "Behavior strategies for eating."

Adding non-white foods to the diet

- Eggs: See if the child can be enticed to eat scrambled eggs made with enough milk to enhance the whiteness.

- Fruits: Add small amounts of pureed fruits to yogurt or ice cream, perhaps one berry at a time in an attempt to get pale pinks, blues and purples into the diet. Gradually increase the amount of fruit and color.

- Vegetables: The color green may be the trickiest. Honeydew melon may be of use to get color acceptance. Another strategy is to put small amounts of vegetable puree into pasta, rice or scrambled eggs.

- Accepting colors: Get a supply of organic multi-colored lollipops (preferably small in size and low in sugar) and use these as treats and as a strategy to introduce new colors and fruit flavors.

PICKY EATING: MEALTIME STRATEGIES

Calming the body before a meal

Don't forget to give the child heavy work prior to eating. It helps to decrease food anxiety.

When/How often: Prior to meals

Amount of time: 15 minutes

Materials: Heavy balls, body sock, knotted rope, and so on

Method
In the OT gym, I have children play hard before eating therapy. Favorite activities are swinging from a trapeze, gliding on a zip line, jumping on a trampoline and climbing. At home, a parent can set up an area with play and exercise equipment that can provide that same calming input. The strongest effect comes from working the upper body, so think of activities such as monkey bars, playing with a weighted ball, tug-of-war with a knotted rope, pull-ups, push-ups, wall push-ups, wheel-barrel walks and animal walks. Older children can benefit from exercise and yoga programs.

Calming the mouth before a meal

These methods help reduce the impact of textures in the sensitive mouth.

When/How often: Prior to meals

Amount of time: A few minutes

Materials: Nuk Brush, Z-Vibe or a small chewable vibration toy, vibrating tooth brush

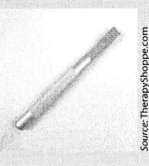

Source: TherapyShoppe.com

Method:
Stimulate the gums, edge of tongue and the inside of cheeks with pressure or vibration for a few minutes prior to eating. When working with a small child, put a sweet or strong taste on to the tip of the device and make a game of putting the device into his mouth so that he is not frightened by the procedure.

Playing with food

Keep eating therapy light by having fun with food. Let the child explore a food's physical qualities like texture and hardness. Playing with food helps set expectations for what the food will feel like in his mouth.

Setting: Kitchen or dinner table

Materials: Sauces, jellies, mustard, catsup

Method:
1. Use the food on the plate to make a picture such as a face, house or dog. This helps the child to touch foods without alarm.
2. Tell the child to write a letter of the alphabet or draw a picture in sauces and pureed foods.
3. Decorate breads, waffles and pancakes with icing, sprinkles or jelly.
4. Dip foods such as pasta, carrot sticks, grapes, hot dog chunks and French fries into catsup, mustard, jellies and other colorful sauces, and then paint pictures with them on a plate or table top.

Helping to cook

An excellent way to get children interested in eating more foods is to have them help prepare meals and treats. Cooking can help the child to acclimate to strong smells, tastes and other sensory aspects of foods that they find offensive.

Setting: Kitchen

Materials: Foods of all types, child's cookbook, cooking bowls, pots, utensils

Method:

Have children help with the following tasks:

1. Selecting recipes from a child's cook book.
2. Finding ingredients for recipes in cupboards and fridge.
3. Washing, peeling and cutting fruits and veggies.
4. Measuring ingredients.
5. Stirring a bowl or a pot (and licking it!).
6. Pouring batter into pans.
7. Setting the timer and checking on the food.
8. Assisting with cleanup.

Sitting at dinner with an option to eat

This describes a way to implement good behavior at the dinner table.

Setting: The dinner table

Materials: A timer and token system materials such as chips or tickets

Method:

1. Set the clock for 20 minutes or however long the child is expected to sit at the table.
2. The child must sit politely. He does not have to eat.
3. When the timer rings, he is excused.
4. If he does not eat, he receives no additional food until the next meal.

Source: TherapyShoppe.com

If compliance is an issue, use a rewards system such as a token economy in which the child is given points for meeting expectations. The points are used to gain rewards. Here is an abbreviated version of token economy.

1. He is given points for sitting nicely at the table.
2. He is optionally given points for eating portions of the food on his plate. This should be spelled out clearly so that there is no need for debate. For example: two forks full of food = five points.
3. Once points are earned, they are not taken away. As with the token system, the child can cash in his points for a reward.

Timed play

Add this procedure to the method above for the child who likes to play with food. As noted above, playing with food can have a value when it helps to overcome food issues. But playing with food is discouraged when others are at the table.

Setting: The dinner table

Materials: A timer such as an egg timer or a visual timer

Method:
1. Seat the child at the table first.
2. Set the timer for 3-5 minutes. Explain to the child that she can play for a few minutes, but then must begin to eat (or sit quietly) when the timer "is done" (rings or reaches zero) and others come to the table to eat.
3. If parents are using a points system such as the token system, the child gains points if she stops play in a timely manner and eats appropriately.

Getting down to eating

This intervention pieces together several techniques to help a small child acquire self-regulation for sensory issues. The goal is to move from playing with food to eating it.

Setting: Kitchen or dinner table

Age: Young child

When/How often: Mealtime

Method:
Children who prefer to play with food rather than to eat it can be given time and opportunity for play prior to meal time. Put a bib on the child, set a visual timer for five minutes, then let her play with foods or food-safe messy substances. Also try using an oral-motor protocol of massage or pressure on the gums, lips, tongue and cheeks prior to a meal. This can be done with gloved fingers, a Nuk brush or a vibrator (use a vibrating toothbrush). When the five minutes are up, it is time to eat. A visual schedule can be used to delineate play from eating.

PICKY EATING: BEHAVIORAL STRATEGIES

Behavioral therapy is used not only to improve eating behaviors but also to increase food variety and quantity. As mentioned earlier, sorting through eating issues can feel like detective work. To clarify the issues, a behavioral therapist performs a functional analysis of the child's behaviors and eating habits prior to establishing an intervention. When working with children with autism, behavioral therapists are especially sensitive to rigid eating habits such as the self-selected "white foods" diet. They also focus on poor attention to task and decreased motivation to eat.

The following two case studies illustrate different behavioral approaches to poor eating habits. The first uses positive reinforcement and a "hierarchical exposure to foods" method similar to Kay Toomey's work. The second uses "escape extinction" along with parental education aimed at eliminating negative reinforcement of disruptive and inflexible behaviors.

Case 1

The first case comes from Koegel, et al (2011). The team's intention was to increase the number of accepted foods for three boys ages 6-8. Fifteen foods were selected to be added to the boys' diets during a 22-week study. After establishing the baseline condition for each boy's eating behaviors over two sessions, therapy was started.

During the study, the boys were expected to work through a hierarchy of steps with each food item. Here is the hierarchy:

1. Touches the food
2. Puts food to the lips
3. Bites the food
4. Puts the food in mouth but does not swallow it
5. Chews the food and spits it out
6. Swallows the food reluctantly
7. Accepts the food without signs of displeasure

At the beginning of each session, each boy was asked what reward (an activity, object or food item) he wanted to earn, and was told what he must do to get it. For his reward, one boy wanted a French fry. He was told he must touch the new food with his finger to get the French fry. When he performed the stated task three times in a row without disruptive behavior, he was advanced to the next level. Once he completed all seven levels, he was introduced to a new food and the process started again.

Another boy, Daniel, ate only six foods at the start of the study: a specific brand of pizza, French fries, chicken nuggets, ground beef, ketchup, and vanilla ice cream. When new foods were presented, he acted out with screaming, crying and running away. By the end of the study, Daniel had accepted eight new foods. He went on to accept another eight foods in the weeks immediately following the study. He no longer needed a reward to move through the hierarchy of steps, but was able to successfully work for verbal praise.

While noting that the hierarchical method employed in the study has sensory underpinnings, the authors claim that motivation rather than sensory strategies are more important in getting past eating rigidity in autism. They also emphasize that their method of positive reinforcement was strong enough to extinguish disruptive behaviors without resorting to the more intrusive methods of negative reinforcement.

Case 2

This case comes from research by Gale et al (2010). The team looked at three boys with eating behaviors and poor acceptance of food textures and flavors. The purpose of their study was to eliminate the disruptive behaviors (such as shouting, gagging and pushing food away) that enabled the child to avoid eating. Analysis of the family's eating behaviors revealed that all parents were inadvertently maintaining their son's escape behaviors by giving rewards after food refusal as a way of calming the child. The authors decided to focus on eliminating this type of negative reinforcement.

As you read the technique, note that the parent or therapist is not forcing the child to eat, but simply presenting food. The parent or therapist is not reacting to the child's behavior, which can give the child negative reward. Instead he or she chooses a demeanor (smiling is fine) and sticks with it no matter what the child does.

The therapy method included three behavioral techniques: non-contingent negative reinforcement (a fixed- time intervention), positive reinforcement, and extinction of disruption.

At the time of the intervention, two of the three boys were being spoon-fed from jars of baby food. The third was self-feeding. The intervention consisted of the parent holding a spoonful of food ¼ inch from the child's mouth for 30 seconds. Parents were instructed to hold the spoon in place, without reacting, no matter what the child's response. If the child did eat the food, however, the spoon was removed and he was rewarded with preferred foods for the remainder of the 30 seconds. If the child attempted to push away the spoon, his arms were held down for the remainder of the 30-second period and then released. A feeding session consisted of a total of 20 trials. Five sessions occurred each day at times that did not interfere with the child's regular mealtimes.

At the end of the study, the two boys who were spoon-fed demonstrated few disruptions and achieved good food acceptance. The self-feeder made measureable gains, as well.

These cases show that behavioral therapy can be an excellent adjunct to traditional eating therapy.

Dinner time, social time

Dinner time does not have to be a battle ground. Two widely different approaches can create peace at the dinner table. In the first approach, dinner is treated as special family time. It is a peaceful ritual which focuses on the social aspects of the meal. If the child is getting eating therapy, that work is done at breakfast, lunch or during snacks. The child eats accepted foods at the dinner table.

In the second approach, eating therapy is conducted at the meal, but behavioral methods are in place to help limit disruptions. Here is a look at both methods.

Method 1: Dinner as a special family time
This approach is useful for children who act out at mealtimes. It can be used in conjunction with sensory strategies listed above.

- Dinner is treated as a special occasion. The whole family makes an effort to be at the sit-down meal at a table. Stories of the day are shared with an emphasis on positive stories and polite behavior. The goal is to give the child (and the rest of the family) a pleasant eating experience rather than a food battle.
- Parents stick to a fixed time for meals so that the child is able to regulate hunger and expectations.
- The child is given foods he is known to enjoy, even if the food is crackers or popcorn. Other foods can also be put on his plate. He is expected to stay at the table, but not required to eat anything.
- He can elect not to eat. Parents do not judge non-eating behaviors. A simple question such as, "Are you sure you aren't hungry, we don't eat again until breakfast," is a gentle reminder of the consequences. Indeed, there are consequences. He receives no other

foods or snacks until the next meal, whether that is a regularly scheduled evening snack or breakfast. In this way, he comes to the table hungry and with motivation to eat.

- If the child is unable to sit at the table without reaction to the sight of foods or the sounds of the table, use the sensory strategies described earlier in this section.
- Alternative: Parents feed the picky eater in a quiet setting prior to the family meal and then invite the child to join the family for dessert or accepted foods.

Method 2: Therapy at dinner

The second approach to family dinner is functional. Parents follow through with the child's feeding programs at the dinner table, but are careful not to react when the child displays negative behaviors. They also instruct other children not to react to the child's outbursts. A calm upbeat manner guides the family through the meal. Typically, a parent will make use of behavioral therapy techniques described above (or others outlined in the chapter on autism). These methods help to eliminate dysfunctional behaviors, provide rewards for success and, with older children, teach self-management skills.

THE IMPACT OF FOOD SENSITIVITIES

Food sensitivities are known to affect children with autism, ADHD and other disorders to a greater degree than their typical peers. Unlike food allergies, food sensitivities are not easily discovered through testing, and so children often suffer with a wide range of symptoms before the source is found (if it ever is).

Here are some signs that are common in children (and adults) with food sensitivities.

- Eczema (red scaly patches) on the skin
- Dark circles under the eyes
- GERD symptoms such as belching and reflux (spitting up)
- A cycle of diarrhea and constipation (irritable bowel)
- Constant constipation or constant diarrhea
- Anxious behaviors

The foods most commonly associated with food intolerances are milk products, foods with gluten (including wheat, rye, barley, spelt, and possibly oats), eggs, soy, and corn. In addition, studies have indicated that 2-3% of children are sensitive to food dyes and additives.

Dairy foods account for most problems. A child may have milk intolerance due to any one of several factors including lactase enzyme deficiency. In a classic study with children with autism, Harvard Medical School (Kushak, 2011) reported insufficient lactase enzyme to digest the lactose in milk in 58-65% of children with autism. Six percent of those children were also found to have an inflamed gut that was attributed in part to lactose intolerance.

To determine a child's food sensitivities, Dr. Stanford Newmark (2010) suggests implementing a multi-food elimination diet for two weeks. The diet completely eliminates dairy, wheat, corn, soy, eggs, nuts, citrus and any products containing food coloring, additives and preservatives. Foods are added back into the diet, one-by-one, with three days spacing between each type of food. If a newly added food type causes changes in behavior, or gastric symptoms such as pain or bloating or changes in the makeup of stools, then remove the offending food group from the diet. Dr. Newmark recommends that this process be conducted under a doctor's supervision.

A feeding team made up of a GI doctor, dietician, a feeding therapist and a sensory therapist can be helpful when implementing a new diet, especially for a child with autism. Feeding teams are often found in hospital outpatient clinics. Optionally, look for an experienced feeding therapist who understands diets, picky eating and how to work with children with autism. This individual will typically be an occupational therapist, speech therapist or behavioral therapist.

A number of cookbooks provide good recipes and tips to parents who must implement special diets for their children. (See the resource section, pp. 186-188).

SLEEP HABITS

Sleep

Getting tired

The best assurance of a good night's sleep is a tired body and calm mind. Children who exercise their muscles with physical play in backyards and playgrounds, participate in sports, or have daily exercise and yoga routines will establish a healthy level of fatigue. Children with sensory sensitivities, ADHD and autism may miss out on opportunities to romp on playground equipment and to engage in sports due to poor socialization skills. While the child may not do well in group sports or noisy gyms, he can still get a good workout on a bicycle, on skates or a skateboard, in a pool or on the track. Martial arts programs are an excellent choice for children with sensory sensitivities, ADHD and autism. Along with a good workout, martial arts give the child with poor social skills a formal structure for interacting with others and that structure can reduce social anxiety.

The child with leftover energy in his muscles may have a hard time falling asleep. Ten minutes of stretching or yoga before bedtime can drain strength from his muscles and help him to relax.

The bedtime routine

Sleep experts stress the importance of a bedtime routine:

- Finish up homework or other activities and put things away.
- Prepare for the next day by laying out clothes and schoolwork.
- Do a few minutes of light exercise, stretching or yoga.
- Take a warm bath. Epsom salts may be especially relaxing.
- Read a story.

Some activities should not be done before bedtime because they are alerting to the brain's sleep mechanism. When darkness comes, the hormone melatonin is released by the pineal gland, causing sleepiness. Strong input in the form of light, noise, tactile sensations and excitement can cause melatonin levels to decrease and prevent sleep. The child remains restlessly awake even though she might be quite tired. The melatonin cycle will eventually start up again and provide the hormone necessary for sleep, but that might take up to 90 minutes.

A similar problem can occur when children wake up in the middle of the night. Typically, melatonin in the brain helps them return to sleep. But if they are alerted by a bright light or loud noise, the melatonin levels can drop and be insufficient for them to return to sleep.

Melatonin is available over-the-counter in pill and liquid forms. It can be given to children to help them return to sleep. Research says that this remedy is safe and effective at inducing sleep; however, it does not work to keep the child asleep. Parents should give melatonin only after consulting with their child's doctor.

Getting to sleep, staying asleep

Here are strategies that can help a child fall asleep or prevent her from awakening in the middle of the night:

- A child who finds water exciting, as do some children with autism, may become overly alert when taking a bath just before bedtime. Try giving the bath at least 90 minutes before bedtime. Or skip the evening bath and instead shower in the morning.
- Bright light can alert a child. In particular, avoid light from the blue-light spectrum before bedtime. Compact fluorescent bulbs use the blue-light spectrum. Consider using LED lights instead. Avoid blue night-lights.
- TV, computers, electronic devices and games are backlit with blue light. Children should avoid these devices beginning 90 minutes before bedtime.
- Loud noises from music devices, TV, and excited play or rough-housing may keep a child awake. Again, the child should avoid noisy input beginning 90 minutes before bedtime.

- Environmental sounds such as trains, traffic or a parent opening the child's bedroom door may cause the child to wake up and become alert. Consider using a white-noise machine for a few minutes at bedtime. If the child awakens, use it again to mask sounds as he goes back to sleep. Have the child select the type of white noise (ocean waves, rippling streams, etc.) used by the device.

- Bedclothes that are rough, tight or itchy may keep a child awake. The touch-sensitive child may need knitted PJs without seams. Optionally, turn PJs inside-out so that the seams do not rub the skin.

- Don't forget the bedtime routine. The child needs a consistent routine that cues her brain for sleep. This may include putting away toys, preparing clothes and book bag for the next day, taking a bath, putting on pajamas, reading a story (or being read to), and for little ones, a lullaby.

Autism Speaks' guide to sleep

Autism Speaks has an eight-page booklet containing strategies for improving sleep in children with autism. Strategies cover bedtime routine, sensory matters, sleeping alone, getting the correct amount of sleep and other important topics. The booklet also includes visual schedule pictures for a sample bedtime routine that can be cut out and used as a bedtime aid. Consider using the content in the booklet to put together an hour-long sleep-education session for parents. You can locate the web page by searching "Autism Speaks sleep toolkit." The URL is: http://www.autismspeaks.org/science/resources-programs/autism-treatment-network/tools-you-can-use/sleep-tool-kit.

Body scan for sleep

When an older child has trouble getting to sleep, have him listen to the UCLA podcast, Body Scan for Sleep *as he lies in bed. Don't be surprised if he is sound asleep long before the audio clip has finished playing.*

Materials: The *Body Scan for Sleep* audio clip, and an iPod or small computer. To obtain the clip for iPod, go to iTunes store and search "UCLA body scan for sleep." To obtain it for a PC product, go to UCLA's site, Marc.UCLA.edu., click on the Free Guided Meditations link and download *Body Scan for Sleep* from the list of audio clips.

Setting: In bed

When/How Often: Nightly

Amount of time: 15-20 minutes

Method:
1. Play the clip once the child is lying in bed and ready for sleep.
2. Have him follow the instructions for relaxing his body. He starts by relaxing his toes and then moves up to his face and down to his fingers.
3. The child may fall asleep before the audio clip is finished.

1. Cobra

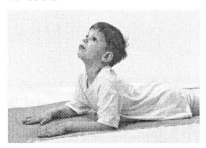

2. Bow Pose

3. Child's Pose

Bedtime yoga

Try yoga stretches before bedtime to release stored energy in wiggly muscles.

Setting: A quiet space.

Group/Individual: Alone or with the family.

When/How often: Bedtime.

Amount of time: 5-10 minutes.

Materials: Yoga mat or carpeted floor, picture of poses.

Method:
1. Have the child do the cobra, locust and curl poses in order. Hold each pose for a few seconds.
2. Repeat the set of poses until the child's body is quiet.
3. Lay in corpse pose for a few minutes.

Bedtime yoga for toddlers

You'll be doing the work of getting the child into the pose.

Method:
Have the child hold each of these poses for a few seconds. Repeat a few times if the child's body is not calm.

1. Have the child lie down on her back and gently extend her limbs. Tell her to reach with her toes and fingers.
2. Have her lie on her belly. Put your arm below her shoulders and gently push up so that her back arches a little. Tell her to stretch.
3. Help her into a downward dog pose.

BOWEL AND BLADDER CONTROL

There are a variety of reasons that a child may have poor bowel and bladder control. Here are a few strategies to help.

Sensing a wet diaper

This technique, attributed to Anat Baniel in The Autism Revolution, *is helpful for the child who does not sense when his bottom is wet.*

Materials: two washcloths, one wet, the other dry

Method:
1. Lightly rub the child's face with the dry cloth saying, "Dry towel."
2. Do the same with the wet cloth saying, "Wet towel."
3. Have him close his eyes and guess which is which when you rub one of them on his face.
4. Now repeat the process on the child's bottom. This will bring awareness to the sensation of wet and dry which, as Anat Baniel found, was all that was needed for the child to figure out the mystery of wet diapers.

iCan Toilet Training Program

This app for iPod costs 99 cents and includes a schedule with fun alarms, games to play while sitting on the toilet and audio/visual rewards for success.

Autism Speaks: ATN/AIR-P Guide to Toilet Training

Autism Speaks' guide has nine pages of advice and method and includes four pictures for a visual schedule that the parent can cut out and use. Locate the website by searching on the words "Autism Speaks toilet training." The page's name is "ATN/AIR-P Parent's Guide to Toilet Training in Autism."

Qigong massage

Dr. Louisa Silva, M.D., has developed a technique to help increase sensory regulation and overall function in children including calming, social skills and improved bowel and bladder control.

Parents massage their child in the prescribed manner for 15 minutes before bedtime. This program is done for five months. It's a long time, but it does produce significant results.

Silva's extensive research shows that this technique works on children ages 3-6 with autism and sensory issues.

She teaches the qigong technique in a workshop setting in Salem, OR to those who have experience working with children with autism. Parents can optionally learn it from the book/DVD *Qigong Massage for Your Child with Autism*. Her web site is QSTI.org.

CHAPTER 5

Emotions and Emotional Regulation

Emotional self-regulation can be considered from a variety of perspectives: the range of emotions themselves, the intensity and duration of emotional experiences, the strategies for regulating emotions, the characteristics of brain regulation of emotions, and the makeup of the parts of the brain that process both emotions and their regulation. In this chapter, we consider the underlying emotional characteristics of children with autism, ADHD and sensory modulation disorder, along with the challenges they face with their emotional makeup.

FOUNDATIONS OF EMOTIONS

The basic emotions

Experts list up to eight basic emotions: happiness and joy, anger and rage, fear and terror, disgust and contempt, shame and humiliation, distress and anguish, interest and excitement, along with sadness and surprise. Notice that these basic emotions include more negative than positive ones. The positive is often buried under the negative, as when shame or humiliation overwhelms pride of self or when distress or anguish prevails over ease and contentment. Researchers typically focus on the negative states because that is where pain, suffering and self-defeating behaviors cluster. The negative states can teach us about the nature of dysfunction. For our purposes, though, we want to focus more on the positive states because the intention of our interventions is to grow or enhance the positive states while decreasing the negative ones.

Traits, moods and states

Our emotional makeup has three aspects: trait, mood and state. Consider a child who feels joyful when she sees a puppy. She smiles for a few minutes and is in a happy *state*. If she maintains that happy state all day, she is in a good *mood*. If she is generally a happy person, that is her *trait*.

These three aspects—trait, mood and state—are layered over one another and influence each other. As you observe a child, think of his underlying personality trait. Is he agreeable, impatient, shy or anxious? Now consider his overlying present mood—let us say it is sadness. Did something happen earlier—a missed birthday party or the breaking of a toy—to change his mood? Finally, look at the state he is in at this moment. Was he able to overcome his sadness to show excitement when his father came home from work?

Moods can be dysfunctional and ongoing. For example, a person with a persistent state of anxiety, depression, and mania has a mood disorder. Children with autism, ADHD and sensory sensitivities have a high co-occurrence of anxiety. It is important to have a psychological perspective on the nature of negative moods.

Like many adults, some children can be stuck emotionally in negative moods and outlooks. They are quick to feel deprived, refused, controlled, and criticized. They can chronically be quite rejecting, even hateful, of themselves and others. It is as if a surly or sour disposition is their emotional default position. Often, the kids—again, like many adults—can be unaware of how negative they are. And they do not realize or do not seem to care about the challenges that others have in dealing with them.

A lot of research has shown how negative emotions can burden our intelligence and impair our health. It appears that children and adults have inner psychological programming that tempts us, if not compels us, to revisit certain negative memories and associations and to hold on to these feelings even when they are painful. It greatly helps us to understand this inner tendency as we attempt to shift away from such negative states of mind and emotions into neutral if not positive outlooks.

Emotional style

Our emotional building blocks make each of us unique. Psychophysiologist Richard Davidson, who maps emotional signals in the brain using MRI and fMRI imaging, has proposed six characteristics that make up the dimensions of our *emotional style*.

Resilience: How quickly does the child recover from disappointment, a devastating life event or some other form of adversity?

Outlook: Is the child's disposition positive, negative or somewhere in between?

Social intuition: How well does the child pick up quickly on social cues?

Self-awareness: Is the child in touch with his body, emotions and mind? Is he over-focused on himself?

Sensitivity to context: Does the child understand which behaviors are acceptable or unacceptable in a particular environment?

Attention: Is the child able to focus well on the task at hand in spite of sensory stimulation, activities in the environment and thoughts in his head?

Dr. Davidson says that these characteristics of emotional style come together and are expressed as the personality traits that are unique to each of us. The table below charts a few of his examples.

	Extrovert	Shy	Impulsive	Anxious	Agreeable	Unhappy
Resilience	Fast to recover	Slow to recover		Slow to recover	Fast to recover	Slow to recover
Outlook	Positive			Negative	Positive	Negative
Social intuition						
Self-awareness			Low	High		
Sensitivity to context		Tuned out			Tuned in	
Attention			Unfocused	Unfocused		

When we consider the general characteristics of children with autism, ADHD and sensory issues, we can map the underlying emotional styles. Although each child with autism, ADHD and sensory sensitivities is unique, each is disordered and predisposed to emotional issues in a way that can be mapped to general characteristics. And all of the disorders are linked to anxiety.

The following chart shows how emotional styles correlate to these disorders and to anxiety and depression.

	Autism	**Sensory Sensitive**	**ADHD**	**Anxiety**	**Depression**
Resilience	Slow to recover	Slow to recover	Slow to recover	Slow to recover	Can be slow to recover
Outlook		Negative		Negative	Negative
Social intuition	Poor				
Self-awareness	High	High	Low	High	
Sensitivity to context	Tuned-out				Can be tuned-out
Attention	Unfocused	Hyper-focused	Unfocused	Unfocused	

As we think of emotional styles, we need to remember that each style is a continuum, with "just right" in the middle and the problematic experiences extending outward in both directions toward the extremes of dysfunction. An outlook that is too positive can be just as problematic as one that is too negative. For example, the Pollyanna personality is reluctant to look at adversity or reality and respond appropriately to life's challenges.

Is it possible for children stuck in the extremes of one of these emotional styles to learn moderation through therapy? For example, can therapy help a child who lacks social intuition to learn those skills? Dr. Davidson has demonstrated that interventions such as emotional reappraisal (below), mindfulness training (Chapter 6) and certain visualization exercises can produce physical changes in key areas of the brain. As this research progresses, other types of interventions are likely to be validated as well.

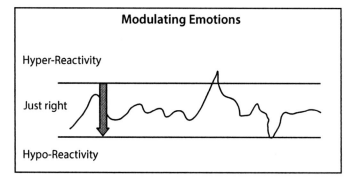

Emotional regulation

Emotional self-regulation is a complex process. It can be defined as " . . . the ability to respond to the ongoing demands of experience with the range of emotions in a manner that is socially tolerable and sufficiently flexible to permit spontaneous reaction as well as the ability to delay spontaneous reactions as needed" (Cole, Michel and Teti, 1994).

In other words, successful self-regulation involves expressing our emotions as the situation demands, while doing so in a way that is socially acceptable and that allows us to regain our balance when the difficult moment has passed. We can simplify our understanding of emotional self-regulation by looking at it as the process of trying, with some degree of success, to stay in the just-right zone.

The developmental process

The foundation of self-regulation is based in childhood development. By age three, we usually start to observe feelings in ourselves and others (e.g., "Why is Jessie sad?"). By age five, we understand how external events can cause us to feel emotions. We also learn the useful strategy of walking away from a difficult situation so that it disappears from sight and we can feel better. Around the age of seven, we begin to use cognitive strategies, such as reappraisal, for emotional regulation. We continue over the years, of course, to develop our cognitive abilities (Eisenberg & Sulk, 2012).

People employ multiple strategies to bring their feelings back to neutral or to positive states. These include three mental or emotional approaches that children as well as adults use for handling strong emotions: concealment, tolerance, and reappraisal (adjustment).

Concealment: The child occupies himself with other activities so that he doesn't have to face his emotions. He puts on a neutral face (is stoic) in front of others.

Hiding one's emotions can work temporarily, but concealment is a poor strategy for the long run. It backfires when we finally have to face the emotion and are not prepared for it. We can also develop tight muscles from the strain of not releasing our feelings, and this tension can cause physical pain, chronic ailments and even disease to develop.

Tolerance: The child exhibits strong emotions, yet he is able to tolerate the feelings and accept the resulting behavior, even though others may feel that he is overreacting and possibly out of control. The child may say to himself: "I know I got upset, but I had a right to be upset because of the circumstances. Now I feel better and I'm back to normal."

A child with this wide range of emotional expression may be able to manage that range with good resilience, yet his resulting behaviors can do damage to social relationships.

Reappraisal: The child uses rational thinking to put a positive spin on a situation or create a positive outcome for himself. He does this to reduce the intensity of the emotion, or to change the emotion, and perhaps to delay its expression. Positive reappraisal is a good strategy and produces better outcomes for the child.

Example 1: "Jared told me there's no way I can use his new video game. Maybe I'll go to Nathan's house and play with him instead."

Example 2: "Maybe mom was just angry because the dog broke a bowl in the kitchen. I was in the wrong place at the wrong time."

Davis, Levine and Lench (2010) performed two studies with 5-6 year-old children. In the first, they asked the children to describe what a character in a story could do to feel better after a mishap. In the second, they asked the children to describe ways that they could make themselves feel better when they were sad, angry or scared. The children's responses were surprisingly sophisticated. The types of strategies they used are listed below along with example situations similar to the ones in the Davis, et al paper.

Strategies to change an outcome:

1. Change the goal.
2. Change the situation.
3. Ask someone to intervene and change the situation.

Example: Jimmy wants to play baseball, but hurt his leg and now is stuck inside the house. Strategies for Jimmy:

    a. He can exercise his leg so he can play soon again.
    b. He can invite his friend over to play a game.
    c. He can ask his mom if he can play fetch with the dog outside.

Adjustments to thoughts about what happened:

1. Forget about it.
2. Change emotional state by going to sleep.
3. Pretend that things have gone right and enjoy those thoughts.

Example: Brandy's mother is ill and so Brandy had to cancel her sleepover for this weekend. Strategies for Brandy:

    a. She could call her friends, and then watch her favorite cartoons.
    b. She could go to bed early. When you are sad, sleeping makes you feel better.
    c. She could remember how nice her friends are and how much they like her.

Adjustments when a goal cannot be met:

1. Do the thing that he doesn't like, reasoning that with time he may learn to like it.
2. Give up the primary goal and try to like another (lesser) outcome instead.
3. Decide that he doesn't want the outcome after all.
4. Talk it out with someone.

Example: Darrell wants a new video game. Darrell's dad told him *no* because he plays too many video games. Dad wants him to read more and tells him that he can have a new book instead. Darrell doesn't like to read.
Darrell's strategies:

    a. "I guess I'll ask for the new Wimpy Kid book. My friend Lamont has been talking about it and wants it. Maybe it's good."
    b. "I guess I have a lot of fun video games. I don't really need a new one."

    c. "The new video game is probably not that great anyway. I can always play it at Cedrick's house."

    d. Darrell asks his older brother, D'Jahn what to do. D'Jahn tells him that Dad goes through these phases every so often and that Darrell should wait a few months and ask again.

EMOTIONAL CHALLENGES

Emotional regulation is challenging for children with autism, sensory modulation or ADHD issues. Let's look at these three groups separately.

Autism

Children with autism typically lack the skill to recognize the emotions in another person's face and to mirror those emotions. This contributes to poor affect.

    Emotional reactions to change can be major concerns for children with autism. Typically, the child with autism does not like change. She acclimates to the status quo of the daily schedule, finding safety in familiarity. She is often not paying attention to the world around her, and so she is surprised by an unexpected occurrence. Change is troubling, often fear-inducing, and it can lead to behavioral reactions. Children with autism can continue to associate fear with a particular object or incident (or person or place) long after a typical child would. The fear can turn into fearful memories that provide the material for repeated upsets (South, 2012). We can slowly desensitize the child to change by incorporating into her day surprises that are paired with calming strategies. We can work to increase her awareness of her environment and her interactions with others with the aid of therapies such as DIRfloortime, P.L.A.Y. Project, or Early Start Denver Model (see Resources, pp. 186-188). These therapy methods help in building play skills and relationships, and they help to reduce rigid and reactive behaviors in children.

Sensory

Children with sensory sensitivities (without autism) have a different type of challenge. Their experience of sensory bombardment can cause them to suffer. As a result, they may become cranky or moody. Children with auditory, touch or proprioceptive sensitivities tend to sit in a state of hyper-vigilance during social situations, waiting for the next distressing experience. Fight-or-flight behaviors can result, leading to more intense emotional experiences. We can help these children with education and with strategies to handle emotional situations.

ADHD

Children with ADHD may experience delayed development of their brain cortical tissue, causing their emotional regulation (and other self-regulation) skills to be developmentally delayed by several years (NIMH, 2007). As they are ready for it, they need for us to support them with opportunities for emotional and social development. A simple strategy is to help the child find appropriate playmates who are younger than he is and who are going through the same developmental stages. When a child with ADHD is hyperactive or impulsive, he may lack attention to his own internal emotional states and so fail to learn the emotional lessons that are available to him. He may be emotionally immature, have poor self-esteem and make behavioral choices that come back to haunt him. We can support him by using positive parenting, teaching and mentoring techniques. (These are described in the chapter on ADHD.)

Anxiety

Anxiety is a major problem for children with sensory issues, ADHD and autism. Anxiety comes from many sources:

- Social anxiety or social unpreparedness.
- Personality-derived stress such as perfectionism.
- External child stressors such as poor grades, being bullied, and feeling overwhelmed.
- Strong persistent sensory input.
- Reactions to food sensitivities, including dyes and additives.
- Family stressors such as moving, divorce and parental job loss.

High levels of anxiety make it more difficult for the child to handle other emotions. This overall weak emotional regulation in turn impacts the child's ability to handle social situations. A vicious cycle ensues: when social situations go awry, anxiety escalates and paves the way for even greater anxiety.

In addition, anxiety can lead to stress which predisposes a child to fight-or-flight patterns of behavior. This can make it difficult for him to keep a positive disposition through the ups-and-downs of the day. As a result, he may develop tag-along behaviors such as melt-downs, crankiness, a negative disposition, anger and other negative emotions.

Intensity

Children with strong traits such as perfectionism, or with rigid behaviors or stubbornness, can benefit from heavy work and activities that are grounding such as those provided in the next section.

Reappraisal revisited – silver linings

When the outcome of a situation is out of the child's control, help her to rethink how less-desired outcomes might still be okay. In this way, she can more easily accept what is to come, whatever the future holds.

<h2 style="text-align:center">THE INTERVENTIONS</h2>

The following interventions focus on decreasing anxiety, enhancing the feeling of being grounded and releasing negative emotions. Included is a section on working with emotions in children with autism.

<h3 style="text-align:center">INTERVENTIONS: GETTING EMOTIONALLY GROUNDED</h3>

<h3 style="text-align:center">Grounding foods</h3>

The art of eating to stay grounded requires the avoidance of artificial ingredients, food dyes and taste additives. Eating heavy foods such as whole grains and meat also helps in this process. The following foods are both heavy in the belly and slow to digest, giving children an ongoing steady supply of nutrition and energy.

Foods to eat:
1. Whole grains such as brown rice, oatmeal, whole wheat and barley.
2. Root vegetables: potatoes, onions, beets, parsnips, turnips. Carrots are good, but cook them to release some of the sugars.
3. Turkey (think of the sleepy feeling you get after eating a turkey dinner). Breakfast with turkey sausage or turkey bacon is a good start to the day.
4. Red meat: an occasional hamburger is very grounding.
5. These ingredients in combination produce soups, stews or roasted dinners.

Foods to avoid:
1. Sugary foods burn carbs too quickly and leave the child depleted.
2. Food dyes and additives. Studies have shown they produce ADHD-like symptoms in 2-3% of children.
3. In addition, if the child has a history of stomach pains and/or bowel irregularities, suggest that parents consult with their child's doctor about the possibility of food intolerances which can be a factor in anxiety.

<h3 style="text-align:center">Grounding anxiety with chores</h3>

Children with ADHD tend to be forgetful and prone to social faux pas. They are less likely than their peers to learn from self-reflection on their experiences and actions. It is not surprising they have a 25% higher rate of anxiety than their peers. A long work session can pull out much of this anxiety and get them grounded for a day or two.

Here are some ways to help them burn off the anxiety and become grounded.

Setting: Home

When/How often: Daily or as often as is possible

How long: 5-30 minutes

Materials: Yard tools

Types of chores:
1. Outside work: Dig in the garden, rake leaves, shovel snow, mow the lawn.
2. Inside work: Stack dining room chairs, sweep and mop floors, vacuum carpets.
3. Younger children can help carry things. A two-year-old can carry up to two pounds.

Feel your feet

A child who toe-walks needs to stretch out the gastroc muscles in the back of the leg, as well as bring awareness to his or her feet.

Materials: Ramp made of a wide board (12 inches wide or more) placed on blocks or bricks. Start by angling the ramp at a small angle. With time, increase the angle by propping the board higher. Put the ramp alongside a wall so that the child can use the wall for balance.

Setting: Anywhere

How long: 5-10 minutes

Materials: Ramp

Method:
Tell the child to:

1. Walk heel-to-toe (with the heel of the foot in front touching the toe of the foot in back) up the ramp. See how many steps she can take without losing balance.
2. Play catch with a partner while walking up the ramp. One toss for each step.
3. Walk backwards down the ramp, again heel-to-toe.

Games to get grounded

These exercises and games keep the child's focus on her feet and produce a sense of solid connection to the ground.

Setting: Anywhere

How long: 5-10 minutes

Materials: Various

Games and activities:
1. Hopscotch, jump rope, jumping jacks.
2. Soccer, kick-ball.
3. Martial arts.
4. Jumping: Scatter color carpet squares or color disks. When a color is called out, the child jumps to that square.
5. Jumping for the older child: Mark distances and compete for longest jump, or have the child try to break his previous record.

Become a tree

If possible, have the child do this grounding exercise outside in bare feet.

Setting: Anywhere, but done outdoors when possible

Group/Individual: Either

How long: 5-10 minutes

Method:
This script induces a feeling of "growing roots." Tell the child to:

1. Take off your shoes.
2. Wiggle toes on the ground, feel your feet.
3. Feel the soles of your feet on the ground. (Do this for about 30 seconds.)
4. Now imagine that your feet have roots! Feel the little tiny roots popping out of the bottoms of your feet. (Do this for about 30 seconds.)
5. Imagine that these little roots are growing. They are one inch long and getting longer. (For little children, use your fingers or hands to show "this much.")
6. Now they are three inches long. Do you think they can grow down to one foot?
7. Now make the roots longer yet. How long do they have to be before you feel stuck on the ground?
8. Feel how sturdy you are, just like a tree.
9. Now, lift up your feet *and roots* and walk a little. Keep those roots long. They can stretch and move with you, but don't let them shrink!
10. Let the child know that a sense of connection to the ground (or the earth) is a good thing.

Tree pose from yoga

With its focus on the body, yoga can be very grounding. In the tree pose, the child balances on one foot, with hands on hips. The arms then move together over the head, pointing at the sky. This posture requires the child to focus on balance and on the foot that is providing all the support. This pose is easier for the child who can feel "tree roots" into the ground as in the "Become a tree" exercise.

Setting: Near a wall

Group/Individual: Either

How long: 5-10 minutes

Materials: Pictures of the tree poses. (See p. 39)

Method:
Show the child the pictures, or demonstrate the poses. Do this near a wall so the child can find support if he starts to fall. Instruct the child:

1. Stand straight with feet together, with hands on your hips.
2. Lift one foot up and steady it on the calf of the other leg. Hold it there as long as you can.

3. In this position, move your hands slowly and put palms together in front of chest, as in a praying position. Hold this pose as long as you can.
4. Still on one leg, move your hands slowly over your head and press the palms together. Hold this pose as long as you can.
5. Switch to the other foot and repeat all three poses.

INTERVENTIONS: WORKING WITH INTENSE EMOTIONS

Emotional Freedom Technique (EFT)

The Emotional Freedom Technique is one of a number of Western-style therapies that incorporate acupressure. The goal of this technique is to reduce the intensity of difficult emotions and take the sting out of unpleasant memories and recurring thoughts.

EFT has three components: a difficult emotion or memory, an affirmation that you create to counter that emotion or memory, and tapping on the body (a form of acupressure). In this procedure, the person actively remembers a challenging situation fraught with vivid emotional feelings, at the same time that he taps (does acupressure) on his upper body, while intermittently repeating a relevant affirmation. The stock affirmation is "*Even though I am (sad, angry, lonely), I deeply and completely accept myself.*"

The tapping is done with the fingertips for a few seconds on the head, face, upper body and hands. Typically, several rounds of tapping on these locations of the body are done in a single sitting. The work is complete once the emotions have subsided and the person can recollect the challenging memory or incident without emotional pain or other intense feelings.

Example: Joey, who has ADHD, gets angry at his swim coach and curses at him in the heat of the moment. He is thrown off the team for the year. Joey is devastated. He loves swimming and was hoping to win an all-city medal this year. He would do anything to take the moment back, but instead he is stuck with regrets and self-criticism.

Joey sees an EFT-certified psychologist who helps him to manage his emotions. Together they create an affirmation: "Even though I have strong emotions and outbursts, I deeply and completely accept myself." The psychologist has Joey revisit the incident and talk about it out loud while tapping in the prescribed manner. Every so often, she has him interrupt his story to recite his affirmation. After four rounds of tapping, his emotional intensity subsides and he is able to look at the incident objectively and use it as a learning experience.

Learning more

The EFT Manual, by Gary Craig (2011), provides a good introduction to EFT. Both the technique (with illustrations) and the evidence from conducted research are discussed in the book. A number of YouTube videos demonstrate the technique and show how it can be used with children. One video shows a child using a "Magic Button Bear" with buttons on the tapping points to show her where to tap as she works through the rounds with the help of a therapist.

Rod Sherwin of Australia has produced an excellent series of videos. One of these, titled "The Shortcut Method," is a variation on the original method and is easy to do. You can find this video by searching for "YouTube EFT Rod Sherwin Shortcut Method."

Information about certification is available at a number of places, including Craig's website, EFTUniverse.com.

This technique is potent, so be sure you do not take it lightly. Do not try, for instance, to use it to help friends with serious issues. Emotions are layered. Sadness can mask rage, for example, and that rage can emerge if the sadness is removed by EFT. You do not want to be surprised by a loaded situation that you are unable to handle.

Softening anger with a smile

An invisible smile with the lips barely turned up can often break through anger.

How long: 5-10 minutes

Materials: None

Method:
1. When the child is angry have her turn her lips up slightly in a small smile that is barely noticeable.
2. Watch as the anger fades into another emotion. (This is the "emotion behind the emotion.")
3. Ask her to try to feel that new emotion. It could be sadness, disappointment, or grief. Have her tune into that emotion until it fades.
4. Breathe slowly for a minute or two.

Breathing with anger

This tried-and-true method for dampening anger works anyplace, anytime.

Method:
1. When a child is angry, have him take a slow, deep breath through his nose all the way into his belly.
2. Slowly exhale.
3. Repeat a few times.

Reappraisal: Taking the intensity out of a story

This simple reappraisal technique can be used to reduce emotional intensity after a difficult experience or explosive outburst. It can also be used to decrease obsessive worrying. The method involves having the child explain the situation as if it happened to someone else. As he gives the scenario in the second person, he gets some perspective on the matter. This is especially useful for a child caught in rigid thinking.

Example:

Andrew is kicking his soccer ball on the playground when Bobby asks if he can join in. When Andrew says no, Bobby kicks the ball as hard as he can, ridiculing Andrew for playing like a girl.

The ball lands in the bushes, and Andrew gets scratched retrieving it. Back in the classroom, Andrew punches Bobby in the arm and screams at him. Andrew is sent to the school office for fighting. When told he might get suspended for fighting, his anger flares us and he screams that it is all unfair.

A school counselor intervenes and has him relate the story of what occurred as if it happened to another boy. She helps Andrew get started by suggesting the opening statement: "This boy was playing with a soccer ball in the playground and another boy came over and said . . . " As Andrew tells the tale in the second person, he begins to realize that he has overreacted.

The counselor next asks Andrew questions about how he perceives the boy's feelings at different points in the story. Andrew says that the boy was embarrassed when the other boy called him a girl.

Method:

1. Have the child tell the story of what happened, as the child perceives it, in the second person.

2. At the end of the recitation, have the child say what feelings he felt at key points of the story. Again, do this in the second person.

INTERVENTIONS: ART AND MUSIC

Art and music have built-in self-regulation properties. Here are a few techniques to make use of them in therapeutic ways.

Daily art therapy

Have a child release the day's tension by drawing pictures. This is especially useful for the child who holds everything in all day at school and then comes home and erupts with negative emotions and behaviors. Art therapy helps to reduce the overall level of accumulated emotional baggage.

Setting: A quiet place

Group/Individual: Individual

How long: 15 minutes

Materials: Butcher-block paper, or a stack of blank white paper. Crayons, markers, paints, colored pencils. A snack

Method:
1. Set up the paper and markers over a table in the kitchen.
2. Place a snack nearby.
3. Ask the child to describe his day in a picture. He may or may not want to verbalize the experience as he draws. Working in silence is okay. The parent is nearby but does not interfere. There is no need to judge or comment on the artwork.

Coloring mosaics (design coloring books)

Coloring books offer another way to let out emotions with art. I recommend books with nature designs or geometric mosaics that offer freedom in color choice and allow intense feelings to be expressed.

Setting: A quiet place

Group/Individual: Individual

Materials: Coloring books, colored pencils or crayons. A snack

Resources for coloring books:
1. www.mindwar.com: search on "coloring books".
2. *Dover Design Coloring Book* series (online and in bookstores).
3. *Ruth Heller's Designs for Coloring series* (online and in bookstores).
4. There are many printable designs available online. Use the phrase *"coloring designs"* for the search.

Method:
1. Create conditions for an hour's uninterrupted work.
2. Encourage the child to think through the colors and to work slowly and neatly. Tell her that she can complete the coloring over a period of days.

Make music playlists (for older children and teens)

Adolescents and teens who become entangled in difficult emotions can be guided through music to a more peaceful mood. Have the person create a playlist of music (using her own favorite music) that starts out with emotional pieces and then gradually moves to calm music. She can listen to the playlist when she finds herself stuck in difficult emotions. The playlists can be set up over a period of several days.

Setting: A quiet place

Group/Individual: Individual

When/How often: As needed

How long: Preparation over several days. Intervention: 30 minutes

Materials: A music device loaded with the child's favorite music

Method:
1. On a day when the child is exhibiting strong emotions (angst, anger, grief, etc.), ask her to name a piece of music that matches her mood.
2. At another time when she is quiet and appears to be in a pleasant state, ask her to name music that matches this mood.
3. These selections constitute the end-posts of a playlist.

4. Have her find music that gently moves from the difficult emotion to the pleasant emotion over 20-30 minutes. For example, the first selection is heavy angst, the second less heavy, and the third lighter still. Working back from the pleasant song at the other end-post, she adds music with increased emotional feeling until the two sides meet in the middle.
5. Remind her to listen to the playlist when she is moody. Tell her that it is important that she not grow attached to wanting or needing depressed feelings. She should instead feel the angst long enough to let out feelings, and then move on to a more positive place.
6. Consider making multiple playlists, one or more for each mood.

Variation for young children

A younger child may not be able to come up with songs for a playlist, so you will need to make the selections. For the emotional start of a playlist, try stormy music. The second track of Sacred Earth Drums by David and Stephen Gordon (see description below) works well for tantrums and stormy moods. For the pleasant end-post, try calm classical music or perhaps classical guitar or flute. The music playlist for a young child can be shorter than it is for teens. Try 15 minutes of music.

Music to work by

Use the magic of background music to create a mood. Relaxing instrumental music can help the child to settle and focus during the school day, evening homework and whenever anxiety arises.

Music for alerting and focusing

Music with a solid beat, either fast or slow, helps to pace an activity. Match the rhythm of the music to the pace of the task at hand. And be playful with the child; these activities can be good fun! Make sure you omit tunes with lyrics when the child is doing schoolwork.

Music ideas:
1. J.S. Bach
2. "No Worries: Songs for Sensory Modulation," by Genevieve Jereb
3. "Cool Bananas," by Genevieve Jereb
4. The marching music of John Philip Sousa (try marching in place or around the room).

Calm music

Calm music can create a pleasant atmosphere and improve attention and regulation skills. Check that children can tolerate the music by playing it on days when they are calm. If the children enjoy music, play it throughout the day. It can help to keep their anxieties low and their focus strong. Make sure that the music is either neutral or positive in mood.

Setting: Anywhere

When/How often: As needed

Transition technique: Yes

Amount of time: 10 minutes or more

Materials: Music device, music

Music ideas:

1. "Sacred Earth Drums," by David and Stephen Gordon.
   This is an excellent remedy for a tantrum. Track two is awesome! The music combines drums, bird songs, throbbing rhythms and a flute.
2. "Mozart for Modulation," by The Oberlin Conservatory of Music.
3. "Baroque for Modulation," by The Oberlin Conservatory of Music.
4. Classical music of all kinds, especially classical guitar.
5. Ethnic music such as Indian Ragas, Celtic harp, African drums (for focus).

Our need to avoid emotional reactivity

Even as we are involved in a compassionate or empathetic way with our charges, we need to practice a certain emotional detachment that protects us from negative influences and helps us to prevent burnout.

Therapists and teachers can expect, at least occasionally, to have adverse inner reactions to the challenging situations we face on a daily basis. It happens all the time, even when we attempt to maintain an emotional distance. When it occurs, we can inadvertently react with inappropriate behaviors and words or with painful feelings. Sometimes this emotional reaction can be quite subtle, and we hardly know it is happening. We can, for instance, be doing good work with a difficult child, even as we are having a troublesome inner reaction. Our reaction can be immediate or it might be delayed. It is common for a therapist or teacher to go home after work and take out her frustration on her family members, not realizing where her bad temper is coming from.

When we are dealing with a difficult child or when we become tired after a long day or long week, we can slip into the painful feeling of being hopelessly ineffective. Nothing we try seems to work the way we hoped. When our best attempts appear to be failing, we can easily start to feel powerless or helpless. Even when we are practicing our skills at a high level, we can still have these kinds of emotional reactions when children respond poorly to our efforts.

Perhaps our most common emotional reactions involve feeling overwhelmed and discouraged. Of course, we do not want a child's incomprehension and resistance to wear us down. The trick is to avoid criticizing ourselves or doubting ourselves. Many people have a nasty inner critic that can belittle them and find fault with much of what they do.

This inner dynamic is behind a lot of self-criticism. It is common for the inner critic to accuse us of not being good enough at what we do, especially when, in dealing with such challenging situations, the benefits of our efforts are not immediately apparent.

We can also feel this criticism if we begin to imagine that the parents of our charges are feeling or expressing dissatisfaction with our work. Sometimes we can imagine that such criticism is occurring, when in fact it is not. Other times, the parents may indeed be critical of our efforts. Some parents have critical personalities, and it is up to us to recognize when this is the case so we do not take personally what they are dishing out. If what they are saying does have some validity, we want to try objectively, without regret or self-recrimination, to consider how we might be able to improve our skills or knowledge.

By maintaining some amount of emotional detachment, we can decrease our susceptibility to emotional reactions that over time lead to burnout.

AUTISM AND EMOTION

Although children with autism may have a flat affect, they are not necessarily displaying a lack of emotions. Children with autism are unable to copy facial and body muscle movements—the emotional signaling—that others display. They also fail to recognize or interpret the social intent of those muscle movements.

Because of this deficit, we must teach them about emotions using tools like emoticons or Kimochees™ and performing exercises such as imitating facial expressions in a mirror. We teach them to recognize our emotions and to replicate them, just as we help them to understand the social context for expressing emotions. This work is typically done by parents, or by teachers and therapists, in early intervention programs. It is important for children to receive emotional training at a young age. Studies have shown that emotional skills play a role in the development of the nervous system, which in turn affects the child's ability to handle social situations without anxiety. The nervous system matures in the early years, and it is more difficult in later years to make changes in how the nervous system responds to the environment and to the people around us.

Interventions for emotional self-regulation can also be found in the section on Polyvagal theory and in the chapter on autism.

CHAPTER 6

Executive Function and ADHD

In earlier chapters, we looked at how emotions, stress and sensations from the environment and the body can challenge a child's ability to stay self-regulated. We followed that with interventions that:

1. Modify the environment so that raw sensation (of sound, for example) is easier for her to tolerate.

2. Increase the child's ability to process emotional or sensory input without a negative reaction.

3. Teach the child strategies (such as performing isometric exercises when stressed) for coping with difficult situations. We also teach her ways to stay grounded and focused with support of an ongoing program of heavy work or exercise.

These methods are more passive in that, once a program for self-regulation is set up, the child is able to maintain self-regulation.

In this chapter, the focus changes from passive to active response. That is, the child uses her executive-function skills to actively change her behaviors to meet the demands of the situation. Teachers and therapists can help facilitate this process the better they understand it.

EXECUTIVE FUNCTION

Psychologist Russell Barkley has put together a large-scale theory of executive function that encompasses self-regulation skills. These skills range from our ability to respond to raw sensory and emotional input to our ability to participate productively in the growth of our political system, society and culture (2013). ADHD, Barkley claims, is the chief disorder of the executive-function (EF) system. He equates EF with self-regulation (SR) and expresses that relationship as EF = SR.

Barkley's theory describes five levels of EF, which are listed here and described below. They are:

1. Pre-EF
2. Self-directed EF
3. Self-reliant EF
4. Tactical-reciprocal EF
5. Strategic-cooperative EF

The levels are arranged to match the developmental process from infant to mature adult. With time and experience we move into higher levels of EF, and we also develop greater skill within current levels. Here is an overview of these levels:

1. Pre-EF provides us with our auto-pilot or automatic processes:

1. Attention, awareness

2. Visual-spatial reasoning

3. Perception of raw emotions

4. Memory

5. Sensory perception

6. Language

7. Movement

Pre-EF underlies true EF in the brain. This is our raw sensing and response, which is not regulated. Barkley uses psychophysiologist James J. Gross's *modal model* (2006) to describe how pre-EF operates. Gross created the modal model to describe emotional regulation, and the model works well to describe other types of regulation. It is a four-step process involving situation, attention, appraisal, and response.

Situation: *Something has happened*
   -> Attention: *I take notice*
      -> Appraisal: *I assess its impact*
         -> Response: *I automatically respond*

Here is an example using Pre-EF functions: *I hear my alarm clock at 6 AM*
   -> *I attend to that sound*
      -> *I realize that it is my alarm clock and it is time to get up. I also realize that it will not stop unless I take action.*
         -> *I roll over and turn it off, then get out of bed.*

Here is another example: As Julie's mother reads a sad story out loud to the family, Julie's emotions arise and tears well up.

Julie's mother is reading her a sad story
   -> *Julie listens intently*
      -> *She thinks how awful is the fate of the main character*
         -> *Tears well up in Julie's eyes*

Note that Pre-EF entails a passive response to the environment. We do not try to change our response. That comes with the next level.

Thoughts

One can make a case that thoughts be included on the list of pre-EF automatic processes. As with other sensory and emotional processes, simple thoughts can present themselves unbidden into our consciousness.

The special case of reflexes

A layer of reflexive action can be teased out of the sensory-motor aspect of pre-EF. Reflexes form our lowest level of response to input, since they comprise direct connection from the sense to the motor response. For example, when someone hears a booming noise, he or she likely experiences a reflexive fight-flight response. The arm muscles (for fight) or the leg muscles (for flight) are energized. We also have simple motor reflexes such as the patellar (knee) reflex: when your doctor taps on your knee, you reflexively produce a kicking motion.

When reflexes are oversensitive or do not work, they disrupt our lowest level of EF functionality. In worst cases, they compromise our fight-flight response which is a necessary component of our nervous system, as well as being a precursor to EF.

Interventions for ADHD at the pre-EF level

Interventions at this level focus primarily on the underlying elements of executive function such as working memory, timing, self-monitoring and self-stopping.

2. Self-directed EF is the first level of true EF. This level allows us to regulate our response to our body, emotions and environmental input (via our senses). The functions are:

1. Self-awareness
2. Self-restraint (inhibition)
3. Sensory-motor actions
4. Private speech or self-talk
5. Appraisal including calculating the emotional cost of an action
6. Play, reconstitution of memories and thoughts, and problem-solving.

With this set of skills we create our first set of reactions to what is happening within us and around us. These reactions are directed inward rather than outward to others. To the degree that we keep our body still and hide our emotions, no one is privy to them. For example, if I am confused and don't want anyone to know, and keep my face from showing confusion, no one will likely know.

The combination of pre-EF and EF allows us to govern ourselves. Barkley claims that the combination of pre-EF and self-directed EF is conscious thought or our mind function.

Pre-EF and EF operate in a similar manner. With EF, however, we gain control over the response. This drastically changes the four-step pre-EF response process (situation, attention, appraisal, response). The self-directed EF process has five steps or stages and is not automated. The child can take action at any point. In the initial situation, she can react with any one of five responses. The first two responses are proactive choices; the remaining three are reactive choices.

Situation selection: *I can choose to stay or leave*
   -> Situation modification: *I can modify the situation so that it has a different outcome*
      -> Attention: *I can choose to place my attention elsewhere*
         -> Appraisal: *I can think things over and come to terms with them*
            -> Response: *I can choose my response*

Let us continue with the example of Julie and the sad story that produced her tears. Julie was embarrassed by the tears. She also did not like the story. She thinks through her options. The next time her mother gets the book out, she can proceed in a pre-EF mode and listen to the story or she can opt to take an action, either proactive or reactive, to change her outcome. Here are sample options for her:

1. Situation selection: She can announce that she has homework and needs to skip the story tonight.

2. Situation modification: She could make light of the story out loud by dramatizing the events and making up a silly ending.

3. Attention: She can sit with others while the story is read, but divert most of her attention to a game she is playing on a hand-held device.

4. Appraisal: She can decide that listening to sad stories is good for her, and so she plans to "tough it out."

5. Response: She can listen to the story and fight back the tears when her mother gets to the next sad passage.

Children sitting in a school classroom or in a structured setting are typically working from the self-directed EF level. They are trying to make whatever change, at an internal level, they feel they need. As we mature, we gain greater skill for operating at this level.

Interventions for ADHD at the self-directed EF level

Interventions at this level primarily focus on independent functioning.

- Children can learn to talk themselves through a difficult situation by using "out-loud" speech. (Refer to the intervention later in this chapter.)

- An older child can learn to continuously monitor himself and to use external strategies to help compensate for poor executive-function skill.

- A child can use external strategies for self-regulation such as timers, alarms, check-in apps, reminders.

3. Self-reliant EF gives us the self-management skills necessary to be independent with activities of daily living (ADLS) such as dressing, preparing food, eating and so on. Barkley compares the person operating at this level to Robinson Crusoe who was able to manage his life on his own without social support. However, at this level, we may find ourselves occasionally competing for resources. People operating at this level are performing in a social context, but it is "everyone for themselves." A child at this level will be competing for toys or play-space during parallel play, or competing with a sibling for a parent's affection.

At this level, we begin to problem-solve, create plans, and take action. We may make use of to-do lists and other organizing tools, or make sketches for plans and ideas. Gratification can be delayed, because we see the benefit of long-term goals. We can imitate others (mirroring). We learn as we observe others accomplishing a task (vicarious learning). We are not yet working with others cooperatively to accomplish our goals; that practice comes in the next level. For now, we compete with others and may prey on them to achieve our goals.

Here are examples of how a child may operate at the self-reliant EF level:

- At school on the playground, a young child observes another child on a climbing structure and thus learns how to navigate it.
- A third-grader gets points if he completes his homework in 30 minutes. He realizes he has five or ten minutes to spare and is restless, so he sets a timer for a five-minute break and pulls out his video game.
- An eighth-grader makes plans for a party by making four lists: who to invite, what food and drink to buy, what decorations to make, and what activities to engage in.
- A 13-year-old girl makes a mental note of how a popular girl has her hair styled, and she asks for the same style at her next hair appointment.
- A 16-year-old boy marks the date of his school prom on his calendar.

At this stage we develop our initial sense of cultural awareness as we observe others. This awareness continues to develop through the remaining levels and, ideally, through our remaining years.

Interventions for ADHD at the self-reliant EF level

Interventions at this level primarily focus on tools for organizing materials, tracking time, problem-solving and describing creative ideas.

The child new to this level is learning early social skills such as parallel play, how to compete, how to be fair and how to avoid being taken advantage of. Early social-skill training is appropriate at this age.

Interventions that focus on being more present (such as mindfulness training, yoga and martial arts) can help a child slow down, watch others, and learn through mirroring and vicarious learning.

Young children can learn good behavior with video modeling (see *p. 32*). This might involve making a video of a child when you see her behaving correctly, and showing it to her daily.

4. Tactical-reciprocal EF: At this level, we use social relationships to achieve our goals. We learn to share and we provide mutual help to friends. We learn what it means to be a friend, and we begin to act accordingly. We begin to regulate our actions, emotions, sensory behaviors, and social behaviors for the purpose of successfully interacting with others. For the first time, moral rules come into play.

At this stage, we also learn to think of solutions to problems in our head and on paper. This ability to play with information and ideas is the basis for complex problem-solving and creative thinking, and normally this ability grows throughout our lives. We learn to think and act strategically and to plan days and weeks ahead. This helps us to achieve longer-term goals.

Here are some examples of children using tactical-reciprocal EF skills:

- Three girls are playing jump-rope. Two girls hold the rope ends, while the third girl jumps. All three benefit when they take turns holding the rope. This is an example of reciprocity.

- Six-year-old Tony knocked over the soccer coach's soda. He asked his friend Evan not to tell on him. When the coach asked who knocked over his soda, Evan (still in the previous stage of self-reliant EF) lied to protect his friend, trusting that his friend would do the same for him. Later, when they are ten years old, something similar occurs. This time Tony admits to causing the accident. He does not want his friend to be blamed. Tony's moral conscience now actively motivates his self-regulation.

Interventions for ADHD at the tactical-reciprocal EF level

At this level, the therapist makes use of interventions that target social skills, improving the ability to regulate behavior in the company of others, moral thinking, and social-emotional skills such as empathy and respect.

5. Strategic-cooperative EF is more an extension of tactical-reciprocal EF than a set of new functions. At this level, our time horizon and the spatial distance we operate within have a larger scope. Now we can include making career decisions, volunteer activities, political or concerned-citizen activities, or organizing a large group for a united goal. The concerns of this level are adult-oriented. But an older teen can begin to work through issues that involve strategic-cooperative EF skills.

Here is an example of a teenager making use of tactical-reciprocal EF skills:

Sixteen-year-old Roger must decide whether to attend a sports camp this summer. He thinks the camp will improve his chances of a sports scholarship. He has been offered free tuition to the camp from his girlfriend Julia's uncle. However, Roger has been considering breaking up with her, and he realizes that this must influence his decision. His other summer option involves getting a job and saving for college. He ponders several questions:

- Should he stay with Julia though fall in order to attend camp without having her feel used?
- Should he talk with Julia's uncle and explain the situation to him?
- Can he qualify for a position on the college team without the camp?
- What are his feelings for Julia?
- Will the money he earns at a summer job be enough to pay for most of his college costs?
- Is playing college sports a good idea? Will it take too much time away from his studies?
- What career is he aiming for?

As he weighs these and other factors, he creates a pros-cons sheet, prioritizing his goals and trying to project five years into the future. He is performing strategic planning as he prioritizes his goals, and he calculates his chances for success in meeting them.

Interventions for ADHD at the strategic-cooperative EF level

The teen and young adult may have a hard time seeing past a six-month time horizon. They will benefit from help with strategic planning. They may also need a rewards schedule that can help them stick to a long-term plan.

Knowing these five levels of executive function can guide those of us who work with children and young adults with ADHD. It helps us select interventions that are appropriate to their EF development level as opposed to their age level. In this way, we can help them move from where they are stuck into the next level of their growth.

ADHD

ADHD in a child is diagnosed symptomatically in the DSM-5. In general, there are three ways a child can meet the criteria for an ADHD diagnosis:

1. The child has inattention alone. This is referred to as ADHD due to inattention.
2. The child has hyperactivity and impulsivity. This is referred to as ADHD due to hyperactivity/impulsivity.
3. The child has all three—inattention, hyperactivity, and impulsivity. This is called the combined form of ADHD.

Some experts think this definition should be changed. Results of brain-imaging studies show that the combined form stems from abnormalities in the prefrontal cortex, while ADHD due to inattention has roots in a different part of the brain. The experts have suggested removing ADHD due to inattention from the ADHD diagnosis and renaming it as a separate disorder. They also suggest removing ADHD due to hyperactivity/impulsivity from the ADHD diagnosis, based on evidence that all persons with ADHD have attention symptoms at some time. Hence, a diagnosis of hyperactivity/impulsivity minus inattention would be unnecessary.

Causes and development of ADHD

ADHD is reported to be caused by genetics, brain injury, environmental factors such maternal smoking or alcohol use during pregnancy, and exposure to lead in old plumbing or paint chips (NIMH, 2013). In addition, 2-3% of children appear to be sensitive to food dyes which may not cause ADHD but may increase its symptoms. We know that poor nutrition and a sugary diet do not cause ADHD but can increase its symptoms. Why do they increase symptoms? The prefrontal cortex is fueled by glucose from the diet. Processed foods and sugary foods are high in glucose. They burn quickly and produce a large blood glucose spike followed by a decrease of both blood glucose and glucose levels in the brain, which reduces energy to the child's prefrontal cortex as well as decreasing his executive-function capability. Better choices of foods are grains, proteins and vegetables. These burn more slowly and help to provide a steady, reliable supply of glucose to the prefrontal cortex where executive function is located (Newmark, 2010).

Children typically show the first signs of ADHD between the ages of three to six. Imaging studies of seven-year-olds with ADHD show that brain maturation is delayed several years in the frontal and temporal (side) areas of the brain. The greatest delays (five years) were in areas that connected sensory to executive function control (NIMH, 2007), which may help to explain some overlap in sensory modulation symptoms and ADHD.

Teens and adults who continue to be hyperactive have greater difficulty managing their lives. They may attempt to do too many things at once and have difficulty completing any of them. They may also opt for short-term fixes to problems rather than thinking through (and following up on) long-term solutions.

A longitudinal study followed more than 200 children with ADHD from the ages of eight to 25. In the group, ADHD symptoms decreased with brain maturation such that, by their teens, about 60% of the children "lost their label." Two-thirds showed no evidence of a mental illness (significant emotional or behavioral problems) by their mid-twenties. Of the remaining one-third who showed symptoms, those who continued to have attention issues in their late teens had the poorest outcomes, including antisocial behavior and substance abuse as adults. The ADHD population of the entire study group had poorer outcomes than their peers in terms of social and psychological adjustment. In addition, only 14% obtained a college degree compared with 51% of typical peers. However, most of the study participants were gainfully employed (Mannuzza, 2000).

A separate longitudinal study found that middle-aged men who had both ongoing and remitted ADHD had structural differences in their brains as compared with typical peers. Brain imaging showed decreased white-matter tracts and structural properties in areas of the brain affecting executive and sensory-motor functions (Cortese, 2013)

ADHD statistics

The occurrence and treatment of ADHD varies widely across the United States. The CDC sponsored a longitudinal study of 10,000 children in North Carolina and Oklahoma to learn about these differences and how children with ADHD developed over time. North Carolina has the highest rate of ADHD in the United States with a rate of 15.6%. In Oklahoma, the rate is 5.6%, one of the lowest in the country. Here are some findings from the study (Visser, et al., 2011).

- The occurrence of other disorders is much higher in children with ADHD than in typical children.
  - 53.4% had at least one other disorder.
  - 44.3% had oppositional defiant disorder.
  - 13.5% had conduct disorder.
  - 16.8% had an affective or anxiety disorder.
- Children with ADHD engage in risky behaviors at a much higher rate than their peers.

  The CDC (2013) also reports:
- Children with ADHD have more difficulty maintaining friendships than their peers.
- Children with ADHD have more peer problems than typical children.
- Approximately 50% of children with ADHD also have a learning disorder.

Assessing ADHD

There are more than 30 disorders and medical issues whose symptoms are similar to those of ADHD. Examples are sleeping disorders, thyroid disease and depression. These 30 disorders and medical issues must be considered as part of the ADHD assessment. This is typically part

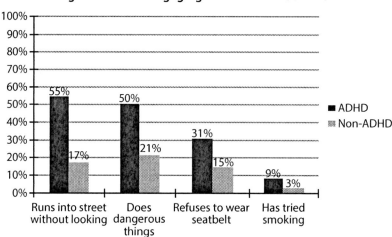

Percentage of Children Engaging in Health Risk Behavior

of a four-to-eight hour assessment that includes observable symptoms, child and family history, and use of standardized assessment tools. The ADHD assessment itself should include a variety of tools and questionnaires relevant to the child's age and development level. The tools need to investigate thoroughly each of the levels of the child's executive-function skills (as described above).

Medication and other options

Once a child has been diagnosed with ADHD, parents are faced with a decision on whether to use ADHD medication. When medication is successful, attention to schoolwork improves and social interactions are easier to manage. Adolescents and adults are better protected from the risk of addictive behaviors.

On the downside, ADHD medications can have adverse side-effects. While stimulant medications, including methylphenidate and amphetamine, have common side-effects such as loss of appetite and poor sleep, these problems are not associated with non-stimulant medications. We have less knowledge of the side-effects of non-stimulant medications, especially long-term effects, since they are newer to the marketplace.

Non-stimulant ADHD medicines are effective for about 24 hours. In contrast, stimulant medications wear off after five-to-eight hours, when the child once again has his full range of symptoms. Parents can opt for 24-hour, time-released capsules, and many parents prefer this choice because it enables them to administer smaller doses of medication. They may opt for their child to be off medication in the evenings and on weekends, which can be a workable strategy for their child. However, when symptoms are disabling, doctors may recommend that the child be administered medication around the clock as a way to give the child and family more relief.

Therapy is recommended along with medication, and studies show that medication and therapeutic interventions, including behavior interventions, are most effective. Some doctors, including Drs. Charles Parker, Sanford Newmark and the late Stanley Greenspan, have recommended that diet and metabolism issues be addressed prior to using medication.

Newmark, an ADHD specialist, recommends trying dietary changes prior to starting medication. He says a child's diet should be rich in grains and vegetables and low in sugars and processed foods, in order to balance energy and sugar levels. Newmark suggests the child take a multivitamin and a probiotic daily, as well as alpha-omega-3 supplements that were shown by Sinn (2007) to significantly decrease ADHD symptoms. (Consult a physician first.) He also recommends performing an elimination diet (laid out in his book, *ADHD Without Drugs*, 2010) to discover food sensitivities. Finally, he recommends checking blood levels of iron, zinc and magnesium.

Greenspan recommended occupational therapy or physical therapy to address any coordination and sensory issues, along with behavioral therapies to help with executive-function and self-reflection issues and counseling for the child or family.

Clearly, parents have much to consider. Each child is unique and there is no one-size-fits-all solution. Some children with ADHD may find help with other types of medicine that target anxiety, OCD (obsessive-compulsive disorder), and behaviors such as self-injury, aggression and tantrums. In these cases, doctors may prescribe a "cocktail" of two or more medications in lower dosages that target the child's symptoms throughout the day.

Medication is not for all children, but for some children it can make all the difference between serious dysfunction and the ability to function more normally. A few years ago, I provided therapy to a sweet seven-year-old boy who had been diagnosed with autism, OCD and ADHD. He was taking a low-dose of an ADHD medication and seeing me for help with gross motor skills, sensory modulation and self-help skills. He made a lot of progress, but after a while his anxiety and OCD behaviors hindered him. When I tried to teach him to tie his shoes, for instance, he created a new OCD ritual around shoe-tying and could not let it go. When not engaged in an OCD ritual, he tended to run around in uncontrolled fashion. I had been hoping to start a rigorous therapy regime with him, but he was not able to attend to that program. His parents took him back to his doctor who adjusted the medication. His anxiety and his OCD symptoms settled down. The boy was able to attend to new programs and we made good progress with social skills, modulation and play skills.

INTERVENTIONS: STRUCTURE AND ORGANIZATION

A child with ADHD struggles to keep his bedroom neat along with study areas, locker, book bag and desk. He is prone to losing his assignments, forgetting when an assignment is due and what time he promised to be home. We now look at simple and fun ways for him to put structure in place in the critical areas of his life. See pp. 61-62 for addition strategies.

General strategies

As a general rule, keep things simple to help children with ADHD to succeed.

1. Keep distractions in the environment to a minimum.
2. Put structure in place to help the child succeed in completing daily routines, schoolwork and home responsibilities.
3. Limit demands on the child. Do not ask him to do more than he is capable of.

Keep it simple: Create a simple environment at home

For the highly distractible child with ADHD, a simple environment free from clutter can help her stay focused. Have the child help with organizing and labeling so she knows where everything is.

Materials: Cupboards or shelves, see-through bins, small removable labels

Age group/Cognitive skill: Fair-good

Setting: Bedroom, play and study areas

When/How often: Do this once, and then revisit seasonally

How long: Put this in place for a few days, then help to maintain the skill with additional days

Set up the space:
1. Remove all clutter from walls. Leave a calendar and one or two calm pictures such as landscapes.
2. Set up a study area for the child that is free of distractions. It should exclude TV, games, radio or phones.
3. Create an area at home where the child's jacket, backpack and lunch bag are stored.

Organize things:
1. Empty out cupboards and drawers. If more space is needed, install shelving.
2. Organize child's belongings into dresser drawers, bins and shelves. If possible, put bins in cupboards or closets. The best containers are see-through plastic.
3. Label bins with small words or pictures. The labels should be small so they do not add to clutter. Put removable labels on closet doors, as well, so items are readily found.

Enforce cleanup with a points program:
1. Use a points program to give positive rewards for keeping spaces neat. (This can be an additional way to gain points if the parents are already using a points program).
2. Create a list of tasks and the number of points each is worth.
3. Identify desirable rewards and the number of points required to get each reward.

Reward List	Points
15 min. extra TV or game time	65
Movie on the weekend	300
Friend overnight	400
Trip for ice cream	65

4. Create a chart such as the one below and put it and the reward list on the refrigerator.
5. Create a cleanup time for straightening the area each day or each week, with a reward to follow the effort. If the parent is using a points program, putting things away will be worth some points.

Cleanup task	Points	Sun	Mon	Tues	Wed	Thurs	Fri	Sat
7:30 room tidy	20	20	20					
4:00 coat on peg	5		5					
6:00 room tidy	20	20	20					
9:00 room tidy	20		20					
9:00 homework in book bag	5	5	5					
clothes in laundry	5		5					
Total	65	45	65					

Organize schoolwork

1. Create organizing helpers in the form of lists, schedules, and reminders. Make it fun by using color pens, and purchase to-do lists with cute illustrations (from a hobby or dollar store).

2. Children in middle school have an especially difficult time being organized. Color code subjects by putting work into different colored folders. Mark subject worksheets, assignments and homework with a dot the same color as the subject folder so that papers are easily sorted. Optionally, put a colored-dot sticker on each paper.

Using technology for the schedule

Find new uses for new or old electronic devices such as a PDA (Palm or Blackberry), phone, smart phone, iPod, iPad, or tablet. Make use of interesting programs and apps involving alarms, reminders, calendars, schedules and lists to help the child stay organized. Remove games, fun apps and other programs that are not allowed in school. Using an electronic organizer makes staying organized more interesting and increases motivation.

Materials: Device with alarms, lists, schedule and calendar

When/How often: Throughout the day, as needed

Age group/Cognitive skill: Age 7 or older, good cognition

Method:
1. Set up the device to be used strictly for organization. Delete games and other distracting apps.
2. Download apps or software with calendars, times, alarms, and lists.
3. Set up tools and apps for the child to use.
4. Teach the child to use the device and its apps.
5. Monitor its use until the child is independent with it.

Create a general schedule

Each season or semester, create a new schedule with regular activities penciled in.

Materials: Paper calendar and/or electronic calendar

When/How often: Create general calendar once, update as needed

Age group/Cognitive skill: Age 7 or older, good cognition

Method:
1. Each season or semester create a new schedule with regular activities penciled in.
2. Put a paper calendar in the kitchen or family area.

Sunday	Monday	Tuesday	Wednesday	Thursday	Friday	Saturday
Church 10:00	Bus 7:30	Bus 7:30	Bus 7:30	Bus 7:30	Bus 7:30	Do nothing!
	School 8:00	School 8:00	School 8:00	School 8:00	School 8:00	
	Out 3:05	Out 3:05	Out 3:05	Out 3:05	Out 3:05	
Homework	Homework	Homework	Homework	Homework	Check homework	
Dinner 5:00	Dinner 6:00	Dinner 6:00	Dinner 6:00	Dinner 6:00	Dinner 6:00	
	Karate 7:00		Karate 7:00			

Keep a calendar

Appointments, dates and special events are penciled into the family calendar. The calendar sits next to the general schedule in the kitchen, den or hallway. Have the child enter dates on the calendar as early as possible to avoid schedule conflicts. (He may have his own electronic calendar, as well.)

Update calendar and set alarms for the week

Every week have the child update electronic calendars with upcoming events and set alarms for each. For important events, it is useful to have two alarms—one that goes off the day before the event and the other just before the time to get ready.

Materials: Electronic organizer (as described above)

When/How often: Weekly, on Sunday evenings for example

Amount of time: 5-10 minutes

Age group/Cognitive skill: Good

Method:

1. As a one-time activity, set up a repeating weekly alarm (possibly on Sunday evening) called "Set weekly alarms." This tells the child it is time to create the coming week's alarms.
2. Weekly: Have the child enter activities and due dates (homework assignments) for the coming week.
3. Create one or two alarms for activities if the child needs to be reminded to gather materials or make plans for the activity.

Create routines

Sticking to a routine is a helpful way to get something done. Here is a way for creating important routines.

Materials: Stiff paper such as poster board, paper and pencil

When/How often: Create once, daily

Age group/Cognitive skill: Age 7 or older, good cognition

Method:

1. Create routines (as seen below) for morning, bedtime, homework, and outside activities.
2. For each routine, create a list of what needs to be done and how long it will take.
3. Move items in the list until the order makes sense and the routine is efficient. Add a five-minute task and place it at the end of the list called "Think."
4. Determine what time the routine needs to be done. Moving backward through the list, figure out at what time each task must be started.
5. Copy the list of tasks and start times on to poster-board and display the board close to where the routines are done.
6. Give points for getting through the routine in a timely fashion. Give extra points for having time for "thinking."

Morning routine	Time
Get up	6:25
Shower + hair	6:25
Dress	6:40
Make breakfast	6:50
Make lunch	6:55
Eat breakfast	7:05
Brush teeth	7:20
Gather things	7:23
Think	7:25
Leave for school	7:30

Channel creative thinking into an ideas notebook

The bright, energetic child with ADHD can use a notebook to jot down her ideas so she doesn't lose them. In more practical terms, using the notebook helps her to channel energy in useful directions.

Materials: Notebook, electronic notes

When/How often: 1 minute

Amount of time: As needed

Age group/Cognitive skill: Age 7 and older, good cognition

Method:
1. Have her create headings on separate pages of the notebook for the categories of ideas that appeal to her:
   a. Great ideas for games.
   b. Inventions for the future.
   c. Videos that can be made.
2. Encourage her to continue to jot down new ideas and title headings.

The stop-think-count mantra

Here is a simple way for the child to check in with himself before moving from one place to another.

Method:
1. Stop.
2. Think – are you ready to go?
3. Count your things before you leave.

Measuring time

Children with ADHD often do not have a functional sense of time. Have them time things for a day to get a better sense of time.

Materials: Timer, notebook, pencil

Setting: Anywhere

When/How often: One day

Amount of time: All day

Method:
1. Explain how to use the timer.
2. Number two sheets of paper. Make two columns: name of activity, amount of time.
3. Have them time everything, including walking from place to place, chatting with a friend, performing an activity, eating, and so on.

INTERVENTIONS: HANDLING COMPLEXITY

The child with ADHD can get overwhelmed by complexity. Here are a few different approaches to helping him simplify problems and solutions.

Out-loud speech for complicated moments

Have the child talk out loud to himself as a way of remembering important information and thinking through problems. Talking through a problem slows down his fast brain. Hearing himself talk gives him another modality (auditory) for processing information. Have the child:

1. Repeat instructions: "If the door is locked, I need to go next door and ask Mrs. Bryant to let me in."
2. Repeat scheduling information: "We meet at 4 o'clock at the bus stop."
3. Count out loud the number of belongings he is taking: "I have four things—jacket, lunch, book bag, and organizer."
4. Repeat the name of someone he just met: "Hi Alan!"
5. Talk out loud through a complex problem (for instance, a math or relationship problem) as a way of making use of auditory memory to support his weak working memory.

Too many things to do

When the child is struggling under the weight of too many things to do or think about, help him to sort it out with this plan of attack.

Materials: Electronic or paper organizers, paper and pencil

Amount of time: 20 minutes

Age group/Cognitive skill: Older child, good cognition

Step 1: Sort it out
Walk the child through the following steps:

1. Make a list that addresses the details of his day.
2. Some of the items may be things to do, some are issues to resolve, perhaps personal issues. Separate these and follow the steps below.

Step 2: Things to do
1. Note when each task is due, and then prioritize the tasks.
2. If any tasks are big, break them into chunks.
3. Plan. For each task or chunk determine:
   a. How much time it will take.
   b. What materials he will need. How he will get the materials.
   c. What challenging aspects are in need of solutions? Is there a simple solution? If not, what is the best way to meet the challenge?

4. For larger items, create a timeline to get them done. Put the tasks and deadlines into his electronic (or paper) organizers, using lists, calendar, alarms, and so on.

Step 3: Issues to resolve
1. For each issue, make lists of:
   a. Things to be considered.
   b. People who are involved. Possible problems regarding their involvement.
   c. Steps to be taken.
   d. Deadline (or multiple deadlines).
   e. If necessary, break this into smaller chunks.
2. Create a timeline to work on the issues, and put the steps to be taken and deadlines into his electronic (or paper) organizers using lists, calendar, alarms and so on.
3. Resolving an issue has its own natural reward, but after a successful completion remind him to stop for a celebratory moment with others who are involved.

Step 4: Self-reflection
Once big items on the list have been worked through, it is time to reflect. Look at the initial plans once again and compare them to the actual process whereby the tasks or issues were resolved.

1. Did things go satisfactorily?
2. Was the time to complete the task faster or slower than expected?
3. Were the challenges and issues different from what were originally expected?
4. What lessons did he learn from the experience?

INTERVENTIONS: WORKING WITH IMPULSIVITY AND HYPERACTIVITY

Here are ways to slow the hyperactive or impulsive mind. There are related interventions in chapter 2 (Staying Calm and Alert) and in the Movement section of the Sensory Modulation chapter. In addition, the last section of this chapter contains an intervention to reduce impulsive "blurting out" in the classroom.

Learning to stop and think

Children with ADHD have difficulty staying present and attentive to what is going on. The following method can literally make them stop and think. It can be lots of fun as a group process.

Setting: Anywhere

When/How often: Regularly to gain practice, and then randomly to maintain skill

Amount of time: 5-15 minutes

Method:
1. While the child is engaged in an activity, say "Freeze" or "Stop." For example:
   a. Have the child pick up a favorite treat and take one small bite. Say "Stop!" and have him hold it in his mouth without any jaw motion.

b. Play freeze. The child moves around but has to stop and hold his position when you say "Freeze!"

c. Have a child (or children in a group) recite a nursery rhyme or verse that she knows. Periodically, tell her to "Freeze!"

2. Quickly ask a random question such as:

   a. What color is your shirt?

   b. Who is standing next to you?

   c. What were you doing?

Learning to wait

These exercises enhance waiting skills. Be playful so that the child does not feel deprived.

Materials: Favorite food, timer or visual timer

Setting: Anywhere

When/How often: Regularly, to gain practice

Amount of time: 5-15 minutes

Age group/Cognitive skill: Any

Activity: Waiting to eat

1. Set a timer for one-to-five minutes, depending on the age and capability of the child. Start with one minute. Use a visual timer for small children or children with poor cognition.

2. Place a small piece of a favorite food in front of the child. Tell him he can have it when the timer goes off.

3. Playfully ask the child, "How long can you wait?"

4. Do this several times in a sitting.

Variation: Waiting to play

1. Place a favorite toy in front of the child, and tell her that she can play with it when the timer goes off.

2. When the timer goes off, let her play with the toy.

3. Reset the timer after a few minutes and repeat. Do this several times in a sitting.

Using a mind jar to find focus

The mind jar is an excellent device for on-the-spot calming. Children watch glitter slowly settle to the bottom of a jar filled with a soap and glycerin solution. Put the jar in sunlight and see it sparkle! This works as a short meditative time-out.

Materials: Glycerin (vegetable glycerin is found online for a few dollars), clear dish soap, several colors of glitter, an attractive water-tight jar.

Setting: Anywhere, in sunlight is awesome.

Amount of time: 5-10 minutes

Age group/Cognitive skill: Fair/good

Method:
1. Fill a jar half-full of glycerin.
2. Add about one teaspoon of dark-colored glitter. Blue, green or violet work well for the background color.
3. Sprinkle in the glitter of two different bright colors—red and gold, for example.
4. Stir. The glitter will move very slowly.
5. Add the dish soap, one teaspoon at a time, counting the number of teaspoons. Stir after each addition of dish soap, noting how fast the glitter moves. Stop adding soap when the glitter takes about three minutes to settle.
6. Make up a second batch of the same proportion of glycerin to soap and add it to the jar. Add more glitter, as desired.
7. Shake or stir the jar. Stirring the jar is messier, but showier.

Variation: The Mind Jar app

Wisdom Publications makes an electronic version of the Mind Jar for iPod, iPhone or iPad. It is easy to use and perfect for travel. It is free at iTunes.

Energy management

The hyperactive child needs outlets for her energy. Give her special exercises and calming activities to perform during the day to help her to burn off excess energy and get grounded.

How often: Throughout the day

How long: A few minutes

Calming exercises
1. Yoga or qigong exercises (see below and p. 33).
2. Isometric exercises.
3. Use calming strategies (p. 30).

Sports and heavy work
1. Individual sports such as karate, swimming, gymnastics, track.
2. Push-ups, wall push-ups.
3. Going for long walks or runs.
4. Heavy work (see p. 33).

Express hyperactivity safely in the classroom
1. Stand at desk to work (with a nearby chair as backup).
2. Run an errand.
3. Collect or pass out books for the teacher.

Using high energy productively

The following method is excellent for engaging a hyperactive child (with very good compliance) in therapy or lessons. Instead of asking the child to slow down, the therapist has him work at a high speed. The invigorating speed can produce a hyper-alert focus that leads to good attention-to-task. The method goes fast, so get all the materials ready before starting.

Materials: A stop-watch or timer, materials for 4-5 therapy activities

Setting: Anywhere

When/How often: Regularly for practice

Amount of time: 5-15 minutes, or until *you* run out of energy

Age group/Cognitive skill: Fair-good

Method:
1. Give the child a set of lively and fun physical activities, and tell him he has two minutes to play. This works best in a gym, playground or sensory room. In a smaller setting, try a series of activities such as bouncing balls, jumping jacks, and jumping games. Encourage the child to move from one activity to the next as quickly as possible. The goal is to get him energized and hyper-alert.
2. Using a stop-watch, count down from two minutes: "90 seconds, 60 seconds, 30 seconds, 15 seconds, 5, 4, 3, 2, 1. Come here, now!" Do this energetically to increase his excitement and hyper-attention.
3. Have the child quickly perform a series of 30-second to two-minute tasks that require attention-to-task. Use the stop-watch on each task, announcing the time every 30 seconds. Announce the time at 15 seconds, and then count down from 5: "5, 4, 3, 2, 1. Come here, now!"
4. Give him a second play break if you have the time and energy for it. (This could wear *you* out!) Continue using the stop watch to count down the time.
5. Do additional therapy activities as possible.
6. The result should be good attention-to-task and absorption of the day's lesson, now that he is hyper-alert and open to learning.

Variation: Move fast for teens with low cognition
This variation of sharp attention builds quality performance with task speed.

Method:

1. Have children take turns performing a functional task such as stacking cups, stacking chairs, or sorting toys as fast as they can. Use a stop-watch and countdowns to help increase excitement.
2. Once they get used to performing the tasks quickly, have two teens attempt to do the task together. This builds speed for work as well as social skills.
3. Play music with a solid beat to help improve motivation and to find the rhythmic aspects of the work.

On-the-spot grounding of energy: Become a tree and the Tree pose of yoga

Two exercises—Become a tree and Tree pose of yoga—are good methods for physically grounding a hyperactive child (see p. 122).

INTERVENTIONS: ATTENTION, STRESS REDUCTION, AND MINDFULNESS

Mindfulness training is a powerful tool for children (and adults) with ADHD. It is a free simple technique for increasing attention and decreasing anxiety. It can also help to reduce anxiety in children with sensory issues and high-functioning autism.

Research shows the following benefits:

1. Attention: Following a 12-week program of 15-20 minutes of mindfulness a day, teenagers with ADHD showed a 30% increase in attention, whether or not they were taking ADHD medication.

2. Working memory: A two-week program of mindfulness increased working memory capacity and lessened mind wandering.

3. Compassion: Following an eight-week meditation training, participants were found to be 50% more inclined to help a person in need.

4. Anxiety: Children with ADHD in an ongoing mindfulness program showed a significant decrease in anxiety symptoms.

It is relatively easy to train children to do a mindfulness practice, and there are many resources (including books, DVDs, podcasts, apps and audio clips) for therapists, teachers and parents.

The method is simple: The child sits in a comfortable straight-back chair in a quiet room. She is attentive to her breath as she inhales and exhales for 15-20 minutes. (Stop after five minutes at the first training. Over a few days, ramp up to 15-20 minutes). She is periodically reminded to let go of her thoughts and return her attention to her breath. The technique is that simple. And surprisingly enough, children tend to sit quietly. After the exercise, they appear calm and centered. The repeated gentle focus on the breath is the key to improved attention.

Mindfulness relaxation therapy: Watching the breath

Materials: A straight-back, but comfortable, chair and clock or timer

Setting: A quiet room

Group/Individual: Either is good

When/How often: Morning or evenings work well. Try meditating with the child or group once a week and have participants meditate at home with parent monitoring on other days. Optionally, this process can be done daily in a classroom setting

Amount of time: 15-20 minutes daily

Method:
1. Have children sit comfortably.
2. Set the timer for 15 minutes.
3. Slowly read a mindfulness script to the group. (A script and resources are listed below)
4. Stop after five minutes at the first training. Over a few days, ramp up to 15-20 minutes.

In a classroom: Do this daily and assign the practice as homework for the weekend. Check out the audio clips and apps listed below and see if you can find one that works for your students at home on the weekend.

In a one-time-per-week group: Consider doing the above method each week during your group. The therapist or teacher requires parent support because students need to continue the practice at home. Send home to parents the mindfulness training instructions and an audio clip of a script (or instructions for downloading a clip). Encourage parents to join the child in the practice. For an embattled family, these quiet moments can be vitally important.

Resources:
1. For young children: Kary Lee MacLean's two books, *Peaceful Piggy Meditation* and *Moody Cow Meditates*, explain the whys and how of meditation.
2. For school-aged children: The book, *Mindful Teaching and Teaching Mindfulness* by Deborah Schoenberlein (Wisdom Publications, Boston, 2009) is a good source of mindfulness scripts for a group of young meditators.
3. For older teens and adults: UCLA offers free podcasts of mindfulness training on iTunes (search on meditation), and has similar audio clips on their site, Marc.UCLA.edu. Go to the site, click on the Free Guided Meditations link where a series of audio clips are listed. Choose from:
   a. *Breathing Meditation*: This five-minute clip is used for the first few days.
   b. *Complete Meditation Instructions*: This 19-minute clip can be used next for the first week or so.
4. Apps: Many 5-15 minute mindfulness and meditation apps are available, as well as timer apps.

Mindfulness script

Sit comfortably on a straight-backed chair. Set the timer for 15 minutes. Slowly read this script to the group (your instructions are italicized). The first few times you go through this script, wait about 15 seconds between steps. Stop after five minutes.

1. Gently close your eyes. Listen to the sounds in the room as it grows quiet.

2. *Wait 15 seconds.*

3. Breathe normally. Feel your breath as you breathe in and out. You can feel it at the tip of your nose. You can feel your chest rise and fall. You can feel your belly move up and down. Just breathe normally and gently watch yourself breathe.

4. *Wait a minute or so.*

5. Feel your breath.

6. *Every minute or so, say any one of the following:*

   a. Are you thinking thoughts? We all think thoughts. Don't pay attention to them. Pay attention to your breath.

   b. Are you daydreaming? We all daydream sometimes. Let the daydream go and pay attention to your breath.

   c. Bring your attention back to the breath.

   d. Very gently watch your breath.

   e. Your breath is very precious. It is your connection to your body and to life.

   f. Breathe normally. Feel your breath as you breathe in and out. You can feel it at the tip of your nose. You can feel your chest rise and fall. You can feel your belly move in and out. Just breathe normally and gently watch yourself breathe.

7. *When the time is up, gently ring a bell and tell the children to open their eyes when they are ready.*

Relaxing the belly

Method:
1. As you sit, feel the breath as it goes into your belly.
2. Now soften the belly, let it relax.
3. Breathe again, soften again.

INTERVENTIONS: TIMING THERAPY

Timing and synchronization are crucial to our brain's ability to function. Our brain has a master clock and circuitry devoted to keeping cells and signals synchronized. In addition, each neuron in our brain has a timing component that keeps it in sync with other neurons as they jointly process information. When the timing of this circuitry is imprecise, brain processes can suffer and we experience a degradation of motor skills, senses, cognitive skills, emotional regulation and other functions.

Timing therapy is an approach to re-syncing the brain's timing circuits. It can be done in several ways, most easily by using hands (or other parts of the body) to keep a precise beat over extended periods (20-60 minutes) of time. Although timing therapy is a relatively new intervention, children for a long time have benefited from timing therapy as a byproduct of learning to play a musical instrument. During music lessons, a child attempts to keep a precise beat to the music, often by using a metronome. He gets feedback on his performance from the instructor, or from listening to how well he synced with other players, or from how well his notes matched the metronome beat. This process is similar to the way we implement timing therapy today.

Research has shown that when we regularly practice timing precision, we can repair out-of-sync timing circuitry in the brain, which in turn increases brain and body functionality in a significant way.

Key elements of timing therapy are:

The beat: It should match the natural rhythm of the activity. For example, a simple clapping beat is expressed as 2/4. A steady drop and catch of a ball mimics this beat. This beat can be thought of as a "round" of two counts (1,2; 1,2; 1,2) without pauses. Another example is the 4/4 beat which can be used to play "patty-cake."

The tempo: This is the number of beats per minute. A comfortable clapping speed for most people is a tempo of 54 beats per minute. However, a typical child with ADHD will be more comfortable at a slightly higher tempo. (I use 63 beats per minute). For ball play, increase the tempo to 80-90 beats per minute. A person does best at his or her own comfortable speed.

Precision: It is important that the child attempt to be consistently precise with the beat. Keeping an imprecise beat (or worse, not caring about the beat) will not produce desired results.

Feedback: The most powerful forms of timing therapy provide sensory feedback on how well the beat is being maintained. Our auditory or visual senses provide the best feedback for maintaining the beat. As mentioned, working with an instructor or in a group is a good way to receive feedback.

An excellent product, the Interactive Metronome, gives feedback at the millisecond level. Other products with feedback include games such as Wii-timed activities and Guitar Hero.

With the ball exercise (see below) a child gets feedback from the participation of other children. Children are instructed to see and hear their balls hitting the ground at the same time. The energy of the group motivates them, and they usually make a good effort to bounce their balls precisely.

The amount of time allotted for sessions: It is important for a child to work for sustained periods. I have seen success with sessions as short as 25 minutes. More typically, I try to have a child train for 45-60 minutes at a time, with breaks as needed.

Frequency of practice: The child needs to practice regularly to avoid regression. Here are examples of schedules that work:

1. Twenty-five minutes of timing therapy, weekly over a school year.
2. Fifteen 45-60-minute sessions at the rate of one per week, two per week or three per week.

Total length of time in practice: It is good practice to complete 12-15 hours of timing therapy over a relatively short period of time. It takes hours of practice (nine hours minimum, in my experience) for timing therapy to begin to improve the child's functional skills.

Much of the research in timing therapy has been done in conjunction with the Interactive Metronome. Studies show that children with ADHD who did 15 hours of tapping and clapping exercises using the Interactive Metronome made 30% gains in their executive-function skills. This includes attention skills, working memory, motivation, ability to plan and problem-solve, as well as the ability to stay organized. Children with learning disabilities (often a co-occurrence for children with ADHD) made large and significant gains in reading and math proficiency. All school children gained an average of six IQ points.

Timing therapy exercises

The following exercises are done in groups. They are done to the beat of a metronome set to a comfortable tempo. Beats are selected to match the activity. Children attempt to synchronize their moves as a group. As they improve, they should hear and see hands clap, toes tap, balls hit the floor or balls snap into hands at precisely the same time as their peers. As they synchronize as a group, each child gets feedback on his own performance. When done regularly for 25 or more minutes at a time, this is effective timing therapy.

Children like to play ball to the sound of a metronome. They find the rhythmic sounds calming, and they work hard to "nail" the beat. Metronomes are easy to find, and free metronome apps or programs are available for phones, tables and computers. Old wooden metronomes or new plastic ones also work well. Unless you are a musician, stick to simple functionality as available on free apps. You want to be able to adjust just two features, the tempo and the beat. Settings allow you to match both the tempo and the beat of your activity, giving you a regular rhythm to work by.

Clapping, snapping and tapping exercises

The following are starter exercises.

Materials: Metronome

When/How often: Once or more per week

Amount of time: 10-15 minutes, then move to ball exercises
Use a 1/2 or 2/4 beat for simple tapping or clapping exercises. Start with a tempo of 63 beats per minute for children with ADHD and adjust for their comfort.

1. Alternate among clapping hands, snapping fingers, tapping fingers and tapping feet.
2. Increase or decrease the beat.
3. Change the rhythm.

Ball exercises

Beyond clapping hands, snapping fingers and tapping feet, many other activities can be done to the beat of a metronome. If these are too difficult for a child, toss a sandbag back and forth to a beat until she understands what to do.

Materials: Racket ball, basketball, metronome

When/How often: Once or more per week

Amount of time: Up to 30 minutes of varied activities

Variation: 2/4 beat activities
For ball activities, match the tempo to the natural speed of the activity. The pace should be comfortable for the child. For the ball play described below, 80 beats per minute or higher can work. Set the beat to 2/4 time. Here are some fun ways to do the method:

1. Drop and catch a ball with one hand.
2. Try drop-and-catch with the other (non-dominant) hand.
3. Drop with one hand and catch with the other.
4. Dribble a basketball with each hand separately, then back and forth between hands.
5. Play drop and catch with partners facing one another.

Variation: 3/4 beat activities
1. Set the beat to 3/4 time for the 3-part sequence of:
    a. Drop ball with left hand.
    b. Catch ball with right hand.
    c. Move ball to left hand (and then repeat over and over).
2. Do the same above sequence, passing the ball behind your back.
3. With a partner, stand facing each other about six feet apart.
    a. Bounce the ball with right hand to partner's left hand.
    b. Partner catches the ball, passes it to his right hand and bounces it back.
    c. Catch ball with left hand, pass it to right hand, and repeat the sequence.
4. Children can clap or bounce a ball in time to a metronome while they practice articulation (speech), math tables, spelling words, and so on.

INTERVENTIONS: MANAGING BEHAVIORS

A general approach to behavior management

Therapists working with children with poor executive functioning, such as children with ADHD, need specific behavioral tactics. Rewards-based methods and positive approaches are two examples. Rewards-based methods can motivate improved self-regulation, while positive approaches promote better self-esteem. We discuss these and other aspects of molding children's behavior in the section below.

Selecting goals and behavior methods

Pick a few key behaviors to work on. Too many goals confuse the child. Use rewards, natural consequences, self-management, video modeling (for young children) and other behavior techniques to address those behaviors.

For the remaining behaviors, redirect noxious behaviors and ignore behaviors that are insignificant. When stronger measures are needed, use timeouts and the removal of privileges.

Lecturing a child about how he should behave is usually not helpful because the child with ADHD typically knows what is expected of him. A more effective approach is to use a behavioral method.

About rewards

Use rewards-based behavioral approaches such as the token exchange and self-management programs. Rewards work best when they are given to the child immediately after he has earned them. Once earned, a reward is not taken back because of new act-out behaviors. The incident of bad behavior is treated separately.

Consider using a sliding-scale reward system with rewards costing different amounts of points. The child earns a fixed number of points (let's say 10 points) each time he earns his reward. While many rewards are worth 10 points (which can be immediately rewarded for smaller efforts), other rewards for larger efforts are worth 20, 50 or even 300 points. The child can elect on a given day to cash in or save his points. Having variety and larger rewards in the reward schedule can motivate the child to continue to work on one behavior after another.

A positive approach

A positive approach works best. Try to find ways to compliment the child throughout the day to support self-esteem. Direct some compliments at worthy behaviors in order to reinforce the child's good choices.

Give the child points toward a weekly reward each time he makes a good choice. Be generous in handing out points.

Try not to react to the child's behaviors with unkind words or negative facial expressions and body language. If the child causes you to react emotionally, look into stress-management and relaxation techniques for yourself that can keep you calm and allow you to interact positively with him. If the child decides he doesn't like you, your work with him may become less effective.

Consistency

Be consistent as you reward and discipline the child. For the best efficacy, the child's entire team (therapists, teachers, and parents) needs to use similar methods and have similar goals.

Use a natural setting

Children with ADHD have difficulty generalizing what they learn to other settings. Therefore, when you set up a behavioral program, do so in a familiar setting that is natural to the activity.

Goal maintenance

Reinstate reward-based programs periodically to help maintain behavior gains.

Glucose depletion and self-control

Self-control has been likened to "a muscle that gets tired" (Baumeister, 2007). Self-control or self-regulation can weaken or lapse when we become tired. Contrary to conventional wisdom, we do not have an unlimited supply of will power. When it is depleted in one area of endeavor, we lose the ability to use will power in other ways and places as well. A child who is working hard on behavior programs can benefit from a high-glucose drink (available in pharmacies), a break with social interaction, or a stress-reduction activity such as play, yoga or mindfulness training.

Motivating the child

Counter the child's poor motivation by making tasks more appealing. At school, replace or supplement textbooks with video-based learning, hands-on exercises and computer-based learning. Math computer games can be an excellent form of learning for a child with ADHD, as can video treatments of low-interest topics such as phonics and grammar.

At home, play upbeat music during chore-time and add a natural reward (game or treat) at the end. Consider ways to make her study space more inviting by adding a bean-bag or swivel chair to the room. Help her to structure her study time in two ways:

1. Have her determine how much time she needs to complete her homework; then have her identify a reward for herself if she completes the work on time. A natural reward (such as free time, TV, or time on social media) is best.

2. Have her make a checklist of all of her homework tasks so that she can check them off and feel a sense of completion when she is done.

A source of advice to the therapist or teacher

Teachers, therapists and parents can get on-the-spot advice for working with a child's behaviors from a product called Parent Coach Cards. Twenty types of common behavior issues are covered, including inflexibility, reactivity, poor organization skills, impulsive speech, and other ADHD-related behaviors.

Each card has a cute picture and pithy saying. The back side of the card contains short phrases that a parent or therapist can use to guide the child. For example, a therapist could say to a hyperactive child: "Finding your brakes means using your 'thinking side' to control your energy."

Content is provided on the backside of the card for the child to read. This content includes short pieces of advice such as, "I need my 'thinking side' even when I'm having fun." The content is written in the first-person and so works for children with high-functioning autism.

Cards and coloring books are available at www.ParentCoachCards.com.

INTERVENTIONS: SELF-MANAGEMENT

Self-management is a behavioral method that puts the onus on a child to monitor her own behaviors as she works towards a goal. When she reaches her goal she gives herself a predetermined reward. This is an effective technique that gives children a sense of control over how they act. It is also effective for children who may be inclined to "fudge" the truth of how well they are doing. Although a child may misrepresent her scores, she still is likely making an appreciable effort to meet her goals and so she achieves true gains.

Self-management is often used with a child who is taking ADHD medication. She works on successive goals over a period of time, quickly gaining a set of new behaviors that can support her when her medication is decreased.

The following example illustrates the process of setting up a program: Martin is a 10-year-old boy in fifth grade who is getting poor grades. He has trouble staying in his seat and uses class time to draw little cartoon books. When his teacher, Ms. Roland, points out to him that he is capable of doing much better, he agrees to work on improving his behavior. His teacher offers him the opportunity to work for a reward as part of a self-management program and he accepts. They create the details of the program by following the six-step process below. (We come back to Martin and Ms. Roland further along in this section.)

1. **Create the goals, select the tasks**

   Create one or two goals with the child's input.

2. **Select the time and place**

   Pick a relaxed time in the schedule to start the program so that the child can get practice under less pressure. The place should be the activity's natural setting. He will learn and maintain habits best this way. As he gets accustomed to working with his new behavior goals, his program can be moved to times and places with greater environmental challenges or distractions.

3. Decide on a start-and-stop time for practice

The child ought to practice the program's requirements every day when possible. Select a time-period that is long enough to challenge him without frustrating him. In determining the length of each scoring segment, consider how difficult it will be for him to maintain his improved behavior.

4. Create scoring periods

To reduce the frustration of trying to be good for a prolonged period, divide the practice time into small chunks. An impulsive child whose goal is to increase self-control by not talking out of turn in the classroom may fail unless the time periods are short.

5. Define success

With rare exception, no one expects the child to meet the goal 100% of the time. On the first day, for example, we may challenge him to be on task 60% of the time. For a hard task involving self-control, 40% compliance may be acceptable.

6. Name the reward(s)

The reward should be commensurate with the activity. For instance, the reward for being polite might be smaller than the one a child would get for keeping his hands to himself.

The approach to giving rewards can be flexible. For example, eight-year-old Sara has a different reward target for each day of the week. Monday's reward gives her permission to watch her favorite TV program even though it conflicts with her chore of washing dishes. Friday's reward is a voucher that says, "Mom will braid my hair."

Martin's program

Here is how Ms. Roland and Martin (introduced earlier) set up the details of his program:

1. **Create the goals.** They chose "Stayed in my seat" and "Did my work."

2. **Select the time and place.** Rather than the resource room, they chose the natural setting of the classroom during academics.

3. **Decide on a start and stop time.** Ms. Roland chose 8:00 to 10:30, a 2 ½-hour period that is solid academics.

4. **Create scoring periods.** Martin thought he could stay on task for 30 minutes at a time, and so they divided the 2 ½ hours into five 30-minute periods.

5. **Define success.** With two goals and five time-periods, Martin can earn at most 10 stars during the morning. Ms. Roland suggested that, as a realistic figure, he try to earn seven stars. He agreed to try it on the condition that they could reduce that number to six should the higher number feel too difficult.

6. **Name the reward(s).** Martin said, "If I meet my goal, dad owes me a video game." Martin's father agreed to the plan, and so Martin made up vouchers that said, "Dad owes me a video game."

	Stayed in seat	Did my work
8:00 - 8:30		✓
8:30 - 9:00	✓	✓
9:00 - 9:30	✓	
9:30 - 10:00		✓
10:00 - 10:30	✓	✓

The score sheets and vouchers were copied and stored on a book shelf. Martin was given a silent timer that vibrated when it was time to score (he could also have used a visual timer). During the first week, Mr. Hinckley, a student-teacher, was asked to check occasionally with Martin to see how the program was proceeding. He also monitored Martin occasionally during that time as a way of encouraging him to be honest.

They started the program on a Tuesday. Martin got a fresh copy of the scoring chart and set the timer to 30 minutes. From 8:00 to 8:30, he earned just one star: He had done his work, but he had retrieved his notebook from the back of the classroom without first asking his teacher. At 8:30, he reset the timer. Throughout the morning, he did well and earned seven stars. At lunchtime, he got his reward (the voucher) from the book shelf.

The program continued for three weeks. By then, Martin was successful at independently doing his work without reminders to stay on task. He found that he enjoyed the program, especially the rewards, and so he agreed to continue the program with a new set of behavior goals.

Self-management of impulsive "blurting-out"

Here is a variation of self-management therapy for an impulsive child who blurts out answers and waves her hand wildly in response to a teacher's questions. She often blurts out the wrong answer because she does not take time to think, and this embarrasses her. But without self-reflection, she doesn't learn the lesson, and so the behavior continues. This technique can help her to pause before acting impulsively.

Materials: A card with the number 15 taped to the child's desk, score sheets

Setting: Classroom or similar setting

When/How often: Throughout the school day

How long: Put this in place until the child has the habit. Then keep the card on her desk, but only periodically use a score sheet. Irregular scoring will help her to maintain the habit.

Method, Part 1:
The child is going to train herself to wait before raising her hand. She does this by tapping on her knee 15 times before she raises her hand, giving her time to think. The teacher helps to support this effort by not calling on the child should her hand shoot up too fast.

1. Tape the card with the number 15 in a visible place on the child's desk.
2. Instruct her to tap for 15 counts before she raises her hand.
3. For the first two days, have her tap but not raise her hand as a way of training self-control and patience. Afterwards, she can raise her hand.
4. She scores herself with hatch marks. Each time she taps, she adds to the hatch marks. If her hand shoots up without tapping, she makes a hatch mark under "Forgot to tap".

Class	Tapped 15 times	Forgot to tap
Math	⏤HHH I	II
Language studies		
Spanish		
Social studies		
Science		
"Specials" class		

Method, Part 2:
Once she has learned to pause, shift the behavior goal to: "I do not raise my hand unless I am sure of the answer." Create an "Oops" column on her score sheet. She puts a mark in here if the answer she planned to give the teacher was incorrect.

1. Whenever the child raises her hand, she reflects on whether the answer in her head was correct. If not, she puts a hatch mark in the "Oops" column.
2. At the end of the day, she computes her on-task percentage using this formula:
   (Oops / Raised hand) x 100%.
   In our example, the score is (3/6) x 100 = 50%. If her target percentage is 50% or better, she earns a reward.

Class	Raised hand	Oops
Math	HHH I	III
Language studies		

Case study: David

David is a 12-year-old boy in eighth grade with ADHD. He is a high-energy boy with lots of ideas, projects and desire, and he leaves behind a trail of discarded objects and random ideas. Last year he often left his homework and other materials at home. He often misses school-project due dates. He is impulsive and blurts out answers in the classroom. On the whole, he is a sweet boy, but recently his parents have noticed new negative and act-out behaviors when they ask him to help out at home.

It is early September and his team (teachers, therapists and parents) hope to get him ready for the coming school year. They call a meeting to discuss their approach to working with him. The social worker, Ms. Walker, emphasizes the importance of a positive approach when David acts out and all agree. David's father admits that his son can "push my buttons" at times, and that he (the father) is using self-talk as a way to keep himself from reacting.

Goals

The team agrees on two primary goals for David: to help him learn organization skills and to reduce his impulsivity. David's father expresses his concern about David's new defiant behaviors and asks for the team's advice on a home program.

Organization

Mr. Chamberlain, the school social worker, and Ms. Solvay, the school OT, agree to help David organize his belongings and activities. To facilitate organizing activities, his parents offer use of an old smart phone as an electronic organizer. The school principal later gives permission for David to use it at school as long as the phone is de-activated and stripped of games and music. (Their organization plan is below.)

Impulsivity

The teacher, Mr. Graham, says he has used self-management successfully in the past to help a child with self-control issues; he wants to try a similar approach with David.

David joins the meeting. Asked about his goals for the coming year, he says he is a good swimmer and hopes to get better in order to make the high-school swim team. He wants to attend the middle-school swim classes on Tuesdays, beginning in October, and he also wants to go to the open swimming on Thursdays. He needs a ride to both programs, but he hasn't yet discussed this with his parents. They say they can provide him with a ride on Tuesdays.

The social worker raises the possibility of using a ride on Thursdays as a natural reward for good behavior at home. David's father grins and says, "You know, David, you might be able to earn a ride on Thursdays." The team discusses a rewards points system for use at home. David can earn points for good behaviors and then cash them in for a ride to swimming or to the movies on weekends. His parents agree to be especially generous with points for polite behavior. David agrees to the plan.

David's organization plan

1. Obtain the organizer tools

    a. Paper: To-do lists, calendars, durable lists.

        i. Laminate the lists or

        ii. Put each paper to-do list in zip-lock bags so the entire list is visible. Attach the list to a gym bag or book bag.

    b. Electronic: Old phone, iPod, or Blackberry.

        i. Remove apps that are distracting

        ii. Add organizing apps such as notes, calendars, and to-do lists.

    c. Gym bag, book bag with pockets.

    d. Clip holders.

        i. Make spare keys, label them with paint or color-tape

        ii. Put keys on rings and rings on clips that attach to a book bag.

Swimming

Suit
Goggles
Ear plugs
Towel
Flip flops
Soap
Water bottle

2. Set up repeating schedules and lists including

   a. Clubs and activities

   b. Appointments

   c. Alarms for

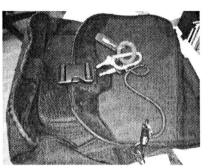

      i. Getting up for school

      ii. Getting out the door (including "think time")

   d. Important contact info: Phone numbers, addresses, Twitter, email, and so on

   e. Set up to-do list

   f. Create the checklist for his morning routine and hang it near the door or somewhere easy to see

   g. Create the two locker checklists (morning and afternoon), and tape them inside the locker

   h. Create a checklist for swimming and attach it to the gym bag.

3. Create a recurring alarm for 7:30 p.m. Sunday to remind David to look at the coming week's schedule

   a. Verify week's schedule has everything in it

   b. Set up the week's reminder alarms

   c. Add to-do lists for the week.

4. Create the morning checklist

(David looks at this before leaving the house during the "five minutes to think" time)

   a. Check and edit the to-do list

   b. Look at check-off list of things often forgotten

      i. Glasses

      ii. Books

      iii. Lunch

      iv. Money

      v. Organizer

      vi. Phone

      vii. Winter – jacket, gloves, hat

      viii. Summer – sunglasses, sunscreen

   c. Count your things before going out the door ("I have four things: backpack, sunglasses, jacket, and lunch").

CHAPTER 7

The Self-Regulated Child

Therapists, teachers and parents perform difficult and noble work in their support of children with ASD, SMD and ADHD. Heroic efforts are also made, of course, by the children themselves. As examples of this valiant effort, let's look at the progress that three children make—and the wisdom their parents acquire—over a period of a year. The children are Brian, 4, who has ASD, Mary, 12, who has sensory issues, and Jake, 8, who has ADHD. We see them in the throes of dysfunction and then take note of the strategies their parents employ to produce developmental progress.

Brian

Brian has been invited to the birthday party of his nine-year-old cousin, Joshua, who he doesn't know very well. Brian's mother, Angela, has been reminding him all week about the party scheduled for Saturday. She shows Brian pictures of Joshua, his mother and their house. Angela tracked down some picture story books about birthday parties and has been reading them to Brian at bedtime. She also wrote a social story with details of what to expect at the party, and she has been reading that to him once or twice a day. He is excited about going to the party for the cake and the party favors. With his autism, Brian isn't drawn to other children for friendships, but he is comfortable around his next-door neighbor, a boy his age, with whom he sometimes plays.

Brian and his mother arrive at the party with a present that Brian, with prompting, gives to Joshua. But reacting to all the children present, Brian quickly makes a dive behind the couch. When Angela tries to coax him out, he begins to wail. His mother complains, "So much preparation gone awry in the first five minutes!" He eventually calms, but he doesn't emerge from behind the couch until all the children leave the family room. He runs to the door wanting to leave and Angela, after saying good-bye to Joshua's mother, takes him home. She wonders what she could have done differently to produce a better experience.

Over the next year, Angela's effort as an involved parent begins to pay off. Brian makes many gains in his pre-school setting. With teachers and therapists, Angela talks through situations that she and Brian encounter on a daily basis. He has learned to use a visual schedule, and they have put together a small sensory space in the basement where he can exert himself with play.

A year later, Brian is again invited to Joshua's birthday party. The week before the event, Angela pulls out the story she wrote the previous year and updates it to include a visual schedule of the party's expected activities (as provided by Joshua's mother). The schedule covers the timing for play, singing happy birthday, eating cake, opening presents, playing again, and then going home. They read the story and review the schedule every day. On the day of the party, she

164

takes Brian to a nearby playground where he plays hard for 30 minutes. They return home, get ready, and then arrive at the party 15 minutes early so Brian can acclimate to the environment before other children arrive. He grins with pleasure when he is brought into the kitchen to see the birthday cake and party favors. Joshua's mother has set up a quiet area in one of the bedrooms as a retreat for Joshua, and Angela takes him there to show what is available to him. Angela hopes to intersperse solitary play time in the bedroom with group party time. She brings a visual timer to use if necessary to help him wait for the birthday cake. Angela's effort pays off. The party is a success for Brian, and a relieved Angela is confident he has made progress and that he is now more likely to have successful experiences in future social situations.

Shania

Shania, 12, has a variety of sensory issues. She touches everything in sight and demands hugs from her mother, yet she can't stand being touched by others. She needs a sense of having constant control over situations in order to feel safe. Other children seem noisy and pushy, and so she has retreated to solitude and books as a refuge. She shies away from crowds of children and her social skills are poor. She has a close friend in the neighborhood named Juana. However, Juana does not go to her school and so Shania gets little social interaction with peers at school.

Each year the school puts on a spring-fest dance for the middle-school children. In the weeks leading up to the dance, Shania thinks of little else. Her mother has made her a pretty dress, and on the evening of the dance she feels like a princess as she leaves for the event. In the hallway outside the gym, she begins to get butterflies in her stomach when she sees other children arrive. The girls walk and cluster in groups, posing and giggling. No one acknowledges her, and Shania begins to wish she hadn't come. The music from the gym is very loud, but a favorite song of hers is playing, and she goes in. She finds a few schoolmates and stands next to them. A boy she doesn't particularly care for asks her to dance, and she does; then she stands with the group once again, not speaking. After 45 minutes, the music is getting on her nerves and she is feeling stressed. At that moment, a nearby student makes a teasing remark about her hair, and Shania shouts at him. She has made a scene and is embarrassed. She leaves the gym in a huff, feeling inadequate and disappointed. In the hallway, close to tears, she phones her parents and asks them to come and get her. For weeks, she had imagined having a good time at the dance, and the outcome now is painful and disappointing. Even as she resolves to stay away from future events of this kind, she wonders what she might have done differently.

The next week, Shania's parents contact a nearby sensory clinic for a sensory evaluation and treatment ideas. After the evaluation, an occupational therapist recommends that Shania's parents sign her up for a three-month sound-therapy and sensory-integration program at the clinic to help her to reduce her reaction to noise and to increase her brain's ability to process sensory information. Shania's parents decide to save money so she can do the program in the fall. In the meantime, the OT gives them general guidance and recommends books and websites that can help Shania with strategies. Shania is told that a regular stress-reduction program in the form of physical exercise, sports, yoga or meditation can help her to decrease anxiety.

Before the start of summer vacation, Shania's parents meet with the school's social worker for suggestions on how to help her make friends. The social worker recommends that she take community education classes or join a teen's volunteer organization when she turns 13 in June.

Shania thinks yoga sounds like fun and mentions it to her friend, Juana, who asks to come along.

That summer, Shania and Juana take yoga classes and practice at each other's' houses. Shania reads online information about sensory sensitivities, and her social difficulties and emotional experiences begin to make sense to her. She starts paying attention to her reactions to noise and begins to recognize early signs of irritation from it. She sees how loud noise can cause her to lose her temper. Her mother suggests that Shania learn to extricate herself from those challenging situations. She can, for instance, offer a simple reason for needing to leave, excuse herself, and go. They practice a number of such scenarios until Shania gets comfortable with the method. Toward the end of summer, Juana has a sleepover with girls from her school that Shania doesn't know. Shania struggles with the prospect of being at a noisy party with unfamiliar faces. Her parents encourage her to go and provide her with ear plugs and headphones. The party goes well, and Shania finds ways to take quiet breaks that involve reading a book for a few minutes or wandering up to the kitchen for water or to the patio (with prior permission from Juana's parents.)

That fall, she attends the sound-therapy and sensory-integration training. By winter, she has begun to make friends with a few girls in her class. She realizes she is more relaxed at school. While she is still uncomfortable in large crowds, she is pleased with her gains, and she plans to attend the coming spring-fest dance with ear plugs hidden under her long hair.

Jake

Jake, 8, is very excited about attending the birthday party of his friend Joshua (the same Joshua who is a cousin to four-year-old Brian). All morning Jake has been racing through his house talking loudly and creating a commotion. Though his parents threaten to keep him home if he doesn't settle down, Jake continues to play loudly in front of the TV and carry on in ceaseless exuberance. At noon, his mother tells him to take a shower and put on fresh clothes. He screams at her that he is fine and that no one is going to care what he looks like. His father, Paul, intervenes, and Jake, after apologizing to his mother for his outburst, takes his shower.

When it's time to go, Jake can't find the birthday card he picked out for Joshua. After 15 minutes of searching, he finds it under his desk. Paul, who is working on positive parenting, restrains his impatience and simply says, "Good work finding the card, Bud. Let's get going." Paul wants to be at the party with Jake but has an important errand to run. He drops Jake off at the house and leaves. Jake is 30 minutes late and feeling frantic. In spite of his father's reminders to take it easy, he runs into the house shouting Joshua's name and asking to see the cake. He calms a bit when he sees parents talking quietly in the living room. But 30 minutes later in Joshua's family room in the basement, he impulsively grabs a balloon and squeezes it so that it breaks with a loud bang. A girl screams. He finds another balloon and chases her with it, tripping over the family's dog and crashing into the table holding the presents, crushing one of them. Joshua yells at Jake, "You're ruining my party!" Joshua's mother intervenes and has Jake help her to put out paper plates and plastic cups. For the remainder of the party, she stays within arm's reach of him while other children keep away. Later he tells his father he had a terrible time.

Jake's parents hear about his behavior at the party and decide it is time to take action. They visit a pediatric psychiatrist who recommends that, before trying medication, they look at nutritional factors such as vitamin and mineral deficiencies and try a diet free of sugar and processed foods and high in grains and vegetables. The specialist also suggests they start therapy that addresses specific areas of executive function. He recommends four or five programs, including timing therapy and memory training. He says there is no hurry to implement these; Jake can do them over a period of several years. His parents opt for a slow steady approach to increasing Jake's executive-function skills, but they take three big steps at once in his therapy plan. First, they sign him up for a six-week timing therapy program at a local clinic. Second, they discuss a self-management program with the school psychologist—to be conducted at school—to help reduce his impulsivity in the classroom. Third, they implement the diet suggested by the doctor and see immediate improvement in impulse control.

When baseball season arrives, Paul buys tickets for a game and has Jake call Joshua to invite him to join the family. It is a way to make up to Joshua for the fiasco at his birthday party. Jake apologizes to Joshua and with his own money buys his friend a baseball cap to replace the present he crushed. The following year, Joshua once again invites Jake to his party. The therapy and behavioral programs and changes in diet have paid off. Though Jake still has plenty of energy, his impulsivity has decreased and he is able to keep himself largely contained while having a good time. At home and school, his energy is channeled in creative ways as he decides to become an inventor. He shares his ideas for new inventions with his teacher and is excited that his father has helped him to learn about patent law.

Three children—three success stories. Love, attention, knowledge and technique can make all the difference between a limited, painful life and a life of growth, discovery and happiness for the growing numbers of children afflicted with ASD, SMD and ADHD. Our professional fulfillment—our happiness, too—lies in doing our very best for them.

Worksheets

Sensory observations throughout the day

Name: _____

Date: _____

When	Problem	Behaviors	Mood	Calm/Alert	Comments

Sensory strategies

Name: _____

Date: _____

Time /Location	Strategy	Overseen By	Comments

Sensory adaptations

Name: _____

Date: _____

Time /Location	Adaptation to child's environment	Overseen By	Comments

Therapy schedule

Name: _____

Date: _____

Day/Time	Location	Activity	Comments

Heavy work/play/exercise schedule

Name:

Date: _____

Day/Time	Location	Activity	Comments

Name: _____

Week of: _____

Sleep Diary	Mon	Tues	Wed	Thurs	Fri	Sat	Sun
Bedtime snack N=none, S=small, M=med, L=large							
Meds today U=Usual, C=Change							
Activity before bed N=none, S=some, L=lots							
How relaxed today (1-10); 1=very relaxed, 10=very agitated							
Time he went to bed							
Amount of time to get to sleep							
Number of times he work up							
Total amount of sleep							
Time he got up							
Naps during the day Number/length							
Comments — use back of page							

Bibliography

Alberto, P. A., & Troutman, A. C. (2003). *Applied Behavior Analysis for Teachers, 6th Edition.* Upper Saddle RIver, NJ: Merril Prentice Hall.

Allen, R., Hill, E., & Heaton, P. (2009). 'Hath charms to soothe . . . ': An exploratory study of how high-functioning adults with ASD experience music. *Autism, 13,* 21-41.

American Psychiatric Association. (2013). *Diagnostic and Statistical Manual Of Mental Disorders* (5th ed.). Washington, DC: American Psychiatric Association.

Attwood, T. (2007). *The Complete Guide to Asperger's Syndrome.* London, U.K.: Jessica Kingsley Publications.

Autism Speaks. (2013). *Learn the signs of autism.* Retrieved Aug. 18, 2013, from Autism Speaks: http://www.autismspeaks.org/what-autism/learn-signs

Ayers, A. J. (2005). *Sensory integration and the child (25th Anniversary ed.).* Los Angeles: Western Psychological Services.

Baker, J. (2008). *No More Meltdowns.* Arlington, TX: Future Horizons.

Barry, L. M., & Messer, J. J. (2003). A practical application of self-management for students diagnosed with attention-deficit/hyperactivity disorder. *Journal of Positive Behavior Interventions,* 238-248.

Barkley, R. (2005). *Taking Charge of ADHD, Revised Edition.* New York: Guilford Press.

Barkley, R. (2012). *Executive Functions: What they are, how they work, and why they evolved.* New York: Guilford Press.

Barkley, R.A., (2011). ADHD: Diagnosis and Subtyping. http://online.pesi.com/catalog/. CMI On Demand.

Bauer, I. M., & Baumeister, R. F. (2011). *Handbook of Self Regulation* (2nd ed.). (K. D. Voys, & R. F. Baumeister, Eds.) New York: The Guilford Press.

Baumeister, R. F., Vohs, K. D., & Tice, D. M. (2007). The Strength Model of Self-Control. *Current Directions in Psychological Science,* 351-355.

Bellini, S. (2006). The development of social anxiety in adolescents with autism spectrum disorders. *Focus on Autism and Other Developmental Disabilities,* 138-145.

Bellini, S., & Akullian, J. (2007). A meta-analysis of video modeling and video self-modeling interventions for children and adolescents with autism spectrum disorder. *Exceptional Children, 73,* 264-287.

Ben-Sasson, A., Cermak, S., Orsmond, G., Tager-Flusberg, H., Kadlec, M., & Carter, A. (2008). Sensory clusters of toddlers with autism spectrum disorders: differences in affective symptoms. *The Journal of Child Psychology and Psychiatry*, 49, 817-825.

Ben-Sasson, A., Cernak, S., Orsmond, G., Tager-Flusberg, H., Carter, A., Kadlec, M., et al. (2007). Extreme sensory modulation behaviors in toddlers with autism spectrum disorders. American *Journal of Occupational Therapy*, 61, 584-592.

Ben-Sasson, A., Hen, L., Fluss, R., Cermak, S., Engel-Yeger, B., & Gal, E. (2009). A meta-analysis of sensory modulation symptoms in individuals with autism spectrum disorders. *Journal of Autism and Developmental Disorders*, 39, 1-11.

Blumenfeld, H. (2002). *Neuroanatomy through Clinical Cases.* Sunderland, MA:Sinaur Associates, Inc..

Bodian, S. (2006). *Meditation for Dummies, 2*nd *Edition.* Wiley Publishing, Inc. Hoboken, NJ.

Bouchard, M. F., Bellinger, D. C., Wright, R. O., & Weisskopf, M. G. (2010). Attention-deficit/hyperactivity disorder and urinary metabolites of organophosphate pesticides. *Pediatrics*, 1270-1277.

Boyd, B. A., McDonough, S. G., Rupp, B., Khan, F., & Bodfish, J. W. (2011). Effects of a family-implemented treatment on the repetitive behaviors of children with autism. *Journal of Autism and Developmental Disorders*, 1330-1341.

Boyd, B. A., McDonough, S. G., F., & Bodfish, J. W. (2012). Evidence-based behavioral interventions for repetitive behaviors in autism. *Journal of Autism and Developmental Disorders*, 1236-1248.

Brimble, M. (2008). Diagnosis and management of ADHD: a new way forward? *Community Practitioner*, 82 (10), 34-37.

Callahan, K., & Rademacher, J. A. (1999). Using self-management strategies to increase the on-task behavior of a student with autism. *Journal of Positive Behavior Interventions*, 1, 117-122.

Carr, Rachel. (1981). Wheel, Camel, Fish and Plow: *Yoga for You.* Englewood Cliffs NJ: Prentice-Hall.

Carter, A., Ben-Sasson, A., & Briggs-Gowan, M. J. (2011). Sensory over-responsivity, psychopathology, and family impairment in school-aged children. *Journal of the American Academy of Child and Adolescent Psychiatry*, 1210-1219.

Case-Smith, J., & Arbesman, M. (2008). Evidence-based review of interventions of autism used in or of relevance to occupational therapy. *The American Journal of Occupational Therapy*, 62, 416-429.

CDC (Centers for Disease Control and Prevention) 2013, April 13. *Attention Deficit / Hyperactivity Disorder.* Retrieved Aug. 5, 2013, from Centers for Disease Control and Prevention: http://www.cdc.gov/ncbddd/adhd/index.html

CDC (Centers for Disease Control and Prevention). 2013. *Autism Spectrum Disorders (ASDs): Data & Statistics.* Retrieved Aug., 18, 2013, from CDC: http://www.cdc.gov/ncbddd/autism/data.html.

Cermak, S. A, Curtin, C., Bandini, L. G. (2010). Food selectivity and sensory sensitivity in children with autism spectrum disorders. *Journal of American Dietetic Association.* 110, 238-246.

Cheung, P. (2009). A comparison of patterns of sensory processing in children with and without developmental disabilities. *Research in Developmental Disabilities*, 30, 1468-1480.

Chuang K-J, Chen H-W, Liu I-J, et al. (2012) The effect of essential oil on heart rate and blood pressure among solus por aqua workers. *Eur J Prevent Cardiol.*

Cole, P. M., Michel, M. K., & Teti, L. O. (1994). *The Development of Emotion Regulation and Dysregulation: A Clinical Perspective.* 59, 73-100. Wiley-Blackwell. Retrieved from http://www.jstor.org/stable/1166139?origin=JSTOR-pdf

Collins, A., & Dworkin, R. J. (2011). Pilot study of the effectiveness of weighted vests. *American Journal of Occupational Therapy*, 65, 688–694.

Corbett, B., Schupp, C., Levine, S., & and Mendoza, S. (2009). Comparing cortisol, stress, and sensory sensitivity in children with autism. *Autism Research*, 2, 39-49.

Cox, S., Fraker, C., & Walbert, L. (2005). *More than Picky: Taking the Fight out of Food with Food Chaining.* Continuing Education Programs of America. Peoria, IL .

Craig, A. D. (2009). Emotional moments across time: A possible neural basis for time perception in the anterior insula. *Philosophical Transactions of the Royal Society of London.* 364, 1933-1942.

Craig, G. (2011). *The EFT Manual.* Energy Psychology Press, Santa Rosa, CA.

Croen, L. A., Grether, J. K., Yoshida, C. K., Odouli, R. & Hendrick, V. (2011). Antidepressant use during pregnancy and childhood autism spectrum disorders. *Archives of General Psychiatry*, 73, 1-9.

Davidson, R. J. (2012). *The Emotional Life of Your Brain.* New York: Hudson Street Press.

Davis, E. L., Levine, L. J., Lench, H. C., & Quas, J. A. (2010). Metacognitive emotion regulation: children's awareness that changing thoughts and goals can alleviate negative emotions. *Emotion*, 498-510.

Dooley, P., Wilczenski, F. L., & Torem, C. (2001). Using an activity schedule to smooth school transitions. *Journal of Positive Behavior Interventions*, 3, 57-61.

Duerden, E. G., Szatmari, P., & Roberts, S. W. (2012). Toward a better understanding of self injurious behaviors in children and adolescents with autism spectrum disorders. *Journal of Autism and Developmental Disorders*, 2515-2518.

Duffy, F. H., Shankardass, A., McAnulty, G. B., & Als, H. (2013). The relationship of Asperger Syndrome to autism: a preliminary EEG coherence study. *BMC Medicine*, 11, 175.

Dunn, W. (2009). Invited commentary on "Sensory sensitivities of gifted children". *American Journal of Occupational Therapy*, 63, 296-300.

Dunn, W., Smith, B. M., & Orr, S. (2002). Sensory-process issues associated with Asperger's Syndrome. *American Journal of Occupational Therapy*, 56, 97-102.

Eisenberg, N., & Sulik, M. J. (2010). Emotion-related self-regulation in children. *Annual Review of Clinical Psychology*, 6, 495-525.

Ellis, E. M., Ala'i-Rosales, S. S., Glenn, S. S., Rosales-Ruiz, J., & Greenspoon, J. (2006). The effects of graduated exposure, modeling, and contingent social attention on tolerance to skin care products with two children with autism. *Research in Developmental Disabilities*, 27, 585-598.

Ermer, J. & Dunn, W. (1997). A sensory profile: A discriminant analysis of children with and without disabilities. *American Journal of Occupational Therapy*, 4, 283-290.

Escalona, A., Field, T., Singer-Straunck, R., Collum, C., & Hartshorn, K. (2001). Brief report: Improvements in the behavior of children with autism following massage therapy. *Journal of Autism and Developmental Disorders*, 31, 513-516.

Fertel-Daly, D., Bedell, G., & Hinojosa, J. (2003). Effects of a weighted vest on attention to task and self-stimulatory behaviors in preschoolers with pervasive developmental disorders. In C. B. Royeen, *Pediatric Issues in Occupational Therapy*, 215-229. Bethesda, MD: AOTA Press.

Fitzgerald, M. (2009). Kenneth Aitken: Dietary interventions in autism spectrum disorders: Why they work when they do, why they don't when they don't. *Journal of Autism and Developmental Disorders*, 39, 819-820.

Frick, S. M., & Hacker, C. (2009). *Listening with the whole body.* Madison, WI: Vital Links.

Gere, D., Capps, S., Mitchell, D., & Grubbs, E. (2009). Sensory sensitivities of gifted children. *American Journal of Occupational Therapy*, 63, 288-295.

Gray, C. (2004). Social stories 10.0. *Jenison Autism Journal*, 15, 3-21.

Grandin, T., & Panek, R. (2013). *The Autistic Brain: Thinking Across the Brain.* Boston: Houghton Mifflin Harcourt.

Green, S. A., Ben-Sasson, A., Soto, T. W., & Carter, A. S. (2011). Anxiety and sensory over-responsivity in toddlers with autism spectrum disorders: bidirectional affects across time. *Journal of Autism and Developmental Disorders.*

Greenspan, S. I., & Greenspan, J. (2009). *Overcoming ADHD.* Cambridge, MA: Da Capo Press.

Gross, J. J. (2007). Emotional Regulation: Conceptual Foundations. In J. J. Gross, *Handbook of Emotional Regulation* (3rd ed., 3-24). New York: Guilford Press.

Gross, J. J., & Barrett, L. F. (2011, January 3). Emotional generation and emotional regulation: One or two depends on your point of view. (Author Manuscript). NIH Public Access. Retrieved Aug. 5, 2013, from http://www.ncbi.nlm.nih.gov/pmc/articles/PMC3072688/.

Hall, L., & Case-Smith, J. (2007). The effect of sound-based intervention on children with sensory processing disorders and visual-motor delays. *The American Journal of Occupational Therapy*, 61, 209-215.

Hallmeyer, J., Cleveland, S., Torres, A. Phillips, J., Cohen, B., Torigoe, T., Miller, J., Fedele, A., Collins, J., Smith, K., Lotspeich, L., Croen, L., Ozonoff, S., Lajonchere, C., Grether, J., K., & Risch, N. (2011). Genetic heritability and shared environmental factors among twin pairs with autism. *Archives of General Psychiatry*, published online July 4, 2011.

Hanson, B., Cerban, B. M., Slater, C. M., Caccamo, L. M., Bacic, J., & Chan, E. (2013). Brief Report: Prevalence of Attention Deficit/Hyperactivity Disorder Among Individuals with an Autism Spectrum Disorder. *Journal of Autism and Developmental Disorders*, 1459-1464.

Heckmann, S. M., Hujoel, P., Habiger, S., Friess, W., Wichmann, M., Heckmann, J. G., et al. (2005). Zinc gluconate in the treatment of dysgeusia—a randomized clinical trial. *Journal of Dental Research,*, 35-38.

Herbert, M., & Weintraub, K. (2012). *The Autism Revolution.* New York: Ballantine Books.

Heuer, L., Ashwood, P., Schauer, J., Goines, P., Krakowiak, P., Hertz-Picciotto, I. (2008). Reduced levels of immunoglobulin in children with autism correlates with behavioral symptoms. *Autism Research*, 1, 275-283.

Hofmann, S. G., & Kashdan, T. B. (2010). The Affective Style Questionnaire: development and psychometric properties. *Journal of Pathological Behavior Assessment*, 255-263.

Howard, A. l., Robinson, M., Smith, G. J., Ambrosini, G. L., Piek, J. P., Oddy, W. H. (2011). ADHD is associated with a "western" dietary pattern in adolescents. *Journal of Attention Disorders*, 15, 403-441.

Jaksch, M. (2012). Start Over: Create the Life You Want. GoodLifeZen.com.

Kalyva, E. (2009). Comparison of eating attitudes between adolescent girls with and without Asperger's Syndrome: Daughters and mothers' reports. *Journal of Autism and Developmental Disorders*, 480-486.

Kim, J., Wigram, T., & Gold, C. (2009). Emotional, motivational and interpersonal responsiveness of children with autism in improvisational music therapy. *Autism*, 13, 389-409.

Kimball, J., Lynch, K., Stewart, K., Williams, N., Thomas, M., & Atwood, K. (2007). Using salivary cortisol to measure the effects of a Wilbarger protocol-based procedure on sympathetic arousal: A pilot study. *American Journal of Occupational Therapy*, 61, 406-413.

Kinnealey, M., Pfeiffer, B., Miller, J., Roan, C., Shoener, R., & Ellner, M. L. (2012). Effect of Classroom Modification on Attention and Engagement of Students With Autism or Dyspraxia. *American Journal of Occupational Therapy*, 511-519.

Kleinhans, N., Richards, T., Weaver, K., Liang, O., Dawson, G., & Aylward, E. (2009). Brief Report: Biochemical correlates of clinical impairment in high functioning autism and Asperger's disorder. *Journal of Autism and Developmental Disorders*, 39, 1079-1086.

Koegel, R. L., Bharoocha, A. A., Ribnick, C. B., Ribnick, R. C., Bucio, M. O., Fredeen, R. M., et al. (2012). Using individualized reinforcers and hierarchical exposure to increase food flexibility in children with autism spectrum. *Journal of Autism and Developmental Disorders*, 1574-1581.

Kushak, R. I., Lauwers, G. Y., Winter, H. S., & Buie, T. M. (2011). Intestinal disaccharidase activity in patients with autism: Effect of age, gender and intestinal inflammation. *Autism*, 3, 285-294.

Kutscher, M. L. (2008). *ADHD: Living without brakes.* Philadelphia: Jessica Kingsley Publishers.

Llewellyn, N., Dolcos, S., Iordan, A. D., Rudolph, K. D., & Dolcos, F. (2013). Reappraisal and suppression mediate the contribution of regulatory focus to anxiety in healthy adults. *Emotion.*

Lorimer, P. A., Simpson, R. L., Smith, B., & Ganz, J. B. (2002). The use of social stories as a preventative behavioral intervention in a home setting with a child with autism. *Journal of Positive Behavior Interventions*, 53-60.

MacDonald, J. (2009). Articles on autism. Retrieved from Communicating Partners: http://jamesdmacdonald.org/Articles/MacDonaldStart.html

MacLean, K. L. (2009). *Moody Cow Meditates.* Somerville, MA: Wisdom Publications.

MacLean, K. L. (2004). *Peaceful Piggy Meditation.* Morton Grove, IL: Albert Whitman & Co.

McAfee, J. (2002). *Navigating the Social World.* Arlington, TX: Future Horizons.

McCann, D., Barrett, A., Cooper, A., Crumpler, D., Dalen, L., Grimshaw, K., et al. (2007). Food additives and hyperactive behaviour in 3-year-old and 8/9-year-old children in the community: a randomised, double-blinded, placebo-controlled trial. *The Lancet*, 1560-1567.

McGrew, K., & Vegas, A. (2009). *The efficacy of rhythm-based (mental timing) treatments with subjects with a variety of clinic disorders: A brief review of theoretical, diagnostic and treatment research.* Institute for Applied Psychometrics. St. Paul, MN.

McNair, P. J., Heine, P. J. (1999). Trunk proprioception: enhancement through lumbar bracing. *Archives of Physical Medicine and Rehabilitation.* 80, 96-99.

Miller, L. J., Nielson, D. M., & Schoe, S. A. (2012). Attention deficit hyperactivity disorder and sensory modulation disorder: A comparison of behavior and physiology. *Research in Developmental Disabilities*, 804-818.

Miller, L. J. (2006). *Sensational Kids.* New York: Penguin Group.

Miller, L., Anzalone, M., Lane, S., Cermak, S., & Osten, E. (2007). Concept evolution in sensory integration: A proposed nosology for diagnosis. *American Journal of Occupational Therapy*, 61, 135-140.

Miller, L., Coll, J., & Schoen, S. (2007). A randomized controlled pilot study of the effectiveness of occupational therapy for children with sensory modulation disorder. *American Journal of Occupational Therapy*, 61, 228-237.

Miller, L., Neilsen, D. M., & Schoen, S. (2012). Attention deficit hyperactivity disorder and sensory modulation disorder: A comparison of behavior and physiology. *Research in Developmental Disabilities*, 804-818.

Miller L. J., Reisman J. E., McIntosh D. N., Simon J. (2001). An ecological model of sensory modulation: performance of children with fragile X syndrome, autistic disorder, attention-deficit/hyperactivity disorder, and sensory modulation dysfunction. In *Understanding the Nature of Sensory Integration with Diverse Populations*, Smith S. Roley, Blanche E. I., Schaaf R. C., editors, (San Antonio, TX, The Psychological Corporation), 57–88.

Ming, X., Brimacombe, M., Malek, J. H., Jani, N. & Wagner, G. C. (2011) Autism spectrum disorders and identified toxic landfills: Co-occurrence across states. *Environmental Health Insights, 2*, 55-59.

Myles, B. S., & Southwick, J. (2005). *Asperger's Syndrome and Difficult Moments.* Shawnee Mission, KS: Autism Asperger Publishing Co.

Myles, B. S., Trautman, M. L., & Schelvan, R. L. (2004). *The Hidden Curriculum.* Shawnee Mission, KS: Autism Asperger Publishing Co.

NIMH. (2007, Nov. 12). *Brain Matures a Few Years Late in ADHD, But Follows Normal Pattern.* Retrieved on Aug. 21, 2011 from: http://www.nimh.nih.gov/science-news/2007/brain-matures-a-few-years-late-in-adhd-but-follows-normal-pattern.shtml

NIMH. (2008, Aug. 27). *Antipsychotic Does Not Harm—and May Improve—Cognitive Skills in Children with Autism.* Retrieved Feb. 15, 2010, from National Institute of Mental Health: http://www.nimh.nih.gov/science-news/2008/antipsychotic-does-not-harm-and-may-improve-cognitive-skills-in-children-with-autism.shtml

National Autism Center. (2009). *National Standard's Report.* Randolph, MA: National Autism Center.

National Cancer Institute. (2012, 10 16). *Aromatherapy and essential oils (PDQ®).* Retrieved Oct. 10, 2013, from National Cancer Institute: http://www.cancer.gov/cancertopics/pdq/cam/aromatherapy/patient/page2

Newmark, S. (2010). *ADHD Without Drugs.* Tucson, AZ: Nurtured Heart Publications.

Nikolov, R. N., Bearss, K. E., Lettinga, J., Erickson, C., Rodowski, M., Aman, M. G., et al. (2008). Gastrointestinal symptoms in a sample of children with pervasive developmental disorders. *Journal of Autism and Developmental Disorders*, 405-413.

NIMH (National Institute of Mental Health). (2012). *Attention Deficit Hyperactivity Disorder.* Retrieved Aug. 5, 2013, from National Institute of Mental Health: http://www.nimh.nih.gov/health/publications/attention-deficit-hyperactivity-disorder/index.shtml

Norall, C. L. (2009). *Quirky, Yes Hopeless, No.* New York: St. Martin's Griffin.

Nwora, A., & Gee, B. (2009). A case study of a five-year-old child with pervasive developmental disorder—not otherwise specified using sound-based interventions. *Occupational Therapy International, 16*, 25-43.

Palo, M. B. (2005). *Video Modeling.* Retrieved 2011, from Dan Marino Child Nett.TV: www.childnett.tv/videos/lectures/mary_beth_palo_video_modeling

Palo, M. B. (2010). *Video Modeling.* Retrieved 2011, from Watch Me Learn: http://www.watchmelearn.com/autism-videos-people.shtml

Parker, C. (2010, 2 10). *Predictable Solutions For the Ten Biggest Problems with ADHD MEds.* Retrieved Feb. 14, 2011, from CorePsych Blog: www.CorePsychBlog Porges, S. (2011, November). Somatic Perspectives on Psychotherapy. (S. Prengel, Interviewer).

Pessler, L. M., Frankena, K., J, T., F, S. H., Dubois, A. E., Pereira, R. R., et al. (2011). Effects of a restricted elimination diet on the behaviour of children with attention-deficit hyperactivity disorder (INCA study): a randomised controlled trial. *The Lancet*, 494-503.

Pfeiffer, B., Henry, A., Miller, S., & Witherell, S. (2008). Effectiveness of disc "O" Sit Cushions on attention to task in second-grade students with attention difficulties. *American Journal of Occupational Therapy*, 62, 274-281.

Porges S. W. (1993). *The infant's sixth sense: Awareness and regulation of bodily processes.* Zero to Three: Bulletin of the National Center for Clinical Infant Programs 14, 12-16.

Porges, S. W. (2001). The polyvagal theory: phylogenetic substrates of a social nervous system. *International Journal of Psychophysiology, 42, 123-146.*

Porges, S. W. (2008, February). The Polyvagal Perspective. *NIH Public Access*, PMC1868418.

Preston, D., & Carter, M. (2009). A review of the efficacy of the picture exchange communication system intervention. *Journal of Autism and Developmental Disorders*, 39, 1471-1486.

Reynolds, S., & Lane, S. (2009). Sensory overresponsivity and anxiety in children with ADHD. *American Journal of Occupational Therapy*, 63, 433-440.

Rodgers, J., Glod, M., Connolly, B., & McConachie, H. (2012). The relationship between anxiety and repetitive behaviors in autism spectrum disorder. *Journal of Autism and Developmental Disorders*, 2404-2409.

Rood, G. H., & Miller, L. J. (1997). *Leiter International.* Wood Dale, IL: Stoelting Co.

Rosenblatt, A. I., & Carbone, P. S. (2013). *Autism Spectrum Disorders: What Every Parent Needs to Know.* Elk Grove Village, IL: American Academy of Pediatricians.

Rossignol, D. A., & Frye, R. E. (2012). A review of research trends in physiological abnormalities in autism spectrum disorders: immune dysregulation, inflammation, oxidative stress, mitochondrial dysfunction and environmental toxicant exposures. *Molecular Psychiatry*, 4, 389-401.

Rydell, A. M., Berlin, L., & Bohlin, G. (2003). Emotionality, Emotion Regulation, and Adaptation Among 5- to 8-Year-Old Children. *Emotion*, 3, 30-47.

Sansosti, F. J., Powell-Smith, K. A., & Kincaid, D. (2004). A research synthesis of social story interventions for children with autism spectrum disorders. *Focus on Autism and Other Developmental Disabilities*, 19, 194-204.

Schaaf, R. C., Benevides, T., Blanche, E. I., Brett-Green, B. A., Burke, J. P., Cohn, E.S., et al. Parasympathetic functions in children with sensory processing disorder. *Frontiers in Integrative Neuroscience.* 2010; 4, 4. Published online 2010 March 9. doi: 10.3389/fnint.2010.00004

Schmidt, R. J., Hansen, R. L., Hartiala, J., Allayee, H., Schmidt, L. C., Tancredi, D. J., et al. (2011). Prenatal vitamins, one-carbon metabolism gene variants, and risk for autism. *Epidemiology*, 4, 476-85.

Schwartz, C. R., Henderson, H. A., Inge, A. P., Zahka, N. E., Coman, D. C., Kojkowski, N. M., et al. (2009). Temperment as a predictor of symptomology and adaptive functioning in adolescents with high functioning autism. *Journal of Autism and Developmental Disorders*, 842-855.

Shaffer, R. J., Jacokes, L. E., Cassily, J. F., Greenspan, S. I., Tuchman, R. F. (2008). Effects of Interactive Metronome™ training on children with ADHD. *American Journal of Occupational Therapy*, 155-162.

Siegel, M., & Beaulieu, A. A. (2012). Psychotropic medications in children with autism spectrum disorders: A systematic review and synthesis for evidenced-based practice. *Journal of Autism and Devlopmental Disorders*, 1592-1605.

Silva, L. M., & Schalock, M. (2012). Sense and Self-Regulation Checklist, a measure of comorbid autism symptom: initial psychometric evidence. *American Journal of Occupational Therapy*, 177-186.

Silva, L., Schalock, M., Ayres, R., Bunse, C., & Budden, S. (2009). Qigong massage treatment for sensory and self-regulation problems in young children with autism: A randomized controlled trial. *American Journal of Occupational Therapy*, 63, 423-432.

Sinn, N., & Bryan, J. (2007). The effect of supplementation with polyunsaturated fatty acids and micronutrients on learning and behavior problems associated with child ADHD. *Journal of Developmental and Behavioral Pediatrics*, 82-91.

Smith, R., Farnworth, H., Wright, B., & Allgar, V. (2009). Are there more bowel symptoms in children with autism compared to normal children and children with other developmental and neurological disorders? A case control study. *Autism*, 13, 343-355.

South, M., Newton, T., & Chamberlain, P. D. (2012). Delayed reversal learning and association with repetitive behavior in autism spectrum disorders. *Autism Research*, 6, 398-406.

Strickland, E. (2009). *Eating for Autism*. Cambridge: Da Capo Press.

The National Autistic Society. (2009). Sleep and autism: Helping your child. Retrieved 2009, from The National Autistic Society website: http://www.nas.org.uk/nas/jsp/polopoly.jsp?d=2427&a=3376

Tomchek, S., & Dunn, W. (2007). Sensory processing in children with and without autism: A comparative study using the short sensory profile. *American Journal of Occupational Therapy*, 61, 190-200.

Tuckman, A. (2010). Six Simple Rules: Fundamental Strategies to Overcome Inattention, Hyperactivity and Impulsivity. *Virtual ADHD Conference.* ADD Management Group.

Turner, Alice. (1973). *Yoga for Beginners*. New York: Franklin Watts.

Visser, S. N., Danielson, M., Cuffe, S. P., McKeown, R. E., Bitsko, R. H., Claussen, A. H. (2011). Health Risk Behaviors over Time among Youth with ADHD. Toronto. Retrieved Aug. 2013, from http://www.cdc.gov/ncbddd/adhd/play2.html

Volkow, N. D., Kollins, S. H., Wigal, T. L., Newcorn, J.H., Telang, F., Fowler, J. S., et al (2010) Evaluating dopamine reward pathway in ADHD. *Journal of the American Medical Association, 303 (3), 232-234.*

Weeks, S., Boshoff, K., & Stewart, H. (2012). Systematic review of the effectiveness of the Wilbarger protocol with children. *Pediatric Health, Medicine and Therapeutics*, 3, 79-89.

Wells, A. M., Chasnoff, I. J., Schmidt, C. A., Telford, E., & Schwartz, L. D. (2012). Neurocognitive habilitation therapy for children with fetal alcohol spectrum disorders: An adaptation of the Alert Program. *American Journal of Occupational Therapy*, 1, 24-34.

White, S., & Roberson-Nay, R. (2009). Anxiety, social deficits and loneliness in youth with autism spectrum disorders. *Journal of Autism and Developmental Disorders*, 39, 1006-1013.

White, S. W., Bray, B. C., & Ollendick, T. H. (2012). Examined shared and unique aspects of social anxiety disorder and autism spectrum disorder using factor analysis. *Journal of Autism and Developmental Disorders*, 874-884.

Wilbarger, P., & Willbarger, J. (2011). Integrated Treatment Approach for Sensory Defensiveness. *Sensory Defensiveness: A Comprehensive Treatment Approach,* 34-61. Santa Barbara, CA: Avanit Educational Programs.

Williams, M. S., & Shellenberger, S. (1996). *Introduction to How Does Your Engine Run: The Alert Program for Self-Regulation.* Albuquerque, NM: Therapy Works, Inc.

Williamson, G., & Anzalone, M. (2001). *Sensory Integration and Self-Regulation in Infants and Toddlers: Helping Very Young Children with Their Environment.* Washington, D.C.: One, Two, Three: National Center for Infants, Toddlers and Families.

Woo, C. C., & Leon, M. (2013). Environmental enrichment as an effective treatment for autism: A randomized control trial. *Behavioral Neuroscience*, 4, 487-497.

Woodruff, T. J., Zota, A. R., Schwartz. J. M. (2011). Environmental chemicals in pregnant women in the United States: NHANES *2003-2004. Environmental Health Perspectives*, 6, 878-885.

Zylowska, L., Ackerman, D. L., Yang, M. H., Futrell, J. L., Horton, N. L., Hale, T. S. (2008). Mindfulness Meditation Training in Adults and Adolescents With ADHD. *Journal of Attention Disorders*, 734-746.

Resources

Autism References

1. *The Autism Revolution,* M. Herbert, New York: Ballantine Books, 2012.

2. *Be Different: My Adventures with Asperger's and My Advice for Fellow Aspergians, Misfits, Families, and Teachers,* John Elder Robinson, New York: Random House, 2011.

3. *No More Meltdowns,* Jed Baker, Arlington, TX, Future Horizons, 2008.

4. *Autism Speaks,* AutismSpeaks.org.

5. *Early Start Denver Model for Young Children with Autism: Promoting Language, Learning, and Engagement,* Rogers, S. (2010).

6. *The Complete Guide to Asperger's Syndrome,* Tony Attwood. London: Jessica Kingsley Publications, 2007.

7. *Cutting Edge Therapies for Autism,* K. Siri & T. Lyons, New York: Skyhorse Publishing, 2012.

8. *Engaging Autism,* Stanley Greenspan, M.D., and Serena Wieder, PhD., Perseus Books, Cambridge, MA, 2006.

9. *Thinking in Pictures,* 2nd ed., Temple Grandin, New York: Vintage Books, 2006.

10. *Social stories 10.0,* Gray, C. (2004).

11. Model Me Kids: modelmekids.com.

12. Watch Me Learn: watchmelearn.com/autism-videos-people.shtml.

Broad-focus Therapy Programs for Autism

1. Early Start Denver Model (ESDM), http://www.ucdmc.ucdavis.edu/mindinstitute/research/esdm/

2. DIRfloortime, http://www.icdl.com/dirFloortime/overview/

3. P.L.A.Y. Project, http://www.playproject.org/

Sensory Modulation References

1. *Sensational Kids*, Lucy Jane Miller, New York: Penguin Group, 2006.

2. The SPD Foundation, SDPFoundation.net.

3. *Sensory Integration and the Child, 25*th *Edition*, A. Jean Ayres. Los Angeles: Western Publishing Company, 2005.

4. *Raising a Sensory Smart Child*, Lindsey Biel and Nancy Peske, New York: Penguin Group, 2005.

5. *Answers to Questions Teachers Ask about Sensory Integration*, Jane Koomar, Carol Kranowitz, Stacey Szklut, et al., Arlington, TX,: Future Horizons, 2007.

6. *The Out-of-Sync Child Series*, Carol Kranowitz, New York: Perigee Penguin, 2005.

7. *Listening With the Whole Body*, Sheila Frick & C. Hacker, Madison, WI: Vital Links, 2009.

Eating, sleeping

1. *Eating for Autism*, E. Strickland, Cambridge, MA: Da Capo Press, 2009.

2. *Deceptively delicious: simple secrets to getting your kids eating good food*, J. Seinfeld, New York: Collins, 2008.

3. *Autism sleep toolkit, http://www.autismspeaks.org/science/resources-programs/autism-treatment-network/tools-you-can-use/sleep-tool-kit.*

Executive function and ADHD references

1. *Executive Functions,* R. Barkley, New York: Guilford Press, 2012.

2. *Taking Charge of ADHD*, R. Barkley, New York: Guilford Press, 2005.

3. *Overcoming ADHD*, S. Greenspan, & J. Greenspan, Cambridge, MA: Da Capo Press., 2010.

4. *ADHD: Living Without Brakes*, M. L. Kutscher, Philadelphia: Jessica Kingsley Publishers, 2008.

5. *An ADHD primer.* G. DuPaul & G. White, National Society of School Psychologists: nasponline.org/resources/principals/nassp_adhd.aspx, 2004.

6. *Mindful Teaching and Teaching Mindfulness,* D. Schoenberlein, Boston: Wisdom Pubs., 2009.

7. *Peaceful Piggy Meditates*, MacLean, K. E., Morton Grove, IL: Albert Whitman & Co., 2004.

8. *Moody Cow Meditates*, MacLean, K. E., Somerville, MA: Wisdom Publications, 2009.

Therapy Methods

1. Astronaut Board Program, astronautboards.com/.
2. Bal-A-Vis-X, Bal-A-Vis-X.com.
3. DIR/Floortime, icdl.com/dirFloortime/overview/ .
4. EFT
   a. Rod Sherwin, Tap4Health.com.
   b. EFTUniverse.
5. Infant massage from Parents magazine:
   parents.com/baby/care/newborn/how-to-massage-baby/.
6. Interactive Metronome, InteractiveMetronome.com.
7. MeMoves, ThinkingMoves.com.
8. Sound Therapies
   a. Berard AIT, aitinstitute.org.
   b. EASe, Vision-Audio.com.
   c. iLs, integratedListening.com.
   d. Therapeutic Listening, VitalLinks.com.
   e. The Listening Program, www.thelisteningprogram.com.
9. UCLA Mindfulness Resources, *Marc.UCLA.edu.*
10. Wilbarger Protocol training: Avanti-ed.com.

Therapy catalogs

1. Abilitations.com
2. FunAndFunction.com
3. SouthPawEnterprises.com
4. SensoryJunction.com
5. Therapro.com
6. TherapyShoppe.com

Index